Embracing
Shared Ministry

EMBRACING SHARED MINISTRY

POWER *and* STATUS *in the* EARLY CHURCH *and* WHY IT MATTERS TODAY

Joseph H. Hellerman

Kregel
Ministry

Embracing Shared Ministry: Power and Status in the Early Church and Why It Matters Today

© 2013 Joseph H. Hellerman

Published by Kregel Publications, a division of Kregel, Inc., P.O. Box 2607, Grand Rapids, MI 49501.

The Greek font GraecaU is available from www.linguistsoftware.com/lgku. htm, +1-425-775-1130.

ISBN 978-0-8254-4264-3

Printed in the United States of America
13 14 15 16 17 / 5 4 3 2 1

To Brandon,
Ed,
Carlos,
Dan,
Denny,
John,
Michael,
and Stan,
my fellow pastor-elders
of Oceanside Christian Fellowship

CONTENTS

ABBREVIATIONS

Periodicals and Reference Works

ACCS	Ancient Christian Commentary on Scripture
BBR	*Bulletin for Biblical Research*
BJRL	*Bulletin of the John Rylands Library*
BTB	*Biblical Theology Bulletin*
CIL	*Corpus inscriptionum latinarum*
ILS	*Inscriptiones latinae selectae*
JBL	*Journal of Biblical Literature*
JETS	*Journal of the Evangelical Theological Society*
NICNT	New International Commentary on the New Testament
NIGTC	New International Greek Testament Commentary
SIG	*Sylloge inscriptionum graecarum*
SNTSMS	Society for New Testament Studies Monograph Series
WUNT	*Wissenschaftliche Untersuchungen zum Neuen Testament*

Greek and Latin Authors

Appian
BCiv.	*The Civil Wars*

Apuleius
Met.	*Metamorphoses (a.k.a. The Golden Ass)*

Cicero
Fam.	*Epistulae ad Familiares (Letters to Friends)*
Tusc.	*Tusculan Disputations*
2 Verr.	*Against Verres, Part Two*

Dio Chrysostom
Or.	*Orations*

Eusebius

    Hist. eccl.   *Historia ecclesiastica*

Marcus Cornelius Fronto

    Ad Pium   *Ad Antoninum Pium*

Philo

    Leg.   *De Legatione ad Gaium (On the Embassy to Gaius)*

Plautus

    Bacch.   *Bacchides (The Two Bacchises)*

    Mil. Glor.   *Miles Gloriosys (The Braggart Warrior)*

Pliny the Younger

    Ep.   *Epistulae (Letters)*

Plutarch

    Brut.   *Brutus*

    Crass.   *Crassus*

    Pomp.   *Pompey*

Porphery

    Abst.   *De abstentia*

Suetonius

    Aug.   *The Deified Augustus*

    Claud.   *The Deified Claudius*

Symmachus

    Ep.   *Epistulae (Letters)*

Tacitus

    Ann.   *The Annals*

Charting Our Course Together

Many local church ministers are emotionally well-balanced Christian leaders with the purest of motives—persons who consistently exercise their pastoral authority in encouraging and nurturing ways.

This book is about those who are not.

Embracing Shared Ministry finds its conceptual origins in an academic monograph published in 2005.[1] I sought to demonstrate that Paul, in his letter to the Philippians, intentionally subverts the social values of the dominant culture in the Roman colony at Philippi in order to create a radically different relational environment among the Philippian Christians.

Surviving archaeological evidence from the site portrays Roman elites and non-elites alike using their financial resources and social capital in the service of their own personal and familial agendas. Paul, in stark contrast, shows Jesus using his status and authority solely in the service of others (Phil 2:6–11).

The grand narrative of Christ's humiliation and exaltation came alive for me anew when I recognized that Paul's designs in the passage were not primarily christological. They were ecclesiological. Or, perhaps more accurately, what we have in Philippians 2:6–11 is Christology in the service of an overarching ecclesiological agenda.

---

1. Joseph H. Hellerman, *Reconstructing Honor in Roman Philippi: Carmen Christi as* Cursus Pudorum, SNTSMS 132 (Cambridge: Cambridge University Press, 2005).

Accordingly, Paul's primary point in verse 6 is not that Christ was somehow ontologically "God" before the incarnation, though one can certainly find ample support in the text for the doctrine of the deity of Christ.

Paul's aim, rather, is to inform his readers that Christ enjoyed "equality with God" with respect to power and status. And it is Christ's attitude toward his privileged position that Paul draws upon in the text to encourage the Philippians—particularly those church members with status and social privilege—to act similarly in their mutual relations in the Jesus community in the colony (v. 5).

Until the fall of 2009, I was content to allow my research on Paul and Roman Philippi to remain in an academic format, leaving it to others, perhaps, to draw upon the findings and contextualize them for broader reading audiences. God used the first semester of the 2009–10 academic year to change my mind.

A World of Hurt

I had come off a much needed spring sabbatical at Talbot School of Theology and was teaching a full load and preaching every Sunday at church. One of my classes that semester was an elective in ecclesiology, titled *The Church as Family*.

The goal for the course is a simple one: to challenge students to exchange the institutional view of church that many had brought with them to seminary for a markedly relational—and much more biblical—perspective on Christian community and pastoral ministry.

Course materials that semester stirred up an inordinate amount of hurt and heartache among my students. I had numbers of them in my office detailing incidents of abuse they had experienced at the hands of pastors and other authority figures in their churches.

Some of these students were in associate staff positions. Others were volunteers. Still others had seen family members manipulated and mistreated by persons in authority in their home churches.

I found myself doing damage control in the lives of students throughout the semester. It became painfully apparent that the pastors in these churches were not using their authority in the service of others, after the example of Jesus in Philippians 2.

The narratives were in some ways quite distinct. Asian students ran headlong into a highly stratified honor culture that facilitates the misuse of power by older persons in positions of leadership. The authority of these Korean senior pastors typically cannot be challenged by the younger leaders and church members under their charge.

Students in large Anglo churches struggled with a corporate mentality that views the senior pastor as a CEO and his associate staff as employees. Add an emotionally dysfunctional senior pastor to the mix in either cultural setting and the result is a recipe for relational disaster.

Different cultures. Different stories. The same results: egregious mistreatment of junior staff and parishioners by pastors who ought to know—and do—better.

Janice's Story

One interaction, in particular, caught me quite off guard. The graduate course described above is a demanding one. A student I will call Janice rose to the occasion.

I had taught Janice second-year Greek while she was an undergraduate Bible major at Biola University, and I was not surprised that she was doing well in seminary. Janice's written responses to the required readings, as well as the questions she raised in class, were consistently incisive and thought-provoking for her professor and fellow students alike. I sensed that God was going to use this young woman in some mighty ways in his kingdom plan.

One day Janice stayed around after class to ask a question: *What do you say to someone who is cynical about church and who doesn't have much hope that the things we are learning about the church as a family could ever really happen?*

Now I naively assumed that Janice was talking about someone

else—a friend, perhaps, or a fellow student who harbored negative feelings towards institutional Christianity. So I proceeded to respond accordingly.

It soon became clear that I had completely misinterpreted the question. Janice's inquiry was not about a friend or fellow student. Janice was describing herself. Janice was the one who was "cynical about church." It was Janice who seriously wondered whether "church as a family could ever really happen."

To my surprise and dismay I discovered that this brilliant, God-loving Bible student was just about ready to give up on the local church, and understandably so, given her personal pilgrimage in the body of Christ.

During her formative years as a high-schooler and young adult, Janice had experienced the heartache of a church split. The months that followed saw Janice's congregation bearing the brunt of highly dysfunctional leadership under the authority of a heavy-handed senior pastor. Janice's father, an elder in the church, was caught in the middle throughout.

By the time she arrived in class in September 2009, the abuse of spiritual authority had taken its toll on Janice, the members of her immediate family, and numbers of persons in her church. Little wonder that Janice was more than a bit skeptical toward her professor's convictions that the church ought to function—and really could function—as a healthy surrogate family.

As that fall semester unfolded it became increasingly clear that what we know about Paul, the social world of Roman Philippi, and Paul's letter to the Philippians has a timely message for contemporary church leaders. In the chapters to follow, I hope to demonstrate that Paul's cruciform vision for authentic spiritual leadership—epitomized in the humiliation and exaltation of Christ in Philippians 2—has much to say to pastors and others in positions of authority in our churches in America today.

Below is an outline of the book. But first a word about a word: "cruciform."

The term surfaced some time ago, in academic circles, as a catchword for Paul's other-centered approach to Christian life and ministry. "Cruciform" literally means "in the shape of the cross."

Now most academic jargon is better left in the ivory tower, in articles and books written *by* biblical scholars *for* biblical scholars. "Cruciform," however, is a word we should co-opt for popular consumption. Why? Because, properly understood, "cruciform" communicates so very much that is at the heart of the gospel.

The cross of Christ is all about self-denial, sacrifice, living and dying in the service of others: "If anyone wants to be My follower, he must deny himself, take up his cross, and follow Me" (Mark 8:34). The Christian life, at its essence, is a cruciform life. It is a life that is shaped like—and shaped by—the cross of Jesus Christ. To genuinely know Christ is to be "conformed to His death" (Phil 3:10).

This is especially the case where the use of spiritual power and authority is concerned. Biblical leadership is other-centered leadership—leadership in the shape of the cross. So you can expect to encounter the word *cruciform* quite often in the pages that follow, since it so nicely summarizes Paul's radically countercultural approach to Christian ministry and leadership.

A Road Map for the Chapters to Follow

The book consists of three parts. Part 1 (Power and Authority in the Roman World: The Social Context of the Pauline Mission) outlines the socio-cultural setting of Roman Philippi. This background information sets the stage for our encounter with Paul's markedly alternative vision for leadership in the biblical materials.

Part 2 (Power and Authority in the Early Church: Paul's Cruciform Vision for Authentic Christian Leadership) interprets Paul's letter to the Philippians, and the apostle's ministry in Philippi, as related by Luke in Acts 16, against the background of Roman social values and behaviors. We will seek to craft a biblical theology of leadership and community that will equip us to address issues of power and authority in our churches today.

An important heads-up: The biblical and historical materials in parts 1 and 2 require serious reflection about a world much different from our own. There are no simple, user-friendly solutions to the unhealthy exercise of authority that plagues so many congregations today. Contemporary sociological and psychological analyses and prescriptions are helpful, but they are not, in the final analysis, fully satisfying.

What is needed is a solid biblical foundation upon which to build a philosophy of ministry that contrasts sharply with the regrettable scenarios of power abuse that play themselves out in our churches. Such an approach necessitates, in turn, thoughtful engagement with the biblical texts in their original socio-cultural settings.

Part 3 (Power and Authority in the Church Today: Cultivating a Social Context for Servant Leadership) concludes the book. Here we consider the implications of Paul's ecclesiology for the exercise of authority by church leaders today.

It is common in evangelical circles for us to encourage one another to respect and submit to the authority figures in our lives. There is, of course, good biblical warrant for doing so. After all, the Christian life finds its beginnings in our submission to the will of our Creator and Redeemer, as we individually and corporately affirm that Jesus is Lord. And then there are passages like Romans 13, which challenge us to submit to the authority of the state, as well.

Numbers of us struggle, however, with uncritical submission or allegiance to authority figures in the human realm. And rightly so. For in many cases our own experiences have taught us to question authority.

Chapter 7 narrates several regrettable instances of the misuse of authority in the local church. These case studies—drawn from firsthand experiences of students and colleagues alike—take us beyond the superficial environment of sanitized Sunday ministry to reveal the unhealthy exercise of pastoral authority that goes on behind the scenes in what I take to be a representative sampling of evangelical churches in America today.

The rest of the book (chaps. 8 and 9) wrestles with what is perhaps the most important question for recapturing in the church today Paul's vision for servant leadership: *What social contexts in our churches will most naturally facilitate a Jesus-like, other-centered approach to pastoral ministry?*

Some ways of doing church readily lend themselves to the healthy exercise of pastoral authority. Others do not. This was true in Paul's day (see chap. 6) and it is true in ours. The corporate culture that has influenced much of church life in America today, for example, tends to inhibit—rather than facilitate—Paul's cruciform vision for authentic Christian leadership.

It is not hard to see why. The business model typically assigns to the pastor sole authority, as the CEO of an institution with a board of directors (generally called elders or deacons) whose ecclesiology is often marked more by the values of the Wall Street Journal than by the letters of Paul.

The pastor in such a setting seldom has a handful of genuine friends in the church who know his strengths and weaknesses and who have permission to speak into his life. An environment like this provides few checks and balances on the potential abuse of pastoral authority.

Please note that I do not wish to minimize the personal responsibility of persons who leverage authority in hurtful ways. Each of us will answer for the ways we lead our people. This is not a book, however, about the inner life of the Christian leader. It is a book about the institutional structures of our churches, structures that often determine the relational contours of our ministry.

I will maintain that the answer to the question of social context (above, in italics) lies in a community of leaders. Ideally the local church should be led by a plurality of pastor-elders who relate to one another first as siblings in Christ, and who function only secondarily—and only within the parameters of that primary relational context—as vision-casting, decision-making leaders for the broader church family. This, in a nutshell, is the central thesis of the book.

The goal here is not to push for a single form of church polity, though some approaches to church government will find it more challenging to implement Paul's values than others. My agenda is broader and more inclusive. I am primarily concerned with function rather than form.

Wherever we land on the scriptural warrant for plurality leadership, and there is room for disagreement, the point here is that a leadership model that is highly relational will most naturally encourage the proper use of authority in local church ministry.

Accordingly, the book concludes by considering in some detail the pragmatic benefits of relational team leadership, for both pastors and their congregations.

The advantages for church leaders are rather straightforward, particularly where authority abuse is concerned. A community of leaders has the ability to maximize a pastor's strengths, while simultaneously intercepting and derailing potential abuses of spiritual authority before irreparable damage is done.

Less obvious, perhaps, but equally significant, are the benefits of team leadership for the broader church family. It is a simple fact that a team of pastors has the ability to model community—and the credibility to challenge their people to live in community—in ways a lone-ranger senior pastor, who answers to no one, will never have.

The social context of pastoral ministry thus has tremendous implications for the relational health of both local church leaders and the congregations in which they serve.

The Way of the Cross

There is a way back to the healthy exercise of authority in the local Christian church. It is the way of the cross. It is the way of Jesus, the most powerful being in the universe, who

> existing in the form of God,
> did not consider equality with God as something to
>   be used for His own advantage.
> Instead He emptied Himself by assuming the form
>   of a slave,

> taking on the likeness of men.
> And when He had come as a man in His external
>   form,
> He humbled Himself by becoming obedient to the
>   point of death
> —even to death on a cross. (Phil 2:6–8)

God intends, of course, for all Christians to follow in the footsteps of Jesus. Paul addressed this remarkable passage to the whole Philippian church, not just to its leaders.

Yet it is interesting to note that Philippians is the only letter in which Paul includes a specific address to community leaders ("the overseers and deacons," 1:1). Given current tendencies toward authority abuse in our churches, pastors and other persons of influence would do well to pay special attention to Philippians 2. Christ's other-centered attitude toward power and status has particular application to those of us in Christian leadership.

Because Jesus led the way to the cross, because he modeled to the extreme the kind of sacrificial, selfless leadership that God desires in his shepherds, God vindicated his Son by exalting him to the highest place, so that every sentient being would publicly acknowledge Jesus's position at the apex of the hierarchy of universal power and authority:

> For this reason God highly exalted Him and gave Him the name that is above every name, so that at the name of Jesus every knee will bow—of those who are in heaven and on earth and under the earth—and every tongue should confess that Jesus Christ is Lord, to the glory of God the Father. (vv. 9–11)

God's exaltation of Jesus assures us today that it is not those of us who minister in self-protective, self-promoting, ultimately hurtful and abusive ways that God will ultimately honor. It is those who follow in the footsteps of Jesus.

Pastors who model their ministries after Paul's cruciform

vision for authentic Christian leadership can shepherd their congregations with the confidence that they will one day hear from their Master the most welcome words a minister of the gospel could ever hope to hear: "Well done, good and faithful slave! . . . Share your master's joy!" (Matt 25:21, 23).

PART ONE

Power and Authority in the Roman World

The Social Context of the Pauline Mission

Putting People in Their Places

Social Stratification in the Roman World

The past is a foreign country: they do things differently there.—L. P. Hartley[1]

We cannot "get" Paul until we get Paul's world. This is particularly true of the apostle's ministry in Roman Philippi and Paul's relationship with the Philippian Christians.

Philippi was unique compared with the other places Paul visited on his missionary journeys. We encounter two distinctives in Luke's narrative of Paul's ministry in the colony in Acts 16 (vv. 12–40).

Note first that Philippi is the only place among Paul's journeys that Luke specifically called "a Roman colony" (Acts 16:12). This should give us pause at the outset. For at least eight other settlements Paul visited in Acts were also Roman colonies, yet Luke apparently did not feel compelled to identify them as such.

Second, when Paul and Silas began to minister in Philippi,

---

1. L. P. Hartley, *The Go-Between* (New York: NYRB Classics, 2002), 17.

local residents accused them of "promoting customs that are not legal for us as Romans to adopt or practice" (16:21).

Now it is fair to assume that the missionaries here promoted the same "customs"—namely, those associated with the gospel message—that they advanced at every stop along Paul's journeys. Only in Philippi, however, was Paul's message specifically described by his opponents as anti-Roman. Apparently for Luke, Philippi was in some ways distinct among the settlements Paul visited.

Philippi's uniqueness can be reduced to a single reality: the town was Roman in ways that other Pauline church-planting locales were not—especially the colony's social values. And familiarity with Roman relational priorities illuminates Paul's agenda in the letter to the Philippians—and the behavior of Paul and Silas in their ministry in Philippi in Acts 16—in some truly remarkable ways.

Social Stratification: A Look at the Pecking Order

One year the Hellerman family won a coveted door prize at our church's New Year's Eve party. A wealthy stockbroker had donated to our raffle a set of four tickets to a Los Angeles Dodgers baseball game.

These were not just any tickets. The tickets were four passes to Dodger Stadium's Dugout Club. The team's official website describes these premium seats as follows:

> The Dugout Club is the most exclusive club at Dodger Stadium and offers the best seats in the house. The Dugout Club is an all-inclusive experience and features access to an adjacent club with a martini lounge, a full bar, and restaurant style seating for an unlimited complimentary high-end buffet of Wolfgang Puck and Levy Restaurants food options and non-alcoholic beverages. You must be a Dugout Club Season Seat Holder to access this area of the stadium.[2]

---

2. Dodger Stadium Information - A to Z Guide, accessed February 1, 2013,

The official price for season tickets to the Dugout Club is not listed on the Dodgers' website. Persons who have purchased the package of 80+ games, however, are currently selling blocks of tickets on the internet for the handsome price of $500 per person, per game.

We went to the ballpark one afternoon the following summer. The Hellermans had a great time that evening experiencing the world of the rich and the famous. We sat tall and proud in those $500 seats, just a few feet from home plate.

But as we sat there, with our bellies stuffed with the free gourmet meal, pampered by attendants who delivered still more goodies at the wave of a hand, one thing was painfully apparent. The Hellermans were out of their league.

Joann and I belong to a completely different social class than the folks in the Dugout Club. Those people pay more for a single ticket to a baseball game than our family sets aside for several months' worth of entertainment.

The Pecking Order Then and Now

We are all familiar with the unequal positions people occupy in relation to others in human society. Different people belong to different classes. Social scientists refer to the phenomenon as social stratification, defined by James Littlejohn as "the name under which sociologists study inequality in society, i.e., the unequal distribution of goods and services, rights and obligations, power and prestige."[3]

All people groups exhibit some social verticality, even American society, as illustrated by the Hellermans' trip to Dodger Stadium. The degree of stratification varies significantly, however, from culture to culture.

Contemporary Western society enjoys a relatively egalitarian social environment compared with more traditional cultures, like

---

http://losangeles.dodgers.mlb.com/la/ballpark/information/index.jsp?content=guide

3. James Littlejohn, *Social Stratification* (London: Allen & Unwin, 1972), 9.

those of the New Testament world. The Romans, in particular, formed a highly stratified society, and they were quite self-conscious about the marked social inequality that characterized their relational universe.

Those at the top of the pecking order jealously guarded their social privileges. "Rank," insisted the Roman statesman Cicero, "must be preserved" (*Pro Plancio* 15). And Romans who possessed rank used their power and authority almost exclusively in the service of their personal and familial agendas.

Persons in the New Testament world divided and subdivided into numerous status groups, with the result that each of these social collectives occupied a very specific place along the Roman hierarchy of honor. In what follows, we will survey these groupings and their respective positions in the empire's pecking order. Then we will examine the resourceful ways in which persons in the ancient world advertised their status to others.

Certain articles of clothing were reserved for specific status groups, for example, so that a person's attire colorfully communicated his or her social standing to others in the public arena. People also sat in order of rank at private dinners and at public spectacles.

Perhaps most revealing is Rome's legal system. The social standing of a person on trial often influenced the outcome of a case more than the evidence itself. And when it came time to punish the guilty, judicial magistrates doled out different sentences for the same crimes, based solely on the rank of the person in view.

The people of Philippi had been socialized for generations to embrace the status-conscious, honor-oriented values of their cultural world. Paul encouraged the Philippians to adopt, instead, the radically alternative servant-oriented approach to human relations exemplified in the attitude and behavior of Jesus of Nazareth. As will become immediately apparent, Paul had his work cut out for him.

Status Groups in the Roman World
The Romans formally distinguished between several status

groups that marked out a person's place in the pecking order. The diagram outlines the primary class divisions in the ancient world at the time of Paul.

ELITES [@ 1,000,000]	
Senators	New Men Nobles
Equestrians	Most Renowned Most Accomplished Excellent
Decurions	Two Manly Men Other Decurions
NON-ELITES [@ 49,000,000]	
Freeborn	Citizens Non-Citizens
Freedmen	Citizens Non-Citizens
Slaves	

The greatest social chasm in the empire divided the population between what social analysts call elites and non-elites. The ancient world was essentially a two-class society in which a small percentage of persons controlled both the means of production and positions of power and influence.

You might recall that this is precisely how the New Testament writers viewed their social world:

Listen, my dear brothers: Didn't God choose the **poor** in this world to be **rich** in faith and heirs of the kingdom that He has promised to those who love Him? Yet you dishonored that **poor** man. Don't the **rich** oppress you and drag you into the courts? (Jas 2:5–6, emphasis mine)

Pagan authors made the same twofold distinction. The Roman senator Tacitus dismissed the non-elite masses as "rabble," reserving for his fellow elites the label "citizens of repute" (*Ann.* 3.36).

Notice, as well, that elites—the senatorial, equestrian, and decurion orders on the diagram (along with their extended families and numbers of hangers-on who rode their coattails of influence)—represented no more than 2 percent of an empire-wide population of some fifty million persons. The overwhelming majority of people were non-elites: slaves, freedpersons (manumitted slaves), and relatively poor freeborn peasants who struggled to survive from one harvest to the next, and who constituted the vast majority of the empire's population.

James had good reason to call these elites "rich." Cross-cultural comparisons of agrarian societies similar to the ancient Mediterranean world indicate that Rome's elite orders, along with the emperor himself, likely together controlled more than half of the empire's annual income. For the rest of the population, the need to depend upon one's god(s) for "daily bread" was hardly a theological abstraction—it was a reality of life.

One Roman satirist compared the chasm between the poor and the rich to the difference between "an ant and a camel" and bemoaned the vast difference in wealth and resources that characterized the two social classes:

> We should be less distressed about it [economic injustice], you may be sure, if we did not see the rich living in such bliss, who, though they have such gold, such silver in their safes, though they have all that clothing and own slaves and carriage-horses and tenements and farms, each and all in large numbers, not only have never shared them with us, but never deign even to notice ordinary people. (Lucian, *Saturnalia* 20)

A great deal of power and wealth was thus concentrated in the hands of a very few families and individuals in the world of the New Testament.

The practical implications of all this for Paul's ministry in Philippi are not insignificant. About five hundred persons of elite decurion status lived in the colony during the first century (the figure includes extended family members).

We will meet some of Philippi's local aristocrats when we survey the inscriptions from the colony in a later chapter. For now it will suffice to note that Paul ministered in a social environment where approximately 3 percent of Philippi's total population of fifteen thousand to twenty thousand persons had a virtual lock on all positions of power and influence. These elite families controlled much of the landed wealth in the colony, as well.

Rome's Elite Orders

Elites themselves subdivided into three distinct social classes: senators, equestrians (knights), and decurions. The early imperial period saw six hundred aristocrats fill the senate, and scholars estimate that approximately twenty thousand men occupied the equestrian order. Some 150,000 to 200,000 decurions, who were the leading citizens in the provinces, held positions of influence in local municipalities.

Rome's senate was replicated in miniature in the decurion councils of towns like Philippi, so it might help to think of the decurions that we will later encounter in Paul's ministry in Philippi as mini-senators (Luke called them "chief magistrates" in Acts 16).

The disdain that elites displayed toward non-elites (see Tacitus's reference to non-elites as "rabble," above) replicated itself when elites compared themselves with members of another—but lower—elite order.

Horace related an entertaining story about a decurion from the municipality of Fundi, who turned out, dressed in all his aristocratic regalia (see below on attire and social status), to greet a senatorial caravan that was traveling from Rome to Brundisium in southern Italy.

This local magistrate, Aufidius Luscus, presumably anticipated a degree of respect in the broader elite world. After all, the man was one of the most distinguished citizens in an important municipality—probably the biggest fish in Fundi's social pond.

Aufidius was sorely disappointed. Instead of esteem and affirmation, the Roman senator and his entourage only howled with laughter as they made their way by the now humiliated civic father (Horace, *Satires* 1.5.34–36).

Aufidius's experience would be rather like a senator from New York intentionally humiliating a local mayor during a public appearance in a small town in the western part of the state. Such an occurrence would be socially inappropriate, of course, in contemporary American society.

Welcome to the very different cultural values and social codes of Roman antiquity. Christianity was born in a world where honor was everything, and where persons in positions of power, like the unnamed senator in the above account, were quick to use their authority publicly to humiliate or abuse their inferiors, if by doing so they thought they could somehow enhance their own status or that of their extended families.

Qualifications for the Elite Orders

How did one become a Roman senator, equestrian, or decurion? The main qualifications were twofold: family of origin and wealth. With few exceptions the ancient world offered little opportunity for social mobility, as we know it in America today. A rural peasant—Jesus' disciple Peter, for example—could hardly aspire someday to enter one of Rome's three elite orders.

Social status in antiquity was determined by ancestry. So, as a general rule, persons were born into the three status groups outlined above. There were also minimum property qualifications for membership in each order:

> Senators — 1,000,000 sesterces
> Equestrians — 400,000 sesterces
> Decurions — 200,000 sesterces

Comparison of ancient and modern monetary values is not an

exact science, but it will help to know that a Roman foot soldier earned an annual pay of 900 sesterces during the New Testament era.

For reasons to be explored in the next chapter, it was extremely important for senators, equestrians, and decurions to meet these financial qualifications, and Roman leaders generally exercised great care to preserve the fiscal integrity of the orders. Claudius, for example, who was emperor when Paul planted the church at Philippi in 49, cleaned house in the Roman senate, ejecting from the order all members whose bankrolls had fallen below the minimum property qualification of one million sesterces (Tacitus, *Ann.* 12.52).

Further Social Stratification among Roman Elites

The social playing field was not level even within each of the elite orders. As the diagram indicates, senators, equestrians, and decurions further subdivided into distinct social categories.

Senators differentiated between men who had come from a long line of senatorial blood and so-called new men, who were the first in their families to ascend to Rome's highest order. The former, known in Latin as *nobiles,* persistently flaunted their superiority.

Thus, Cicero, a "new man" who lacked a noble pedigree, was painfully aware "with what jealousy, with what dislike, the merit and energy of new men are regarded by certain of the nobles" (*2 Verr.* 5.71).

Equestrians, on their part, fell into at least three substrata: "excellent," "most accomplished," and "most renowned." Pontius Pilate, a Roman elite familiar to us from the Gospel narratives, belonged to the "excellent" class of Roman knights.

At the top of the decurion order were the duumviri (from the Latin, meaning "two manly men"), who led local decurion town councils in the provinces. Aufidius Luscus, mentioned above, was likely a duumvir in Fundi. So were the magistrates who ordered Paul and Silas to be beaten with rods in Philippi (Acts 16:22–23).

The Non-Elite Pecking Order

Non-elites inhabited a carefully mapped out social universe, as well. The greatest chasm stood between free persons and slaves. Estimates of the slave population in the empire during the New Testament period vary from two million to as many as ten million (approximately 4 to 20 percent of the population).

Paul's contemporaries made much of the class distinction between slave and free, and the position of slaves in the pecking order of antiquity is particularly relevant to the apostle's strategy in Philippians.

Philippians 2:7 is the only place in Paul's writings where he called Christ a "slave" (Greek, *doulos*). Philippians is also the only letter in which Paul introduced himself as a "slave" (*doulos*), without also including the accompanying designation "apostle" (1:1; compare Rom 1:1). We will explore these informative anomalies in some detail in chapter 4.

The Romans also carefully demarcated between citizens and those who lacked the citizen franchise. This issue also proves illuminating for Paul's relationship with the Philippians, since the population breakdown of Philippi was highly exceptional where Roman citizenship was concerned.

A census in A.D. 47 identified just under seven million citizens, approximately 14 percent of the total population of the empire. Because Augustus had founded Philippi with Roman citizen soldiers (30 B.C.), however, Paul encountered in the colony a settlement that boasted roughly 40 percent Roman citizens. So important was citizen status to the colony's residents that fully one-half of the surviving inscriptions contain some reference to the Roman citizen tribe of the person in view.

This explains why the missionaries' Roman citizenship played a central role as events unfolded during Paul and Silas's activities in the colony (Acts 16:20–21, 35–40). It is no accident, moreover, that only in Philippians did Paul discuss the Christian life in terms of "citizenship." For example, in Philippians 1:27, the Greek verb translated "live your life" (HCSB, NRSV) literally means "live as a citizen." Elsewhere in the letter, we discover that the citizenship Paul has in view is "our citizenship...in heaven" (3:20).

Summary: The Social Hierarchy

Social stratification occurs among humans wherever two or more are gathered. We invariably seek to define ourselves in relation to one another in ways that generate some kind of social pecking order.

As noted above, however, the nature and degree of social verticality vary significantly from culture to culture. Social scientists have determined that advanced agrarian societies, such as ancient Rome, exhibited more in way of social stratification than any other kind of society. Gerhard Lenski notes,

> One fact impresses itself on almost any observer of agrarian societies, especially on one who views them in a broadly comparative perspective. This is the fact of *marked social inequality.* Without exception, one finds pronounced differences in power, privilege, and honor associated with mature agrarian economies.[4]

Such was the world of Mediterranean antiquity. As we have seen, the Roman empire's population divided and subdivided into an ever-increasing array of groups and subgroups, in order to clearly demarcate the social pecking order. And the Romans devised some creative ways to publicly broadcast the social hierarchy, as well.

Putting People in Their Place: Public Marks of Social Status

I have six wooden plaques in my office detailing various university degrees I earned over the years, along with several other

---

4. Gerhard E. Lenski, *Power and Privilege: A Theory of Social Stratification* (New York: McGraw-Hill, 1966), 210. Lenski's italics.

awards from Biola University for scholarship and faculty mentoring. They are my public marks of social status.

I have always struggled, as a Christian leader, to figure out what to do with these tangible indicators of vocational advancement. I suppose I could attach the plaques to a conspicuous wall in my office at the university (at eye level, of course) so that every student who comes to meet with me during office hours would see them. But that strikes me as a blatant exercise in social posturing and intellectual arrogance.

At the other extreme, maybe I ought to stash all my tokens of academic status away in a drawer somewhere and forget about them. That's what I did for a number of years. But that didn't seem quite right either.

So, for now, for better or for worse, my degrees and awards are displayed high up on top of a six-foot bookshelf in my church office. Few people besides me will ever see them there. But they are on display.

My struggle to know what to do with these wooden plaques will resonate with many of my readers. We live in a culture that generally discourages self-promotion. We feel awkward tooting our own horn. And as Christians we are particularly sensitive to the need to be humble about our achievements, and rightly so.

As we will discover, the discomfort that many of us feel about publicly proclaiming our social status was not experienced by the ancient Romans. The Romans delighted in advertising their status and achievements, and they were remarkably resourceful in devising ways to indicate where various individuals fit into the pecking order. Three public marks of social status in particular identified persons according to rank throughout the empire: attire, seating at public and private events, and the judicial system.

Dressed for Success: Clothing as a Mark of Social Status

When I was in the fourth grade, long-sleeved wool shirts boasting pockets with flaps on the front were the rage among my grammar school peers. My parents wondered why in the world a Southern California kid needed a long-sleeved wool shirt to wear to school, but after a whole lot of pleading and cajoling, I finally persuaded them to buy me a Pendleton.

The problem was that my Pendleton was not actually a Pendleton. The name-brand wool shirts were much too expensive for the Hellerman family budget, so Mom bought me a knock-off.

I don't think I even made it to recess that morning before someone noticed. "Hey, Joey, is *that* a Pendleton?" one of my well-heeled schoolmates imperiously inquired. Ouch!

Most of us are quite aware that a relationship exists between clothing and status in American culture today. One look at a fashion magazine like *Bazaar* or *Vogue* reminds us that wealthy people array themselves in ways that the rest of us cannot afford.

The connection between clothing and rank in the ancient world was, in many cases, formally institutionalized, and it was profoundly more significant than is the case in the West today. As an entree into Roman convictions about attire, consider the following story.

The Roman Citizen Toga

At some point while the apostle Paul was engaged in his missionary work in the East, an illuminating debacle erupted in the city of Rome. A trial was in process to determine whether or not a certain individual was a Roman citizen.

Soon, however, the man's citizenship was no longer the major point of contention. His clothing was. It seems that proceedings suddenly ground to a halt when a debate arose between the advocates about whether or not the defendant should be allowed to wear his citizen toga at the trial.

The attorney defending the man's claim to Roman citizenship insisted that his client be allowed the toga. The prosecuting counsel argued the contrary, contending that the man ought to be dressed in a Greek mantle in the Forum, since his citizenship was still in doubt.

The emperor stepped in and resolved the dispute. Claudius, "with the idea of showing absolute impartiality, made him change his garb several times, according as he was accused or defended" (Suetonius, *Claud.* 15).

We chuckle at the emperor's clever solution to a seemingly intractable dilemma. Ancient readers would not have been so easily amused, for the toga functioned as the preeminent visual symbol of Roman citizenship in the ancient world.

Young males first donned the toga during an important rite of passage that marked the transition from childhood to adulthood, when they were formally enrolled in their Roman citizen tribe. A non-citizen wearing a citizen toga was a direct affront to Roman social sensibilities—thus the struggle, in the legal proceedings outlined above, to determine the proper attire for a man whose citizen status was in question.

The toga surfaces often as a status symbol in Roman literature. Augustus, the founder of the colony at Philippi, was particularly concerned to keep his citizens properly attired. The garment figures prominently among a series of reforms instituted by the emperor. The Roman biographer Suetonius claims that Augustus desired also to revive the ancient fashion of dress, and once when he saw in an assembly a throng of men in dark cloaks (the toga was white), he cried out indignantly,

> "Behold them, Romans, lords of the world, the nation clad in the toga," [sarcastically quoting Virgil, *Aenied* 1.282] and he directed the aediles never again to allow anyone to appear in the Forum or its neighbourhood except in the toga and without a cloak. (Suetonius, *Aug.* 40)

Augustus reinforced such legislation with his own dress and propaganda. In an important study of the social power of images in the Roman world, Paul Zanker observes, "It is astonishing how many portraits of Augustus made during his lifetime, both on coins … and as honorific statues, show him veiled in a toga."[5]

---

5. Paul Zanker, *The Power of Images in the Age of Augustus,* trans. Alan Shapiro (Ann Arbor: University of Michigan Press, 1988), 127.

Attire and Roman Status Groups

Rome's citizen toga was further decorated according to the social status of the person wearing it. Members of the senatorial order, for example, wore a toga adorned with a broad purple stripe (Latin, *latus clavus*). By the time of Augustus, the *latus clavus* had become the quintessential public mark of membership in the senatorial class.

Equestrians, too, were easily identified by their attire. Their togas boasted a narrow purple stripe that distinguished them from senators above and from common citizens below. An equestrian also wore a gold ring on his finger to mark out his place in the social hierarchy. Only the knights could wear these rings, and entry into the order was sometimes described in the literature simply as receiving "the honour of the gold ring" (Suetonius, *Galba*, 14).

Nowhere was the connection between rank and attire more vividly apparent than at a senatorial funeral. A funeral provided a man's surviving descendants with an opportunity not only to broadcast the rank of the deceased but also to remind their aristocratic peers of the accomplishments of the family's noble ancestors of generations past. And all this was achieved through the visible vehicle of clothing.

The funeral ceremony was a fascinating one, and I will let the ancient Romans describe it themselves:

> [W]hen any distinguished member of the family dies they [surviving family members] take them [ancestor masks "reproducing with remarkable fidelity both the features and complexion of the deceased"] to the funeral, putting them on men who seem to them to bear the closest resemblance to the original in stature and carriage. These representatives wear togas, with a purple border if the deceased was a consul or praetor, whole purple if he was a censor, and embroidered with gold if he had celebrated a triumph or achieved anything similar. (Polybius, *Histories* 6.53)

> For they employ actors who through a man's whole life have carefully observed his carriage and the several peculiarities of

his appearance. In like fashion each of the dead man's ancestors takes his place in the funeral procession, with such robes and insignia as enable the spectators to distinguish from the portrayal how far each had advanced in the *cursus honorum* [Latin, literally "honors race"] and had had a part in the dignities of the state. (Diodorus of Sicily, *Library of History* 31.25.2)

Harriet Flower, a social historian who has studied Roman funeral practices in some detail, appropriately observes, "The public part of an aristocratic funeral, which comprised the procession of ancestors and the funeral eulogy in the Forum, was reserved for the families of office-holders and set them apart from ordinary citizens in a conspicuous way."[6]

Aristocratic funerals thus served powerfully to reinforce the marked verticality of Rome's social landscape. And clothing played a central role in these ostentatious public displays of status and power.

The connection between rank and clothing was not restricted to the vicinity of Rome. Like other elite values, it was replicated in miniature wherever Rome ruled. In the provinces we encounter lesser elites—and non-elites, as well—donning clothing appropriate to their social status.

Apuleius, in his *Metamorphosis*, narrated an encounter, in Thessaly, between his protagonist Lucius and one of Lucius's old acquaintances. After Lucius was questioned concerning his well-being, he responded, "But what about you? I'm glad you have achieved success. I see, for example, that you have attendants and fasces and clothing which befits a magistrate." "Yes," the man replied, "I'm in charge of the market here; I hold the position of aedile" (Apuleius, *Met.* 1.24–25).

Lucius's friend in the above encounter likely boasted a rank identical to that held by the local magistrates encountered by Paul and Silas in Philippi (Acts 16). His attire graphically communicated his social status to all who passed his way.

---

6. Harriet I. Flower, *Ancestor Masks and Aristocratic Power in Roman Culture* (Oxford: Clarendon, 1996), 127.

Even non-elite freedmen had socially appropriate attire. Just as the gold ring marked entry into the equestrian class, so also a "cap of liberty" symbolized the freedom gained by a slave at manumission.

The Latin term *pilleus*, used to describe a close-fitting felt cap shaped like half an egg, could (like the term "ring" for the equestrian class, above) serve as a synecdoche for the whole idea of a slave acquiring his freedom. Thus, Roman generals at times "summoned the slaves to arms by showing them a cap of liberty" (Valerius Maximus 8.6.2).

Christian Writers on Clothing as a Status Symbol

Christian leaders tried to challenge the connection between attire and status that was so central to their social world. Perhaps most familiar is a passage from the letter of James:

> My brothers, do not show favoritism as you hold on to the faith in our glorious Lord Jesus Christ. For example, a man comes into your meeting wearing a gold ring and dressed in fine clothes, and a poor man dressed in dirty clothes also comes in. If you look with favor on the man wearing the fine clothes and say, "Sit here in a good place," and yet you say to the poor man, "Stand over there," or, "Sit here on the floor by my footstool," haven't you discriminated among yourselves and become judges with evil thoughts? (2:1–4)

The idea of clothing as a public status symbol sheds considerable light on Paul's strategy in a key passage in Philippians. In a world where appearance was inextricably linked to rank, a person who existed in the "form of God," and who then chose to take on the "form of a slave," would have been acting in a manner profoundly at odds with the social values of the dominant culture (Phil 2:6–7).

In ancient literature the term "form" (Greek *morphe*) refers fundamentally to an individual's "outward appearance." A translation like the NIV's "in very nature God" is therefore somewhat misleading, since it implies that Paul was emphasizing the "inside" (ontology) of the preincarnate Christ and not the "outside" (visible appearance).

What Paul was highlighting in the phrase "form of God" is not, first and foremost, the deity of the Christ, although a secondary argument can be made along those lines.

Paul had more directly in view Christ's visible appearance in his preincarnate state. And when persons in Paul's audience thought about outward appearance, what came immediately to mind was the cultural script outlined above, that is, the relationship between attire and social status.

A recent commentator, in fact, paraphrases the phrase "was in the form of God" (Phil 2:6) as follows: "clothed in the garments of divine majesty and splendour."[7] If Peter O'Brien is correct on this point—and many believe that he is—then the correlation between attire and rank in the Roman value system indicates that Paul in Philippians 2:6 sought intentionally to emphasize the exalted social status of the preexistent Christ.

This, in turn, renders Jesus's willingness to divest himself of his robe of glory and don, instead, the garb of "a slave" (v. 7) all the more socially anomalous. We will return to Philippians 2 and expand upon these remarks—and their implications for the use of power and authority in our churches today—in some detail in a later chapter.

Jockeying for Position: Seating at Banquets and Public Events in the Ancient World

The passage from James, above, compels us to consider a second public mark of honor in the ancient world, namely, seating at private and public events.

A host would typically assign seats at a private banquet according to the social status of the persons invited. The seating arrangement thus visibly publicized to all who were present the

---

7. Peter T. O'Brien, *The Epistle to the Philippians,* NIGTC (Grand Rapids: Eerdmans, 1991), 211.

relative status of the guests. When the food was served, it, too, was carefully distributed according to social rank.

Pliny, a consular senator who served in the province of Bithynia, described a dinner party he attended at the villa of a fellow elite:

> The best dishes were set in front of himself [the host] and a select few, and cheap scraps of food before the rest of the company. He had even put the wine into tiny little flasks, divided into three categories, not with the idea of giving his guests the opportunity of choosing, but to make it impossible for them to refuse what they were given. One lot was intended for himself and for us, another for his lesser friends (all his friends are graded) and the third for his and our freedmen. (*Ep.* 2.6)

Can you imagine today hosting a dinner party at which you serve your guests varying qualities of food and drink, depending on how your "friends are graded"?

Hosts from every level of society took care to preserve the social hierarchy at mealtime. We are informed that the emperor Augustus, for example, "gave dinner parties constantly and always formally, with great regard to the rank and personality of his guests" (Suetonius, *Aug.* 74).

A Familiar Passage in an Unfamiliar World

Given such practices at mealtime, we are not surprised to find James and John jockeying for the best seats at the eschatological banquet: "Allow us to sit at Your right and at Your left in Your glory" (Mark 10:37).

Most of us react rather indignantly to what we take to be a brazen request on the part of the two disciples. We are quick to assume that James and John should have known better. After all, we certainly wouldn't ask such a thing.

The opposite is the case. Two thousand years of Christian influence upon Western civilization have equipped us with a deep sensitivity to the need for humility in human relations—a sensitivity wholly lacking among persons socialized to embrace the honor culture of Mediterranean antiquity.

Humility was not a virtue in the Roman world. And we should not be at all surprised at the brothers' request. James and John were doing what their culture had taught them to do from infancy, namely, to do everything within their power to enhance their honor and that of their extended family.

What is striking in Mark 10—what is radically countercultural in the story—is not the disciples' request. It is Jesus's response later in the dialogue: "But it must not be like that among you. On the contrary, whoever wants to become great among you must be your servant, and whoever wants to be first among you must be a slave to all" (Mark 10:43–44).

Jesus's challenge to James and John would have struck Mark's honor-seeking, self-serving Roman readers as utter nonsense—indeed, if put into practice, social suicide.

The Social Function of Meals

Meals establish and reinforce relational boundaries in all cultures, and the study of table fellowship has become something of a cottage industry among New Testament scholars and others interested in Mediterranean social values.

Richard Saller underscores an important difference, however, between modern practices and the way mealtime worked in the ancient world:

> Throughout the ages dining has served as a context for the advertisement of status, but in recent times this has more often been accomplished by the exclusion of unworthies; in Rome humble men were invited, even paid, to attend so that they might pay deference or (from the viewpoint of the jaundiced observer) suffer as victims to displays of *superbia* by their hosts.[8]

---

8. Richard Saller, "Status and Patronage," in *The Cambridge Ancient History,* ed. Alan K. Bowman et al., vol. 11 (Cambridge: Cambridge University Press, 2000), 830.

Saller's point is straightforward. In contemporary society we tend to share meals with people like ourselves. The Romans, in contrast, often invited persons across the social spectrum to their banquets. Aelius Aristides, a Roman elite, tells us why: "the existence of inferiors is an advantage to superiors since they will be able to point out those over whom they are superior" (*Orations* 24.34).

We encounter the reflections of one of Aristides's "inferiors"—the view from below, so to speak—in an excerpt from the Roman satirist Juvenal. Here a non-elite client described how the lower classes are treated at the dinner parties of the rich and famous. The passage drips with sarcasm:

> First of all, remember this: when you are invited to dinner, you are being repaid in full for all your earlier services. Food is your payment for serving as a client to the great. Your master, I mean patron, records these infrequent dinner invitations under "debts discharged." And thus every two months or so, when he feels like using a normally neglected client to fill up an empty spot on the lowest couch, he says: "Come and join us." Your greatest wish is fulfilled! What more can you ask for? . . . Ah, and what a dinner you get! The wine is so bad that even new wool won't absorb it. . . . The bread is so hard you can barely break it, a mouldy crust of petrified dough that you can't bite into without cracking your teeth. Of course, the master of the house is served soft, white bread made from the finest flour. (Juvenal, *Satires* 5.12–22, 24, 25, 67–71)[9]

Front Row Center: Seating at Public Events

When we move from the dining hall to the stadium or the theater, we encounter the same concern to seat persons by rank. The Romans took particular care to ensure that theater patrons were neatly arranged in rows according to social status.

---

9. Jo-Ann Shelton, trans. and ed., *As the Romans Did: A Sourcebook in Roman Social History* (New York: Oxford University Press, 1988), 17.

Senators alone occupied the first row (the orchestra). The next fourteen rows of theater seats were reserved for the equestrian order. Urban citizen commoners sat in yet another location, separated from elites, and set apart from non-citizens, women, and children.

Not all willingly complied. Augustus felt compelled to respond to an incident in a crowded amphitheater at Puteoli, for example, where locals refused to give up their prime seats to a Roman senator. A senatorial decree resulted, which sought to reinforce the social hierarchy in public settings across the empire:

> In consequence of this the senate decreed that, whenever any public show was given anywhere, the first row of seats should be reserved for senators; and at Rome he [Augustus] would not allow the envoys of the free and allied nations to sit in the orchestra, since he was informed that even freedmen were sometimes appointed. He separated the soldiery from the people. He assigned special seats to the married men of the commons, to boys under age their own section and the adjoining one to their preceptors; and he decreed that no one wearing a dark cloak should sit in the middle of the house. (Suetonius, *Aug.* 44)

Notice in the citation the prohibition of orchestral seating for foreign dignitaries of "allied nations." Some decades later, during the reign of Nero, a couple of visiting barbarians nearly got themselves in a world of trouble by brazenly sitting out of rank in Pompey's theater in Rome. The Roman elite, Tacitus, described the events (*Ann.* 13.54).

A Pair of Bold Barbarians

Verritus and Malorix, two ambassadors from the Frisian people of Germany, had traveled to the capital to appeal a recent Roman decree that, in their view, unfairly restricted their tribal boundaries. While waiting to see Nero (this could sometimes take days), the Germans enjoyed a sight-seeing tour of Rome. At one point the visitors entered Pompey's theater while a performance was underway.

The theater in Rome was a massive structure, seating some 17,500 persons, so the Frisian guests likely went unnoticed for some time. Tacitus, with his typical disdain for persons of lower status, assures us that the barbarians "had not sufficient knowledge to be amused by the play." What caught their attention, instead, was the social stratification of the audience, evident in the seating arrangements—what Tacitus called "the distinctions between the orders."

The Frisians began enthusiastically to inquire "where were the knights?—where was the senate?" Then they happened to notice a few men in non-Roman attire (no citizen toga with the broad purple stripe) seated among the senators, and they inquired as to their identity.

Much to their delight the Germans discovered that these oddly dressed men in the orchestra were foreigners like themselves. Tacitus tells us what happened next:

> [O]n hearing that this [permission for foreigners to sit among the senate] was a compliment paid to the envoys of nations distinguished for their courage and for friendship to Rome, [the Frisian visitors] exclaimed that no people in the world ranked before Germans in arms or loyalty, went down, and took their seats among the Fathers.

In a single move the Frisians violated a key aspect of Roman social protocol that had been enshrined in law for generations, and they did so in the presence of thousands of Roman citizens and others who sat "in their places," so to speak, during the performance that day in Pompey's theater.

The drama in the audience was suddenly much more charged with excitement than the drama on the stage. How would the crowd respond to such a bold social insult? How would the emperor and the senatorial elites react?

Because the offenders were barbarians who knew no better, the German visitors got away with it. As Tacitus relates, "The action was taken in good part by the onlookers, as a trait of primitive

45

impetuosity and generous rivalry." Even Nero joined the party, affirming the behavior of the Germans by granting each of the visitors Roman citizenship before finally hearing their appeal and sending them on their way back home (Tacitus, *Ann.* 13.54).

Severe Penalties for Sitting Out of Order

For persons who knew better a completely different set of standards applied. Early in Augustus's reign the emperor noticed a common soldier sitting among the knights in the fourteen rows. He immediately had the man ejected (Suetonius, *Aug.* 14). Even equestrians themselves who had lost their wealth, and who technically no longer qualified for the order, "did not venture to view the games from the fourteen rows through fear of the penalty of the law" (Suetonius, *Aug.* 40).

Regulations in the provinces were equally stringent, and the penalties were at times more severe. When we consider the contextualization of Roman social values in the colony of Philippi in chapter 3, we will confront an informative phenomenon that I label "value replication." Value replication means, in brief, that Rome's social priorities and practices reproduced themselves in miniature in local municipalities throughout the provinces.

Nowhere is value replication more obvious than in the practice of seating according to rank. During the New Testament era, the empire boasted nearly a thousand cities. Although some had a population of less than fifteen thousand residents, even the smallest of these settlements typically had a local theater where, just like at Pompey's theater in Rome, people took their seats according to social status.

Consider the social blueprint for the theater in the Roman colony of Urso, in Spain. In the orchestra sat the decurions (local civic elites), along with any Roman senators who happened to be visiting the settlement. The next set of seats was assigned to full citizens of the colony. Immediately behind the citizens sat noncitizens who dwelt on territory controlled by the colony. The least preferable seats were left for outsiders, generally travelers or inhabitants of nearby settlements.

Most telling are the penalties enforced upon persons who sat out of rank in the theater at Urso. The fine for compromising the social order in the colony's theater was set at a whopping five thousand sesterces.

We gain an immediate appreciation of the severity of the penalty when we recall, again, that a citizen foot soldier in the Roman army was paid a total of nine hundred sesterces per year. Imagine being fined the equivalent of five years' wages for sitting in the wrong section at an NFL football game!

The Romans were obviously quite serious about seating according to rank at public events. As Peter Garnsey and Richard Saller, two noted social historians, observe, "[S]omething more was at stake than getting a good seat to watch the show."[10] That "something," of course, was the proclamation—and preservation—of the social pecking order.

Order in the Court: The Roman Legal System

Trials in Rome had become public spectacles of sorts, where locals gathered in the Forum to hear the greatest forensic orators of their day, and where a bystander in the audience might even venture to join the proceedings and, in some cases, determine the outcome of the trial itself.

On one occasion a large crowd listened intently to a series of witnesses testify against an unnamed defendant. Valerius Maximus (8.5.6), the ancient writer telling the story, failed to name the particular charges against the man, which anyhow proved to be irrelevant to the final verdict in the case.

It seems that a certain Publius Servilius, a Roman senator who happened to be passing by, suddenly interrupted the proceedings and insisted upon taking the witness stand himself. No one dared object. The author of the account tells us why: Publius was an "ex-Consul and ex-Censor, triumphator, who added the surname of Isauricus to the titles of his ancestors."

---

10. Peter Garnsey and Richard Saller, *The Roman Empire: Economy, Society, and Culture* (Berkeley: University of California Press, 1987), 117.

We will consider the significance of these offices in some detail later. For the present we simply note that the titles mark out Publius Servilius as one of the most highly respected aristocrats of his day.

Publius had absolutely nothing to contribute that was directly relevant to the charges against the defendant. He readily admitted as much at the outset: "Gentlemen of the jury, I don't know where this man on trial comes from or what life he has led or how rightly or wrongly he stands accused."

Why, then, we might wonder, did our esteemed Roman senator barge in on the proceedings to begin with? As it turns out, Publius took the witness stand not because of what he knew but because of who he was. And what Publius had to say influenced the outcome of the case far more than any piece of hard evidence.

The aristocrat's comments, along with the response of the jurors, speak volumes about the social function of power and status in the Roman world. Here is what Publius had to say:

> Gentlemen of the jury, I don't know where this man on trial comes from or what life he has led or how rightly or wrongly he stands accused: I know only this much, that when he met me as I was traveling on the Laurentine Way in a pretty narrow passage, he refused to get off his horse. Whether that concerns you as a jury, you will judge. I thought I ought not to keep it back. (Valerius Maximus, 8.5.6)

Really, Mr. Senator? You interrupted the proceedings to tell us that? Modern readers will find the senator's observations wholly immaterial to the case at hand.

Our evaluation only serves to show, however, how far removed we are from Roman social values and priorities. Those presiding over the trial in the Forum that day viewed the testimony of Publius Servilius in markedly different terms.

The jurors immediately declared the anonymous defendant guilty—"almost," Valerius informs us, "without hearing the other witnesses." The reason:

They were impressed by Servilius' eminence and his grave indignation at the neglect of his dignity and believed that someone who did not know how to respect our leading men would rush into any villainy. (Valerius Maximus, 8.5.6)

The unfortunate defendant lost his case because he had dared to insult a member of Rome's esteemed nobility in an incident completely unrelated to the charges at hand.

This narrative grates severely against modern judicial sensibilities, where on paper, at any rate, we insist that all persons are created equal and that equal justice should be available to all. The story makes perfect sense, however, in the socially stratified world of Roman antiquity, where honor counted for everything and where *dignitas* (Latin, "status") often prevailed over *veritas* (Latin, "truth") in court cases like the one related above.

It would be misleading to conclude from stories like the one related above that the Romans failed to consider genuine evidence that might impinge upon the outcome of a trial. Roman magistrates did not ignore the facts. They just took into account more than what we would call "evidence" when they judged a case. That something extra, of course, was social status.

The great orator Cicero insisted accordingly that the courts ought to treat a person "in a manner befitting the justice of his case *and his own position*" (*Fam.* 13.57.2, italics mine). Justice could never be blind in the Roman world. It always had to cast a long glance at the rank of the individuals involved.

Punishment According to Rank

The connection between rank and justice surfaces not only in the influence that an aristocrat like Publius Servilius could exercise on the outcome of a case. The judicial system in Roman antiquity also sentenced the guilty according to social status.

Roman citizens, for example, enjoyed protection against public flogging, torture, and certain kinds of executions (crucifixion, for example). Non-citizens did not.

The legal disadvantage faced by non-citizens surfaces often

in ancient stories about the Christian persecutions. According to tradition, Paul, a Roman citizen, was beheaded. Peter, a non-citizen, was crucified.

In the early second century, Pliny, the governor of Bithynia, executed non-citizens who confessed Jesus as Lord but sent citizens to Rome, where they had an opportunity to appeal to the emperor (*Ep.* 10.96). A later pogrom in Lyons under Marcus Aurelius saw wild animals devour non-citizen Christians in the arena, while Romans who remained faithful to Jesus were summarily beheaded (Eusebius, *Hist. eccl.* 5.1.47).

The themes of justice and citizen status intersect in an illuminating way in the story of Paul's ministry in Philippi (Acts 16). Based on the complaints of the mob (vv. 20–21), Philippi's local decurions apparently assumed that Paul and Silas were not Roman citizens. So they flogged and imprisoned the missionaries for stirring up trouble in the colony (vv. 22–23).

As events unfolded, the magistrates were shocked to discover that the persons they had beaten were, in fact, citizens of Rome. Now we might wonder why Paul and Silas failed to appeal to their citizen status to avoid the beating in the first place, and we will consider this anomaly in chapter 4. Here I simply wish to underscore the sudden and profound change of attitude on the part of the colony's magistrates.

According to Luke, these esteemed local elites "were afraid when they heard that [Paul and Silas] were Roman citizens; so they came and apologized to them. And they took them out and asked them to leave the city" (vv. 38–39). The damage control these city fathers undertook speaks volumes about the legal privileges enjoyed by Roman citizens—and about the trouble a local magistrate could get into if he ignored the difference between citizen and non-citizen while doling out justice in the provinces.

By the second century the divide between citizen and non-citizen had evolved into a legal demarcation between elites (Latin, *honestiores*) and non-elites (Latin, *humiliores*), and harsh penalties once applied only to slaves were now applied to humble free persons. Consider a representative piece of legislation:

Those who break into a temple at night in order to pillage or plunder it are thrown to wild animals. But if they steal some minor object from the temple during the day, if they are *honestiores* they are exiled; if they are *humiliores* they are condemned to the mines. In the case of people accused of violating sepulchers, if they actually drag out the bodies or remove the bones, if they are *humiliores* they are punished with the ultimate torture; if they are *honestiores* they are exiled to an island. For other violations, *honestiores* are expelled and *humiliores* are condemned to the mines. (FIRA 2, p. 405 [Paulus, *Opinions* 5.19–19a])[11]

A modern equivalent might see a college-educated shoplifter receive a small fine for his crime, while an uneducated person gets sentenced to ten years in prison for the same offense. Such a scenario—unthinkable in America today—would make perfect sense to a first-century Roman elite.

Nothing Is More Unequal Than Equality Itself

Pliny, an esteemed Roman senator, colorfully illustrated Rome's unquestioning affirmation of social inequality in a revealing charge he gives to a fellow elite. Pliny exhorted a provincial governor in Spain to take the utmost care in dispensing justice to preserve "the distinctions of orders and dignity." Why? Because, as Pliny insisted, "if these distinctions are confused, nothing is more unequal than equality itself" (*Ep.* 9.5).[12]

Some centuries later Pascal would observe, "Not being able to make that which is just strong, man has made that which is strong just."[13] These sentiments, so offensive to the modern mind, appeared perfectly reasonable to elites in agrarian societies like Pliny's Rome or Pascal's medieval Europe.[14]

---

11. Shelton, *As the Romans Did,* 12-13.
12. Garnsey and Saller, *The Roman Empire,* 118.
13. Pascal, "Pensées," ed. Brunschvieg, fragm. 298 (cited by Lenski, *Power and Privilege,* 43).
14. Pascal, living in a world that had seen more than a millennium of Christian influence, regrets these realities; Pliny affirms them.

Conclusion

Our snapshot look at social stratification in Roman antiquity is now complete. We examined the numerous status groups that occupied distinct positions in the empire's relational hierarchy. And we explored three ways—attire, seating at public and private events, and the judicial system—in which the Romans publicly advertised their rank, and in which ancient elites reinforced the social status quo.

It is not by accident that we have begun what is ultimately a study of the use of power and authority in the Christian church with a chapter on Roman social stratification.

Acute social stratification guaranteed that certain individuals in the ancient world would be highly privileged with respect to power and status, relative to others in their social networks. It is a truism, moreover, that deep disparity in power and authority invites the abuse of such privilege on the part of those who possess it.

We will not be surprised to discover, then, that persons with social capital in the New Testament world tended to leverage their status in the service of their own agendas, generally disregarding the fallout of their behavior in the lives of people beyond the boundaries of their extended kinship groups.

This widespread but regrettable phenomenon manifested itself among Rome's aristocrats, it defined interactions among local elite families in Philippi, and it threatened the relational integrity of the Christian community in the colony, as well.

Paul clearly anticipated the potential damage that these social dynamics could inflict upon the church in Philippi. Building on the life and teachings of Jesus, Paul responded with an understanding of community life—and a vision for church leaders—that intentionally subverted the relational values of the dominant culture, where power, status, and the exercise of authority were concerned.

In chapters 4, 5, and 6, we will unpack Paul's vision in some detail. The final portion of the book then draws upon the biblical materials to address issues of authority abuse in our churches today. Paul's take on Christian leadership and community in ancient Philippi proves to be remarkably relevant for the people of God today.

But we are getting ahead of ourselves. For the present we must remain among Paul's Roman contemporaries to fill out our picture of their social world.

Persons in Mediterranean antiquity vigorously competed with one another for honor and social status in the public arena. The next chapter considers the dynamics of social mobility and the quest for public honor that characterized daily life in the ancient world.

Questions for Reflection

1. Social stratification is not unique to the ancient Romans. To some degree it can be found in every culture. Describe the pecking order of the society in which you live. Who is at the top? Who is at the bottom? Think about your school or place of employment. Is there a formal hierarchy of some kind in that environment? Perhaps a pecking order that is unexpressed but nevertheless present?

2. The Romans reinforced the social order by the way they dressed, where they sat at public and private events, and how they treated one another in the law courts. How can you tell "who's who" in our society? What are the public marks of social status?

3. In a number of ways social stratification in the Roman world was quite different than it is in America today. List as many of these differences as you can from the chapter.

4. Blaise Pascal wrote, "Not being able to make that which is just strong, man has made that which is strong just."[15] How was that true in the ancient Roman world? It what ways is it still true in our culture today?

5. Hellerman claims that "deep disparity in power and authority invites the abuse of such privilege on the part of those who possess it." Do you agree? What have you experienced, in this regard, as you have interacted with persons in authority in your life (parents, teachers, supervisors, pastors)?

---

15. Pascal, "Pensées," ed. Brunschvieg, fragm. 298.

Running the Race for Glory

The *Cursus Honorum* and the Roman Quest for Honor

Aristocratic life often appears to us as a ceaseless, restless quest for distinction in the eyes of one's peers and of posterity. — Jon Lendon[1]

Imagine driving along a busy interstate highway past a large billboard with the following message:

> By nature we yearn and hunger for _____ , and once we have glimpsed, as it were, some part of its radiance, there is nothing we are not prepared to bear and suffer in order to secure it.

---

1. J. E. Lendon, *Empire of Honour: The Art of Government in the Roman World* (Oxford: Clarendon, 1997), 35. I am indebted to Lendon for much of what follows.

How do you think passing drivers would fill in the blank? How would you fill it in?

The romantics among us might opt for the word *love.* The statement would then warmly resonate with much of what we hear and see in popular music and film.

Indeed, "love" is such a semantically expansive term that a passing motorist could interpret it anyway she liked—from the romantic love of a Hollywood movie, to the communal love shared among members of a healthy Christian congregation, to the *agape* love demonstrated in the atoning death of a sacrificing Savior.

Maybe John Lennon had it right after all. All you need is love. Perhaps "love" is what our billboard needs, at any rate.

Others would likely take a more cynical approach: *By nature we yearn and hunger for money!* As one jokester quipped, "Money isn't everything—but it's a long way ahead of what comes next." After all, what society other than ours would put the adjective "almighty" in front of the word *dollar?*

Now let's return to the world of the early Christians. What if one of the Roman magistrates whom we met in the previous chapter came across the billboard on his horse, as he was traveling along the Via Egnatia, just outside of Philippi, during Paul's time? How would he complete the sentence?

As it turns out, the statement comes directly from the writings of just such a person—the great Roman magistrate and statesman Cicero. Here is Cicero's assertion with our blank filled in:

> By nature we yearn and hunger for **honor**, and once we have glimpsed, as it were, some part of its radiance, there is nothing we are not prepared to bear and suffer in order to secure it. (*Tusc.* 2.24.58)

Honor—not money (and certainly not love)—was the most prized social commodity in the Roman world during the New Testament era.

Beyond the basic necessities of life, persons in antiquity did everything possible to defend and augment their honor in the public sphere. Conversely, they did everything in their power to avoid the shame of public dishonor.

The goal of this chapter is twofold. We will learn to appreciate the preeminent position that honor occupied at the apex of the hierarchy of social values in the ancient world. And we will consider specific strategies that individuals and families employed to defend and augment their honor in the public arena.

The Centrality of Honor in the Roman World

Bruce Malina and Jerome Neyrey define honor as "the positive value of a person in his or her own eyes plus the positive appreciation of that person in the eyes of his or her social group."[2]

This is not rocket science. All cultures include honor among their social values. What distinguishes the ancient Mediterranean world from modern Euro-American culture, in this regard, is the relative value assigned to honor—and honor-seeking—compared with the other social and relational priorities of life.

Among persons in the New Testament world, honor was not a secondary value (less important, for example, than wealth), as is the case in the modern West. Honor was a pivotal cultural value. The following pair of observations from the first-century philosopher Dio Chrysostom make this point quite well:

> You will find that there is nothing else [besides honor], at least in the case of the great majority, that incites every man to despise danger, to endure toils, and to scorn the life of pleasure and ease. (*Or.* 31.17)

> However, this much is clear, that neither you nor any others, whether Greeks or barbarians, who are thought to have become great, advanced to glory and power for any other rea-

---

2. Bruce J. Malina and Jerome H. Neyrey, "Honor and Shame in Luke-Acts: Pivotal Values of the Mediterranean World," in *The Social World of Luke-Acts,* ed. Jerome H. Neyrey (Peabody, MA: Hendrickson, 1991), 25–26.

son than because fortune gave to each in succession men who were jealous of honour and regarded their fame in after times as more precious than life. (*Or.* 31.20)

Identity Theft Then and Now

It might help at this juncture to return to the present and reflect for a moment on the widespread phenomenon of identity theft. Why do crooks want to steal a person's identity? The answer is self-evident: money.

Criminals want to get their hands on my identity, so that they can use my social security number to make purchases against credit cards taken out in my name. Why else would anyone want to steal a person's identity?

For honor, perhaps? Identity theft is not just a modern phenomenon. Persons in the Roman world stole the identity of others, but not to get money. The ancients engaged in identity theft to steal another person's honor.

In Paul's social universe the primary determinant of honor was birth status. An individual's honor rating came from his family's honor rating. To steal the identity of another person, to fake one's way into his family, was to acquire his birth status and, by extension, his family's honor rating, in the broader public sphere.

Identity theft of this kind was so widespread that one Roman author, Valerius Maximus, was able to fill several pages with examples of such behavior. He titled the piece, "Of Persons Born in the Lowest Station Who Tried by Falsehood to Thrust Themselves into Illustrious Families" (9.15). Not a particularly economic or elegant title, but you get the point.

Valerius's stories are quite engaging, and they are highly revealing. One fellow—a lowly "horse doctor" (doctors and veterinarians were low-class rabble in the ancient world)—tried to pose as a member of an esteemed senatorial family:

Herophilus, a horse doctor, claimed C. Marius, seven times Consul, as his grandfather and so puffed himself up that a number of colonies of veterans and distinguished municipalities and almost all the clubs adopted him as their patron. What is more, when C. Caesar, after crushing Cn. Pompeius the younger in Spain, admitted the public in his suburban estate, the pretender was greeted on the other side of the column with almost equal enthusiasm by the throng. (Valerius Maximus, 9.15.1)

Roman aristocrats were not at all amused by such antics. It was not long before the nobility figured out our horse doctor's true identity and banished the imposter from Italy. Herophilus was finally "put to death in prison by order of the Fathers [the senate]" (9.15.1).

The point of the story is straightforward. Criminals today engage in identity theft for money. The ancients did it for honor. This is because honor, in the New Testament world, was a social commodity far more valuable than wealth.

Social scientists helpfully distinguish, in this regard, between (a) goals valued in their own right and (b) other goals "sought largely or entirely for their *instrumental* value."[3] The Romans clearly situated honor in the former category, wealth in the latter. As the philosopher Seneca, a contemporary of the apostle Paul, remarked, "the honorable is cherished for no other reason than because it is honorable" (*On Benefits* 4.16.2).

Yale historian Ramsay MacMullen put it like this: "The Romans indeed acknowledged a goddess called Money (*Pecunia*); but . . . her cult was tributary to another, Status (*Philotimia*)."[4]

We see the tributary relationship between wealth and status functioning most prominently in the practice of urban benefaction.

Tooting His Own Horn: Pliny the Younger's Statue Project

A letter from the Roman senator Pliny graphically demonstrates how persons of means in the ancient world leveraged their

---

3. Lenski, *Power and Privilege,* 37.

4. Ramsay MacMullen, *Roman Social Relations: 50 B.C. to A.D. 284* (New Haven: Yale University Press, 1974), 118.

wealth to gain honor. The letter was occasioned by the death of a client who had apparently left Pliny a substantial amount of money. Note carefully what this esteemed Roman elite did with his newfound wealth:

> I have lately purchased with a legacy that was left to me a statue of Corinthian bronze [prized by Roman connoisseurs] . . . . But I did so, not with any intent of placing it in my own house . . . but with a design of fixing it in some conspicuous place in my native province, preferably in the temple of Jupiter; for it is a present well worthy of a temple and a god. Pray, then, undertake this, as readily as you do all my commissions, and give immediate orders for a pedestal to be made. I leave the choice of marble to you, but let my name be engraved upon it, and, if you think proper, my titles. (*Ep.* 3.6)

Pliny used the inheritance to buy a fancy statue. He instructed the recipient of the letter to erect the piece in a "conspicuous" place. Notice—and this is key—that Pliny did not give this gift to his "native province" anonymously. He wanted his name engraved on the pedestal of the statue, along with his "titles."

The "titles" are the names of the public offices Pliny occupied as he ascended the *cursus honorum*. Rome's "honors race" was a carefully scripted series of state offices that functioned as a career path for senatorial aristocrats. Elites like Pliny competed vigorously with one another for these posts, and they delighted in broadcasting their *cursus* honors to others in public inscriptions like the one Pliny requested for the statue, above.

And do not for a second be fooled by the obligatory aside, "if you think proper," near the end of the letter. The whole purpose of the endeavor is to gain a public platform for Pliny to proclaim his social status by listing his titles on the statue. Such was the dynamic of the widespread practice of urban benefaction in the ancient world, whereby persons used their wealth publicly to broadcast their honors to others.

This kind of shameless self-promotion does not set well with modern Americans. We don't take very well to people who brag about their accomplishments. And we rather delight to see a boastful person publicly put in his place.

I will never forget sitting around a lunch table at UCLA some years ago, with an editor from a prestigious publishing house and several of the university's esteemed academics. Among those present were my doctoral adviser in History of Christianity, Scott Bartchy, and a fellow I will call Richard, a highly respected professor from a department elsewhere in the university.

It was soon clear to all but one of us (guess who!) that Richard was rather full of himself. Unfortunately for Richard that day, Scott has a marked distaste for pride and arrogance, and he can smell it a mile away. I could sense Scott's increasing discomfort with Richard as our conversation unfolded.

Things began to get dicey when the discussion turned to the subject of transliterating words in the biblical languages (Greek, Hebrew, Aramaic) into English characters to satisfy the style requirements of certain academic journals (for example, the Greek ἀδελφός ["brother"] becomes *adelphos*). The more prestigious journals don't require transliteration, preferring, instead, to leave the script as it is found in the original text.

After some bantering back and forth on the topic, Richard imperiously remarked, "*I* will no longer even submit *my* scholarship to a journal or publisher that requires me to transliterate."

By this time Scott had had just about enough of his colleague's pomposity. He shot right back, "Well, Richard, how profoundly honored we are to get a glimpse of the soles of your feet as you ascend to heaven!"

It was all that the rest of us could do to contain our laughter.

Richard's self-promotion does not sit well with modern American social sensibilities. But Richard would have fit right in with Roman cultural norms related to honor-seeking and public self-promotion.

On a personal note, it just so happens that the story about Pliny and the statue (above) accentuates for me, in a rather immediate and practical way, the distance between Pliny's first-century honor culture and social priorities in twenty-first-century America.

Like Pliny, I was named in the will of a friend who recently died. Soon I expect to receive ten thousand dollars left to me by a fishing buddy who went to be with the Lord in September 2009.

Here, however, the similarities between me and Pliny end. For I most assuredly will *not* use my inheritance to (a) buy a statue with a marble plaque, (b) engrave my name and titles upon its pedestal, and (c) erect it in some prominent place in my local beach community.

Pliny's statue project, as foreign as it is to our sensibilities, nevertheless illustrates a fundamental reality about ancient social strategy. The most efficient avenue to public recognition for Roman elites was the practice of urban benefaction.

Urban Benefaction: Trading Wealth for Social Status

In the previous chapter you encountered a chart outlining the monetary requirements for membership in the elite orders. There was a reason for this criterion of wealth. Persons who belonged to the Roman senate, and who held honorific posts in Rome and in the provinces, needed to have deep pockets in order to fulfill their roles as public benefactors.

Aristocrats like Pliny engaged in building projects across the empire. For their generosity as patrons, the wealthy received, in turn, various honors, including dedicatory honor inscriptions that gave elites an opportunity to broadcast their achievements in public.

Among Rome's aristocrats, then, wealth served both (a) as a *qualification* for the honor of entering an elite order and (b) as a *vehicle* for accumulating further honor through public benefaction.

Public benefaction will be foreign to most readers. My wife and I recently returned from a trip to the northern part of our state. At several places along the way, California's Department of Transportation (CalTrans) was engaged in road repair. At nearly every juncture a sign was posted: "Your Tax Dollars at Work!"

This is familiar territory to most of us. In our experience, impersonal government agencies take care of necessities like the water supply, the upkeep of municipal buildings, and road repair. And they use our tax dollars to do so.

Things were much different in Paul's day. Taxes collected by Rome's elites and other local dynasts were not earmarked for public works undertaken by faceless government agencies. Those taxes instead became the personal riches of the empire's well-heeled elite minority. These individuals then used their wealth—tremendous amounts of it, in fact—to engage in public works.

The expenditures varied in nature. Elites financed civic banquets, gladiatorial contests, and distributions of money and food to the urban masses. Persons of means also left more permanent monuments attesting to their rank in the social hierarchy.

Wealthy Romans built fountains, erected statues (like Pliny's, above), paved walkways, and repaired temples. Herod the Great's decades-long work on the Jerusalem temple, and the harbor that Herod constructed at Caesarea Maritima, are prime examples of such activity.

We might wonder what could compel a rich Roman aristocrat to cut loose with so much of his money in order to finance a public bath or a theater? By now the answer should be right at hand: public recognition.

By means of such expenditures, Roman aristocrats became the personal patrons of local municipalities. Town fathers responded, in turn, by publicly honoring them for their generosity.

Gaius's Generosity

The town fathers of Spoleto, Italy, honored a generous elite patron named Gaius Torasius Severus. Inscriptions like this could be multiplied a thousand fold:

> Gaius Torasius Severus son of Gaius, of the Horatian tribe, quattuorvir with judicial power, augur, built this [probably the public baths] in his own name and in the name of his son, Publius Meclonius Proculus Torasianus, pontiff, on his own land and at his own expense. He likewise gave the community

for celebrating the birthday of his son 250,000 sesterces, out of the income from which on August 30 annually the decurions are to hold a public banquet and the townspeople who are present receive eight sesterces apiece. Likewise he gave to the board of six priests of Augustus and the priests of the Lares of Augustus and the block captains 120,000 sesterces, so that out of the income from this sum they might have a public repast on the same day. Because of his services to the municipality the council of decurions adopted him as patron of the municipality.[5]

Gaius's provision of public baths and banquets for the populace undoubtedly pleased both the commoners and the town fathers. But for Gaius himself the real payoff was having the above inscription prominently and permanently erected in the center of the town square of Spoleto, so that others could see how he had been honored for his efforts.

The Ultimate Goal of Urban Benefaction

The masses no doubt benefited significantly from many instances of urban patronage. While we might reasonably question the public utility of a statue like Pliny's, we should not underestimate the importance of a new aqueduct, a temple, or a public bath.

We must not lose sight of the fact, though, that Roman elites used positions of power and influence—particularly their wealth—not directly in the service of others but, rather, to augment their own status in the public eye.

Elite generosity was not motivated, to any great degree, by the plight of the masses. Roman aristocrats traded wealth for public acclaim because they valued honor above everything else.

As one elite Roman noted, "the pillar, the inscription, and being set up in bronze are regarded as a high honour by noble men" (Dio Chrysostom, *Or.* 31.20).

---

5. *CIL* 9.4815.

The Public Nature of Honor

The practice of urban benefaction naturally leads us to consider a fundamental aspect of honor in the ancient world: honor was a distinctly public commodity. As one historian recently remarked, "For the Romans, being was being seen."[6] The Roman philosopher Dio Chrysostom elaborates:

> For all men set great store by the outward tokens of high achievement, and not one man in a thousand is willing to agree that what he regards as a noble deed shall have been done for himself alone and that no other man shall have knowledge of it. (*Or.* 31.22)

So much for the countercultural teaching of Jesus: "Don't let your left hand know what your right hand is doing" (Matt 6:3)!

Those who study Mediterranean social values consistently underscore the public nature of honor. As Halvor Moxnes remarks, honor is "fundamentally the *public* recognition of one's social standing."[7] This, in turn, derives from the group-oriented worldview of people in the ancient world:

> Since the group is so important for the identity of a Mediterranean person … it is critical to recognize that honor status comes primarily from *group* recognition. While honor may sometimes be an inner quality, the value of a person in his or her own eyes, it depends ultimately on recognition from significant others in society. It is a public matter. When someone's claim to honor is recognized by the group, honor is confirmed, and the result is a new social status.[8]

---

6. Carlin A. Barton, *Roman Honor: The Fire in the Bones* (Berkeley: University of California Press, 2001), 58.
7. Halvor Moxnes, "Honor and Shame," in *The Social Sciences and New Testament Interpretation,* ed. Richard Rohrbaugh (Peabody, MA: Hendrickson, 1996), 20. Moxnes's italics.
8. Ibid.

Conversely, as Bruce Malina and Richard Rohrbaugh bluntly assert, "To claim honor the community does not recognize is to play the fool."[9]

As a result, the Romans engaged in the various activities of their daily lives with the eye of the public always in view. Dio Chrysostom, again, offers us his insider's perspective:

> Clearly, therefore, if a person is going to be exceedingly anxious to win the praise of the crowd as well, believing that its praise or censure has more weight than his own judgment, his every act and wish will be aimed to show himself the sort of person that the crowd expects. (*Or.* 77/78.24)

Social Mobility and the Dynamics of Honor

Roman elites competed with one another for honor on the battlefield, and they competed with one another for honor in the political arena. On the home front this "struggle for reputation" centered around the honorific offices that constituted Rome's *cursus honorum*, or "race for honors" (Dio Chrysostom, *Or.* 66.18).

We will outline the various steps in Rome's honor's race, and we'll see how *cursus* ideology was replicated in provincial towns like Philippi. First, however, some observations are in order about the nature of public office in the New Testament world.

Public office in antiquity functioned quite differently than it does in America today, and it is important to keep this in view. A pair of stories from the past will make this distinction quite clear.

The first incident finds a senator named Marcus Cornelius Fronto interceding with the emperor on behalf of a friend. In a letter to Antoninus Pius, Fronto requested a procuratorship to "enhance the dignity" of a fellow elite who was advancing in years.

What is interesting here is that Fronto assured the emperor that his friend will, in fact, decline the office. The elderly man simply wanted the honor of being called "procurator"—not the

---

9. Bruce J. Malina and Richard L. Rohrbaugh, *Social-Science Commentary on the Synoptic Gospels* (Minneapolis: Fortress, 1992), 371.

associated responsibilities (*ad Pium* 1.9.2). The aged aristocrat had likely begun to reflect upon the series of honorific titles that would soon adorn his gravestone. Here was an opportunity to add another one to the list.

A second incident finds our friend Pliny attempting to broker an office for an equestrian client named Maturus Arrianus. Pliny was quite frank about the fact that his goal was solely to enhance the man's honor. Pliny informed the emperor that he did not much care what honor was awarded, as long as (a) it was "a distinction" and (b) it did not demand much work (*Ep.* 3.2.6).

Did not demand much work?! Imagine a modern politician openly seeking office with such intentions and priorities: "I would like to be the governor of California, as long as it doesn't demand too much work." We all know how a campaign like that would go over at the ballot box.

The fundamental difference between our understanding of public office and the manner in which the Romans viewed such positions can be concisely summarized: public honor—not public service—was central to office-holding in the Roman world.

This is not to imply that Roman magistrates did not carry out significant tasks. It is to emphasize the secondary nature of such duties. The offices were first and foremost honors—thus the expression *cursus honorum*. The various functions related to these posts were always a secondary consideration.

The balance of this chapter examines the dynamics of Rome's honors race. We will give particular attention to the way in which the social priorities and practices of the senatorial class at Rome (level one) were replicated in miniature among local decurion elites in the provinces (level two) and, finally, in non-elite religious groups throughout the empire (level three).

Value Replication—Level One: Rome's Cursus Honorum

The scripted array of senatorial honors in Rome included, in ascending order, the offices of quaestor, aedile, praetor, consul. Only two men per year shared the office of consul, an honor that few senators achieved during their lifetimes.

Each post in the *cursus* assumed specific responsibilities. Quaestors took care of state finances, including various taxes and payments to the Roman treasury. Aediles personally underwrote building projects in the capital, and they entertained the masses by staging games and other public spectacles.

Praetors, the first rank in the *cursus* to hold *imperium* (Latin, "formal judicial power"), exercised authority in the courts at Rome. Some later served as propraetors, dispensing justice in the provinces. During the Republic, two consuls stood at the apex of the *cursus* hierarchy. Later the emperor was at the top of the heap, often sharing the consulship with another member of the nobility.

Specific limits were placed upon (a) the minimum age at which a person could hold a magistracy, (b) the number of persons holding an office at a given time, and (c) the length of time a position could be occupied by an individual. The offices, and the order in which they were occupied during the Republic (ca. pre-30 B.C.) and the Empire (ca. post-30 B.C.), was as follows: [10]

REPUBLIC	Min. Age	EMPIRE	Min. Age
		Vigintivir	18
Military service		Military tribune	20
Quaestor	30	Quaestor	25
Aedile or Tribune	37	Aedile or Tribune	27
Praetor	40	Praetor	30
		Prefect Propraetor Proconsul Commander of a legion	
Consul	43	Consul	32
Censor		Praefectus urbi Propraetor Proconsul	

---

10. Jona Lendering, "Cursus Honorum," Livius Articles on Ancient History, accessed July 16, 2011, http://www.livius.org/ct-cz/cursus/cursus_honorum.html.

The offices on the chart are the "titles" that Pliny wanted engraved on the base of his statue, in the story related earlier in the chapter. Since Pliny had ascended to the highest rung of the social ladder, the consulship, the honor inscription on the pedestal of his statue would have included, "quaestor, tribune, praetor, propraetor of Bithynia, consul, imperial governor/proconsul of Bithynia-Pontus"—an impressive list of honors that could be matched by only a handful of Pliny's senatorial peers. Little wonder that Pliny wanted the statue set up "in some conspicuous place"!

The one thing today remotely analogous to an ancient honor inscription is a resumé or a *curriculum vitae*. My CV, for example, lists all the degrees I have earned, the university posts I have held, and the publications I have produced.

We do not, however, compile our CVs and resumés publicly to proclaim our honors indiscriminately to every passer-by. In our culture these documents serve the much more utilitarian function of helping us to secure employment or, perhaps (in academia), a speaking engagement or book contract.

Value Replication—Level Two: Cursus Ideology Among Provincial Elites

Those who ascended Rome's *cursus honorum* formed a truly elite group. Only a portion of the six hundred or so men in the senate held positions in the *cursus,* and only a small percentage of these rose to the offices of praetor or consul.

Local municipalities like Philippi, however, adopted Rome's *cursus* ideology, and local decurion elites replicated Roman social practices right down to the very titles they used for some of their honorific offices.

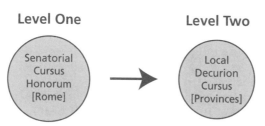

Consider the following town charter from a municipality in Spain (late first century A.D.). The excerpt relates to oaths to be taken by various local dignitaries. Notice, in particular, the titles of some of the offices:

> The incumbent douvirs [sic (duumvirs)] with judicial power in this municipality, likewise the aediles and quaestors now holding office . . . likewise the duovirs, aediles, or quaestors who shall henceforth be elected . . . each of them within the five days next following their entrance upon the office of duovir, aedile, or quaestor, and before a meeting of the decurions . . . is held, shall in a public meeting take oath by Jupiter, by the deified Augustus, by the deified Claudius.[11]

The decurions mentioned near the end of the inscription are the local elites who ran the town. The duumvirs are the two chief men (also decurions) of the municipality.

It might help to think of the decurion council as a local version of the Roman senate and the pair of duumvirs as Rome's twofold consulship replicated in miniature. The rest of the titles represent other honors held by members of the town's local aristocracy.

Notice how some of the honors (aedile, quaestor) parrot the official titles that we encountered in the *cursus* in Rome. The oaths to Augustus and Claudius are also informative. A local *cursus,* titular mimicry, oaths to deified emperors—what we have here reflects the widespread replication and contextualization of Roman social values in this provincial Spanish settlement.

As we might expect, the Roman army had a *cursus* of its own. The military remains highly stratified even in modern Euro-Western societies, and we will not be surprised to find that the same was the case in Rome.

---

11. CIL 2.1963, trans. Naphtali Lewis and Meyer Reinhold, eds., *Roman Civilization: Sourcebook II: The Empire* (New York: Harper Torchbooks, 1966), 322.

We will examine hierarchy and honor in the military in the next chapter. For our purposes here it is illuminating to note that the Roman army provided one of the few avenues for upward mobility from one social order to another.

The inscription below illustrates a scenario that occasionally saw a military career followed by the acquisition of honorific posts in a local municipality. Here a soldier who had risen to the post of town decurion took pains to publicize his *cursus* achievements on the tombstone that would someday adorn his gravesite:

C. Luccius . . . Sabinus, decurion of Beneventum, while still living made [this tomb] for himself, his wife Ofillia Parata, and his brother Luccius Verecundus, and his posterity. He served in the First Urban Cohort at the side of the tribunes, was an attendant (seutor), orderly (optio) of the hospital, orderly of the prison, aid (singularis), clerk of a tribune (beneficiarus), put in charge of the examination of witnesses by Annius Verus, Prefect of the City; he was also officer in charge of the watchword, orderly, standard-bearer, clerk of the treasury, orderly in charge of records, senior clerk of a tribune, clerk of Valerius Asiaticus, Prefect of the City. He was discharged by the emperor Hadrian when Servianus . . . and Vibius Verus were consuls [A.D. 134].[12]

I have officiated over the years at a number of graveside services. I have yet to come across a tombstone covered with titles like the one cited above. You probably haven't seen one either. Yet archaeologists have unearthed hundreds of such gravestones everywhere Rome ruled.

As you can gather from the above inscription, the Romans had a title for just about every social station a person occupied in the military and municipal hierarchies of the ancient world. One cannot help but get the impression that this decurion from Beneventum was rather proud of his honorific offices.

---

12. ILS 2117, trans. Lendon, *Empire of Honour*, 246.

Value Replication—Level Three: Cursus *Ideology Among the* Masses

Local aristocrats still constituted but a small percentage of a town's population, so that only a handful of elite families shared the desirable offices in a local municipality like Beneventum.

In Philippi, for example, only about five hundred people, out of a population of fifteen thousand to twenty thousand residents, belonged to the decurion order. These folks, in turn, were the only ones qualified to seek public office in the colony's municipal *cursus,* as described above.

Non-elites, however, were not to be outdone. As one Roman observed, "Glory drags along the obscure no less than the nobly born bound to her shining chariot" (Horace, *Satires* 1.6.23–4).[13] In yet another expression of the phenomenon of value replication, commoners, too, assumed Roman social practices, constructing their own "honors races" in voluntary associations across the empire.

The activities of non-elite associations prove highly informative for the study of Christian social organization. Like the house churches, voluntary associations consisted of relatively small groups of non-elites (approximately ten to forty members) who gathered together for purposes unrelated to local or state governmental administration.

The associations met for a variety of reasons. Some were religious in orientation, like the early Christians. Others brought together persons who plied the same trade. Burial societies guaranteed their members a decent funeral. Common to all these groups was the replication—now even further down the social hierarchy—of the social stratification and honor-seeking that characterized life among Roman and municipal elites.

The *cursus* that defined the social hierarchy of those devoted to the god Mithras is representative. The Mithras cult was a mystery religion popular among non-elite males—especially Roman soldiers.

---

13. Trans. Lendon, *Empire of Honour,* 97.

The association's honors ran in ascending order as follows: *Corax* (Raven), *Nymphus* (Nymphus), *Miles* (Soldier), *Leo* (Lion), *Perses* (Persian), *Heliodromus* (Sun-Runner), and *Pater* (Father). These seven offices further bifurcated into two substrata. The association recognized persons attaining to the grade of "Lion" as true "participants." Persons in the lower three ranks remained the cult's "underlings" or "servitors."[14]

Another religious cult, the voluntary association of Aesculapius and Hygia from Rome, had Latin terms for offices that included *quinquennalis, pater, mater, immunes, curatores*. Greek cult associations also boasted numerous honorific titles including *hiereus, archiereus, archimystes and archithiasitēs* (or *thiasarchēs*), *pater, mater, presbys, tamias, grammateus, hypēretēs, diakonos,* "and a host of more specialized terms."[15]

We need not pause to translate and explain these Latin and Greek titles. It is sufficient simply to grasp the persistent replication of Roman elite social practices, as non-elites gathered together in their associations and generated their own sets of honorific offices. We can now begin to appreciate the replication of *cursus* ideology and practices across the social spectrum.

Social Mobility Then and Now

The replication of *cursus* ideology and practice at every stratum in the hierarchy helps us grasp the nature of social mobility in the ancient world. In the Roman Empire almost all upward mobility occurred within one's social stratum and not between one status group and another.

Persons in Euro-Western societies often ascend to heights socio-economically that far eclipse the achievements of their

---

14. Roger Beck, "The Mysteries of Mithras," in *Voluntary Associations in the Graeco-Roman World: Issues in Function, Taxonomy, and Membership,* ed. John S. Kloppenborg and Stephen G. Wilson (London: Routledge, 1996), 180–181.

15. John S. Kloppenborg, "Collegia and *Thiasoi,*" in *Voluntary Associations in the Graeco-Roman World: Issues in Function, Taxonomy, and Membership,* ed. John S. Kloppenborg and Stephen G. Wilson (London: Routledge, 1996), 26.

parents and grandparents. My grandfather, for example, was a German Jewish immigrant. My father was a retail clerk with a high school education. I am a university professor with five graduate degrees under my belt. The boundaries between social classes in the modern West are quite porous, relatively speaking.

The opposite was the case in the Roman world. Mobility between elite and non-elite strata was the exception rather than the rule. The reason is easily discerned. Elite orders had a stiff monetary requirement, so that becoming a decurion, for example, demanded a significant increase in wealth. And wealth was usually passed on within families. Social movement of any kind, therefore, was rare among non-elites.

There were always exceptions, though, and soldiers and wealthy freedmen at times enjoyed opportunities for social advancement that others did not. But even here the phenomenon of a non-elite entering an elite order was highly exceptional.

Richard Saller describes the pathway to upward mobility through the military, for example, as "extremely narrow," noting that "only a few tens of thousands out of the empire's many millions were recruited into the legions each year, and only one or two out of the thousands of veterans retiring each year rose to the ranks of procurator."[16]

Social mobility in the Roman world normally consisted, therefore, of advancement *within* the various social strata of a given town or municipality, rather than *across* the strata. The typical *cursus* did not find an army recruit or a local dockworker ascending a series of posts that culminated in admission to the senatorial order.

Instead, a soldier would climb the ranks of his local Mithras cult; a dockworker would seek an honorary position in the "Poseidoniastai of Berytos, Merchants, Shippers and Warehousemen," a "commercial association" on the island of Delos.[17] It was the replication of Rome's *cursus honorum* in these

---

16. Saller, "Status and Patronage," 836.
17. For the Delos Poseidonists see B. Hudson McLean, "The Place of Cult

local, non-elite settings that provided opportunities for social recognition and mobility for the great majority of the empire's population.

One scholar properly observes that "social relations and organization [in such groups] tended to mirror the municipal organization of the public cult of the *polis*," right down to a "formally enrolled 'citizenry,' a governing council," and "the division of members into voting groups."[18]

The Philippian Church as a Voluntary Association

In Philippians, Paul describes the Christian church as a citizen body (1:27; 3:20). As one of a number of voluntary associations in the colony, the temptation was ever present for the church in Philippi to replicate the values of the dominant culture and come up with its own hierarchy of honors, complete with offices, public inscriptions, and the like. In the next chapter we will see that other voluntary religious groups in Philippi did precisely that.

The Philippian church, too, finally caved in to such pressures, long after the apostle Paul had left the scene. Among the burial inscriptions that archaeologists have unearthed at the site, several second-century tombstones have local Christians boasting about the offices they had held in the church during their lifetimes.

The process of accommodation to the values of the dominant culture continued unabated for the next several centuries. By the time Christianity had become the state-sponsored religion in the

---

in Voluntary Associations and Christian Churches on Delos," in *Voluntary Associations in the Graeco-Roman World: Issues in Function, Taxonomy, and Membership,* ed. John S. Kloppenborg and Stephen G. Wilson (London: Routledge, 1996), 197.

18. Sandra Walker-Ramisch, "Graeco-Roman Voluntary Associations and the Damascus Document: A Sociological Analysis," in *Voluntary Associations in the Graeco-Roman World: Issues in Function, Taxonomy, and Membership,* ed. John S. Kloppenborg and Stephen G. Wilson (London: Routledge, 1996), 134.

fourth century A.D., the ascending list of honorific offices in the Christian church pretty much mirrored in principle the *cursus honorum* of the post–Constantinian Roman imperial court.

Paul, Cursus *Ideology, and Honorary Titles*

How did Paul view the Roman honors race, this quest for public notoriety and approval that was replicated in countless social settings, everywhere Rome ruled? You might be surprised to discover that Paul appropriated *cursus* ideology, only to subvert it and turn it completely on its head.

Paul presented his own *cursus honorum* in Philippians 3:5–6. Except for the fact that the honors happen to be Jewish ones, it reads just like a Roman honor inscription:

> circumcised the eighth day;
> of the nation of Israel,
> of the tribe of Benjamin,
> a Hebrew born of Hebrews;
> regarding the law, a Pharisee;
> regarding zeal, persecuting the church;
> regarding the righteousness that is in the law, blameless

This is quite a resumé. Members of the Philippian church who had bought into Rome's self-promoting honor culture would have been impressed. They would have applauded Paul's achievements and the fact that he publicly proclaimed them to others. They would have said to themselves: "Yes, Paul. You go right ahead and leverage your pre-Christian privileges and accomplishments to stake out your position in the church pecking order. We'll do the same. Some of us, you know, are Roman citizens. A couple of us even come from decurion families. That ought to count for something in this group."

Not in Paul's social economy. Paul, you see, was not yet finished with his commentary on Roman *cursus* ideology. In a frontal assault on all such posturing, honor-seeking, and self-promotion, Paul proceeded forcefully and unequivocally to assert,

But everything that was a gain to me, I have considered to be a loss because of Christ. More than that, I also consider everything to be a loss in view of the surpassing value of knowing Christ Jesus my Lord. Because of Him I have suffered the loss of all things and consider them filth, so that I may gain Christ and be found in Him, not having a righteousness of my own from the law, but one that is through faith in Christ—the righteousness from God based on faith. (Phil 3:7–9)

So much for Jewish privilege. So much for Roman citizenship. So much for decurion status. So much for using my social capital—whatever it might be—to build my own empire and serve my own selfish desires.

And what about all those titles that the residents of Philippi found so impressive and attractive? What did our great apostle think of those? Roman social priorities, you will recall, guaranteed that people with titles would make sure that others knew what those titles were—like Pliny did with his statue project.

Paul in Philippians 1:1 did precisely the opposite. He refrained from proclaiming his title, "apostle," and referred to himself and Timothy, instead, as "slaves."

Then, in direct contrast to typical Roman behavior, he honored *others* by addressing them with *their* titles: "overseers and deacons." Paul practiced what he would preach later in the letter: "in humility consider others as more important than yourselves" (2:3).

After Paul and Silas left Philippi, they arrived in Thessalonica, where local agitators claimed, "These men who have turned the world upside down have come here too" (Acts 17:6).

Paul's opponents got that one right. Paul and his gospel really did turn the Roman world upside down, where social relations were concerned. More on this to come!

Conclusion

Like many of us today, people in the ancient world sometimes wondered about the meaning of their dreams. Resident experts on such matters insisted that dreams were to be interpreted according to the social status of the person doing the dreaming.

In the second century A.D., a fellow named Artemidorus wrote a treatise on the interpretation of dreams. If a poor man dreams that he is sleeping on a heap of dung (I'd call that a nightmare!), this means, according to Artemidorus, that the man will become rich. A rich man who has such a dream can be confident that he will gain an important public office (3.52).

A dream with positive connotations for one person could be a negative portent for another of a different rank. Thus, it is a good omen for a rich man—and, interestingly enough, also for a slave—to dream he is attired in a purple robe. For the poor free person such a dream constitutes a grave warning of bad things to come (2.3).[19]

Apparently no aspect of life—not even the interpretation of dreams—was immune to the effects of what Jon Lendon has labeled the "deep structure" of honor and hierarchy in the Roman world.[20]

Our overview of Roman social values is now complete. Chapter 1 uncovered a deeply hierarchical social taxonomy in the ancient world, one which divided and subdivided the population into numerous status groups.

We saw, as well, that people took great care publicly to mark out their positions in the social hierarchy. Clothing, seating at public and private banquets, and treatment in the law courts all differed according to the rank of the persons in view.

The present chapter examined the centrality of honor and honor-seeking in the Roman world. We became acquainted with Rome's aristocratic career path—the *cursus honorum*—and we reflected upon the way in which *cursus* ideology was replicated among non-elite voluntary associations in municipalities across the empire.

---

19. Lendon, *Empire of Honour*, 33.
20. Ibid., 73.

We now narrow our focus to the Roman colony at Philippi, where these same values and behaviors determined social reality for local residents and presented a formidable challenge to anyone who sought to follow in the footsteps of Jesus.

Questions for Reflection

1. What was the most important social commodity in the Roman world? How about your world? How would your friends or coworkers fill in the billboard at the beginning of the chapter?

2. The chapter treats in some detail the quest for honor in the ancient world. Define "honor," as the Romans understood it. What made someone honorable in the Roman world? What brings honor to a person in our culture today?

3. Describe how the Romans turned wealth into honor. How does this differ from the way wealthy persons in our society spend their money?

4. Social mobility—the ability to improve one's social status and standard of living—has been at the heart of the "American dream" for decades. What did social mobility look like in the ancient world?

5. Where would Roman social values and practices have come into conflict with New Testament teachings about relationships in the church? Support your answers with specific New Testament passages.

Power and Status in Philippi

A Culture of Honor and Self-Promotion

> We ran a straight course to Samothrace, the next day to
> Neapolis, and from there to Philippi, a Roman colony.
> —Acts 16:11–12

John F. Kennedy's election to the presidency in 1960 had nearly as much effect on fashion in the United States as it did upon the political process. Here we see value replication—the social values of the upper class influencing the behavior of the masses—colorfully illustrated in our own recent history.

The first lady, Jacqueline Kennedy, was a sophisticated young woman who immediately caught the attention of the fashion-conscious. She set trends with her clothing and with the way she wore her hair.

Jackie's bouffant hairstyle became the rage in Hollywood and continued to be so until the mid-1960s. Her clothes still made the news some four decades later, after Jackie's years in the White House were long over.

In the spring of 2001, New York City's Metropolitan

Museum of Art hosted an exhibit titled, "Jacqueline Kennedy: The White House Years." The exhibit featured more than eighty garments Jackie wore from 1959 to 1963.

A 2001 *People* magazine article about the exhibit identified Jackie as "a fashion icon of the 20th century." "She had a global influence on style," declared designer Carolina Herrera. "Millions of women copied her."[1]

The widespread influence of Jacqueline Kennedy's taste for fashion is a classic example of value replication. Apparently the practice of the masses mimicking one's social betters is as ubiquitous in contemporary America as it was in the world of Paul and the early Christians.

As we have seen, persons in ancient municipalities went to great lengths to replicate in their own social settings the honor-seeking activities of senatorial elites at Rome. We turn now to consider the ways in which value replication determined the social priorities of the population of Roman Philippi.

The Colonization of Philippi

The transition from republic to empire (first century B.C.) consumed more than a half-century of Roman history and cost thousands of lives. For several decades powerful generals with their personal armies violently competed with one another for glory and honor across the Mediterranean world.

The social chaos of Rome's civil wars finally culminated in a series of events that followed the assassination of Julius Caesar in 44 B.C. Two opposing factions struggled to fill the power vacuum left by Caesar's death.

Republican forces rallied around Brutus and Cassius, Caesar's murderers. Octavian (later to become the emperor Augustus) and Mark Antony (of Antony and Cleopatra fame) assembled an opposing group of legions, seeking (so they claimed) to avenge the dictator's death.

---

1. Michelle Tauber, Elizabeth McNeil, and Cathy Nolan, "Jackie's Style," *People* 55:18 (2001): 52.

The two armies faced off near a Greek city called Philippi, in the Roman province of Macedonia. The proximity of Philippi to this decisive battle guaranteed that the town would never be the same again.

Octavian and Antony won the battle of Philippi in 42 B.C., defeating Brutus, Cassius, and the Republican faction. The conquerors partitioned among themselves the vast area that Rome now ruled. Octavian seized Italy and the West. Antony claimed the East.

A pressing challenge immediately confronted the two leaders. The victorious generals needed to retain their soldiers' loyalty by rewarding them for their service. They did so by founding colonies of veterans in various locations throughout Italy and the Greek East—including the town of Philippi.

Dispossessing a Local Population

You would not want the Romans to fight a major battle anywhere near your hometown. For when a conflict was over, Roman generals often indiscriminately drove out local landholders and settled their veterans near the sites where their battles were fought.

For example, after the Romans had conquered a key part of Britain, they founded a colony of veterans at Camulodunum (modern Colchester, in Essex, England), acting "as though they had received a free gift of the entire country, driving the natives from their homes, ejecting them from their lands,—they styled them 'captives' and 'slaves'" (Tacitus, *Ann.* 14.31).

Macedonia suffered a similar fate in 42 B.C. and again a little more than a decade later. At Philippi, while the battle was still raging, Brutus promised his soldiers that "he would turn over to them two cities for plunder and booty, Thessalonica and Lacedaemon" (Plutarch, *Brut.* 46.1). The local residents of these settlements would have no say in the matter.

"Antony and Octavius," we are told, "practised far greater cruelty than this in rewarding their soldiers" (*Brut.* 46.2). After they defeated Brutus and Cassius, Octavian and Antony settled some two or three thousand retired soldiers in the region. Philippi was formally established as a Roman colony.

Octavian later settled more veterans in Philippi, when he defeated Mark Antony in yet another civil war to become Rome's first emperor in 30 B.C. In the process, Octavian and Antony "enriched their supporters, took vengeance on their enemies, and victimized the innocent."[2]

Imagine an army coming to your neighborhood today, confiscating property that had belonged to your family for generations, and not paying you a cent in return. Welcome to the oppressive, rapacious process of Roman colonization.

The Romanization of Philippi

Romans were never the numerical majority in Philippi. The Roman minority, however, immediately became the primary locus of power and influence in the colony.

As we saw in the previous chapters, wealth served as a key requirement for membership in an elite order, such as the decurion class in a municipality like Philippi. Arable land was the primary source of wealth in the ancient world.

When Roman soldiers dispossessed local landowners and confiscated their holdings, the veterans became in a single stroke the wealthiest residents of Philippi. As the colony's newly minted aristocracy, the Roman settlers now qualified for the decurion council, and they proceeded to hold nearly all of the honorific posts in the colony. The result was an influence upon the social world of Philippi which was markedly disproportionate to the raw percentage of Romans in the colony.

Although Romans were not a numerical majority, the cultural atmosphere of Philippi soon became Roman through and through. The trickle-down effect of value replication guaranteed that the relational priorities and behaviors of the colony's Roman elites would ultimately reproduce themselves in miniature in the social patterns of Greeks and other non-elite residents of the colony.

One ancient writer described Roman colonies as "miniatures,

---

2. Edward T. Salmon, *Roman Colonization Under the Republic* (London: Thames & Hudson, 1969), 137–38.

as it were, and in a way copies" of the city of Rome itself (Aulus Gellius, *Noctes Atticae (Attic Nights)* 16.13.8–9).

This was particularly the case for Philippi. The establishment of the colony on the site in 42 B.C., and the special relationship that the retired military veterans shared with Augustus, the colony's founder, guaranteed that Rome's social and religious values would permeate the settlement in some rather exceptional ways. Peter Pilhofer remarks, "A person like Paul who came from the East to Philippi entered another world. Roman colonies could be found also in Asia Minor, but none was so markedly 'Roman' as Philippi."[3]

The biblical authors were not unaware of this, and it was no accident that Philippi was the only place that Luke specifically labeled "a Roman colony" (Acts 16:12), even though Paul stopped at eight other colonies during his journeys in Acts.

Rank in the Military

The importance of rank and title in Rome's highly stratified army sharply informed the social ethos of the veteran colony at Philippi. As was the case in the Roman army, even in relatively egalitarian societies like the United States, the military remains a highly stratified environment where rank carries both privilege and responsibility.

One of the more promising members of the college/career group Joann and I led in the early 1980s was a young Air Force officer named Lansen Conley. I trained Lansen as a Bible teacher and soon shared the teaching with him at our Sunday morning meetings.

The quality of Lansen's character and work ethic was not lost on Uncle Sam. First Lieutenant Conley soon became Captain Conley, became Major Conley, became Lieutenant Colonel Conley, became Colonel Conley. In each case, Lansen was rewarded with these rank increases when he first became eligible for promotion.

---

3. Peter Pilhofer, *Philippi, Band 1: Die erste christliche Gemeinde Europas,* WUNT (Tübingen: J. C. B. Mohr, 1995), 92, my translation.

At one point later in his career, Lansen was working at the Pentagon and attending church in Virginia. Lansen and his wife, Pamela, struggled to find friends in the church. The church members were not the problem. They were friendly enough. The issue was Lansen's position in the Air Force hierarchy.

The congregation was full of Pentagon folks who had great difficulty leaving their military ranks at the door, in order to treat one another as equals in the family of God. Lansen's situation was particularly problematic, since the great majority of men his age occupied positions in the pecking order well below Lansen's.

The result? Few couples in the church felt comfortable treating Lansen and Pamela as a peer brother and sister in the Lord. What had happened here, of course, was that the military hierarchy of the Pentagon had subtly imprinted itself upon the social hierarchy of a local church.

The Military Hierarchy Becomes Philippi's Social Hierarchy

The same dynamic worked itself out in ancient Philippi. Here, however, the military hierarchy did not influence the social hierarchy of a local church, as was the case with Lansen and Pamela.

In Philippi, the military hierarchy influenced the social hierarchy of a whole town—all as a result of Roman colonization. To appreciate how this came about, we must familiarize ourselves with social stratification in the Roman army.

The army had a steeply differentiated pay scale. After the founding of Philippi, Augustus apparently felt the need to give careful attention to military remuneration:

> [Augustus] restricted all the soldiery everywhere to a fixed scale of pay and allowances, designating the duration of their service and the rewards on its completion *according to each man's rank,* in order to keep them from being tempted to revolution after their discharge either by age or poverty. (Suetonius, *Aug.* 49, my italics)

Under Augustus the soldiers were paid as follows (in sesterces):

foot soldier	900
cavalry	1,050
centurion	13,500
primus ordo	27,000
primuspilus	54,000

Notice that the annual salary of a *primuspilus* (Latin, lit. "number one spear-thrower") is sixty times that of the average foot soldier. The chasm between the ranks was huge.

By way of comparison, the top monthly pay rate for a general in the U.S. Army in 2010 was less than six times the monthly pay earned by the lowest-ranked commissioned officer, a first lieutenant. The rank system in the Roman army was much more steeply stratified than is the case in the military in America today.

The physical layout of a Roman camp also spoke volumes about rank and status among the soldiers. The commander—a consul or high-ranking senator—monopolized some 75,000 square feet of the army's encampment. His living quarters boasted rich furnishings, decorated halls, and a peristyle courtyard. A run-of-the-mill legionnaire had to be satisfied, in contrast, with roughly 50 square feet of space.

Finally, in the wake of a major victory, Roman generals also distributed booty according to the rank of the soldiers under their charge. The division of spoils at Pompey's triumph shows how military rank was rewarded and reinforced long after the battle was over:

Staff officer	ca. 800,000 denarii
Legionary tribune	ca. 180,000 denarii
Legionary centurion	ca. 30,000 denarii
Legionary private	ca. 15,000 denarii

Victorious generals also doled out land allotments according to their soldiers' respective ranks in the army during the process of colonization.

Such policies, in turn, determined the social make-up of a colony like Philippi, since high-ranking officers—who received disproportionately large allotments of land—now qualified financially for the honor of public office as decurions, magistrates, and priests in public religious cults.

In this way the military hierarchy was essentially transformed into the social hierarchy of a newly founded colony, as Roman veterans effectively displaced indigenous aristocrats as the leading citizens of these settlements.

We can now add a final component to the diagram introduced in the previous chapter. The new, localized version below reflects the fact that the army hierarchy of retired veterans strongly influenced the social make-up of the elite decurion class of the population of Philippi. This, in turn, had a corresponding effect upon non–elite values in the colony.

Social Value Replication in Roman Philippi

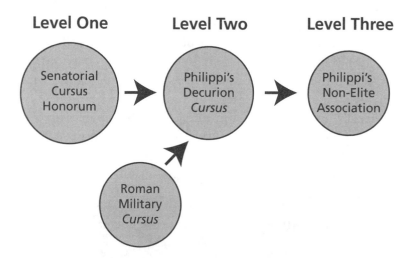

The dynamics of value replication placed residents of Philippi of all classes—including members of Paul's church—under great pressure to conform to Roman social patterns, where rank, status, and honor-seeking were concerned.

Social Status and Honor-Seeking in Philippi

We are now prepared to appreciate some of the archaeological evidence for life in Philippi, when Paul came into the town, as Luke related in Acts 16. We have at our disposal much evidence—in the form of some seven hundred inscriptions unearthed at the site—that shows how Roman cultural values and social codes found expression in the colony.

The material falls conveniently into two sections, corresponding to the great social divide between elites and non-elites, respectively. We will be particularly sensitive to two (often related) phenomena discussed in chapter 2: (1) the publication of one's titles and other honors in *cursus* form, and (2) the practice of benefaction, whereby individuals and families leveraged their financial resources to gain honor and recognition in the public eye.

Elite Honors in Philippi

We begin with an inscription from Philippi which helpfully outlines a full civic *cursus honorum*. Here is the man's resumé, inscribed in stone and erected in a conspicuous place for all passers-by to see:

> Publius Marius Valens, son of Publius, from the tribe Voltinia, honored with the decorations of a decurion, aedile, also decurion of Philippi, priest of the divine Antoninus Pius, duumvir, sponsor of games.[4]

A municipal career formally began with admission to the decurion council, and the office of aedile (or, more likely, quaestor). An aristocrat would then set his sights on the primary honor of the decurion class, namely, the office of duumvir.

Publius also identified himself as "priest of the divine

---

4. 395/L780, p. 397. Inscriptions from Philippi are numbered according to Peter Pilhofer, *Philippi, Band 2: Katalog der Inschriften von Philippi,* WUNT (Tübingen: J. C. B. Mohr, 2000). The English translations are mine, though I closely follow Pilhofer's German.

Antoninus Pius," a second-century Roman emperor. The worship of the emperor formed a key part of civic religion in the colony, and it was a great honor for a person like Publius to be awarded an imperial priesthood by the local decurion council.

Don't for a moment imagine that Publius sought to occupy these offices out of some altruistic desire to serve his fellow citizens. Dio Chrysostom reminds us, once again, of the true motivation. Local elites competed for public office

> not for the sake of what is truly best and in the interest of their country itself, but for the sake of reputation and honours and the possession of greater power than their neighbours, in the pursuit of crowns and precedence and purple robes, fixing their gaze upon these things and staking all upon their attainment. (Dio Chrysostom, *Or.* 34.29)

Notice, as well, the phrase "tribe Voltinia" on Publius's resume. When a man became a Roman citizen, he was enrolled in a specific citizen tribe. Publius's tribe was "Voltinia," as was the case with nearly all of the Roman citizens we are able to identify from Philippi.

Finally, observe the way in which the inscription begins, with Publius drawing attention to his relationship with his father. Almost all of the 700+ inscriptions found at Philippi begin by situating the person to be honored in his or her broader family context. This emphasis upon familial honor will become highly illuminating when we consider Paul's vision for the church as a family in chapter 6.

Elite males representing different kinship groups in the colony competed with one another to gain honor for their extended families through costly works of benefaction. Several inscriptions erected by the Decimii family in Philippi's forum colorfully illustrate this practice.

The most prominent comes from a member of this family who contributed a significant sum of money for the construction of a fountain on the western side of Philippi's forum:

Lucius Decimius Bassus, the son of Lucius, from the tribe Voltinia, aedile of Philippi, has, on the basis of his will, ordered (this fountain) to be made for himself and for Lucius Decimius, the son of Lucius, from the tribe Voltinia, the quaestor and duumvir of Philippi, his father, and for Gaius Decimius Maxsimus, the son of Lucius, out of the tribe Voltinia, his brother, at a cost of 30,000 sesterces.[5]

We gain some perspective about the cost of the endeavor when we recall that the annual pay for an army legionnaire was approximately nine hundred sesterces per year.

The whole Decimii family utilized the fountain as a place to proclaim their honors. The aedile who built the structure (line 1, above: Lucius Decimius Bassus) appears in another inscription adjacent to the fountain: "For Lucius Decimius Bassus, son of Lucius, of the tribe Voltinia, an aedile."[6] So does his brother (listed above as Gaius Decimius Maxsimus) in yet another inscription.[7]

The benefactor's father, also included in the fountain inscription, rose to the top of the civic *cursus*. His attainment of the honor of duumvir (above: "Lucius Decimius...duumvir of Philippi") is proclaimed again in a fourth family inscription, also found near the western fountain:

For Lucius Decimius, son of Lucius, of the tribe Voltinia, quaestor, duumvir.[8]

Don't miss the honorific titles and the references to the person's citizen tribe on the above inscriptions.

Here is a monument in which a member of another family publicly honored a brother for his noteworthy achievements. Note, once again, the extensive list of titles:

---

5. Pilhofer, *Philippi, Band 2*, 213/L347, p. 230.
6. Ibid., 217/L348, p. 234.
7. Ibid., 215/L350, p. 232.
8. Ibid., 214/L349, p. 231.

For Gaius Julius Maximus Mucianus, the son of Gaius, of the tribe Voltinia, a *vir clarissimus*, honored with the *latus clavus* by the divine (Antoninus) Pius, quaestor pro praetore of Pontus and Bithynia, aedile of the grain supply, designated praetor, also decurion of Philippi and in the province of Thracia. Gaius Julius Teres, the Thracharch, father of senators, (has set up this inscription for) his brother in the place determined by a decree of the decurions.[9]

The Latin expressions *vir clarissimus* and *latus clavus* in the inscription refer to the senatorial order. Gaius Julius Teres wanted the world to know that his brother, Gaius Julius Maximus Mucianus, was made a senator by the emperor himself ("the divine [Antoninus] Pius").

This will shed considerable light upon Philippians 2, when we examine the passage in a later chapter. It was a truism in the ancient world that the ability to honor a person—and to make such honor stick in the public eye—was directly proportional to the social status of the individual bestowing the honor.

According to the value system of the dominant culture, the emperor stood at the apex of the social pecking order. The social status of the emperor, in turn, renders the honors he bestows both renowned and incontestable. This is why Gaius, above, made it a point to underscore the fact that it was Antoninus Pius, the emperor of Rome, who made his brother a senator. No one could dispute this claim to honor.

For the early Christians, however, there was someone who occupied a place in the social hierarchy even higher than Rome's emperor. It is not insignificant, in this regard, that Paul, in Philippians 2:9, portrays God—the most esteemed being imaginable—honoring Jesus for his culturally anomalous behavior, as outlined in verses 6–8.

Because of God's status as the supreme being, the honors he bestowed on Jesus would be publicly acknowledged by all: "every

---

9. Ibid., 240/L465, p. 256.

knee will bow . . . and every tongue confess that Jesus Christ [not Caesar] is Lord" (vv. 10–11). The challenge to the colony's social norms could hardly be more direct.

Honor-Seeking Among the Philippian Masses

The masses typically adopted the social values of elites in their local municipalities. According to Ramsay MacMullen, non-elite voluntary associations in provincial towns "ape(d) the high-sounding terminology of larger, municipal bodies, the nomenclature of officialdom . . . and constituted in every detail miniature cities."[10]

This was certainly the case in Philippi. Inscriptions attest to a Bacchus cult, an association devoted to Cybele, a group that met to celebrate the Thracian god Suregethes, a Diana cult, an organization of persons dedicated to Dionysius, and an association that venerated the Egyptian deities Isis and Serapis.[11]

Like the church in Philippi, these were small religious assemblies of less than fifty persons, made up of rural peasants, the urban poor, or other groups of commoners. And nearly all of the inscriptions produced by these associations include references to honorific titles held by their members.

The Worship of Silvanus

The best attested non–elite association in Philippi is the cult of the god Silvanus, the Roman god of the forest.[12] Silvanus worship is illuminating for our purposes, since (a) the cult provides an informative example of value replication in a non-elite religious

---

10. MacMullen, *Roman Social Relations,* 76.
11. Pilhofer, *Philippi, Band 2.* 340/L589, p. 346 (Bacchus); 321/L377, p. 326 (Cybele); 133/G441, p. 134 (Suregethes); 451/L158, p. 439, 519/L245, p. 504 (Diana); 524/L103, 525/L104, 597/G221, p. 511 (Dionysius); 252/L467, 307/G410 (Isis and Serapis).
12. Ibid., 148/L682, p. 150; 163/L002, p. 170; 164/L001, p. 176; 165/L003, p. 179; and 166/L004, p. 181. The Silvanus association is the best attested cult group in Philippi, one which has generated a substantial bibliography (see Pilhofer, *Philippi, Band 1,* 108–13, and *Philippi, Band 2,* 170–83).

group, and (b) the association was in some respects socially analogous to the Jesus community in Philippi.

Peter Dorcey describes Silvanus as follows:

> He qualifies as popular because his cult was restricted to the private domain, remained unconnected with political and civic life, and continued to be of little concern to elite society. Senators and equestrians were not very interested in him and failed to include him in the state calendar. The lettered aristocracy rarely mentioned the god in their writings.[13]

The description could be applied without qualification to Paul's congregations in the East.

There are other similarities. Both the church and the Silvanus cult went against the grain of the sharp social verticality of the dominant culture by including slaves, freedmen, and freeborn persons. The cult's central honor, the office of aedile, for example, was on at least one occasion awarded to a freedman in the Silvanus cult.

Birth status was, in fact, apparently of little concern to members of the association, since an extensive list of members randomly scatters the names of slaves and freedmen among those of non-elite freeborn persons.[14] The early Christians, of course, also sought to shorten the social distance between slave and free in their teachings and social practices.

A final similarity between the church and the Silvanus group relates to the presence of extended households in both voluntary associations. Readers will likely be familiar with the household conversion of the Philippian jailer, as narrated in Acts 16:33–34. Lydia and her household were baptized during Paul's stay in the colony, as well (v. 15).

---

13. Peter F. Dorcey, *The Cult of Silvanus: A Study in Roman Folk Religion* (Leiden: Brill, 1992), 3.
14. Pilhofer, *Philippi, Band 1,* 109–10.

The Silvanus association, too, included whole households. Among the inscriptions from Philippi we encounter a patriarch named Gaius Paccius Mercuriales whose entire family—sons, a freedman, and a slave—belonged to the Silvanus cult in the colony.

So much for the similarities. In other areas the Silvanus cult and the Christian community prove to be quite dissimilar. Ethnically, for example, the worshippers of Silvanus were exclusively Roman.

Nor do any women appear in the Silvanus inscriptions. The cult consisted solely of non-elite males, along with the male members of their extended households.

The Jesus community in the colony was more inclusive with respect to both ethnicity and gender. It has been recently estimated that about one third of those who belonged to the church at Philippi possessed Roman citizenship. The majority of the congregation would have been non-citizen Greeks and others.

We learn from Acts, moreover, that the church at Philippi began with the conversion of a woman (Acts 16:14–15). And we read in Philippians about women in the church who had served alongside Paul and had labored in the ministry of the gospel (4:2–3).

More pertinent to the present discussion are the differences between Silvanus and Christianity with respect to Rome's *cursus* ideology. As we will see below, the non-elite Romans who venerated Silvanus in the colony at Philippi replicated in miniature the preoccupation with honor and status that characterized the lives of their social betters on the local decurion council and in the imperial senate at Rome.

Paul, in his letter to the Philippians, sought, in contrast, to challenge such tendencies in the Christian *ekklēsia* (Greek). We will examine Paul's strategy in some detail in the following chapters. Here it will prove illuminating to consider the ways in which the worshippers of Silvanus appropriated the social values and practices of Philippi's local elites. Here is a summary of our comparison–contrast between Silvanus worshippers and the followers of Jesus at Philippi:

Silvanus Worshippers and the Christian Church in Philippi

SIMILARITIES		
Both were non-elite social groups		
Both downplayed the social hierarchy		
Both included whole households		
Silvanus Group	**DIFFERENCES**	**Jesus Group**
Limited to Romans		Jews, Greeks, and Romans
Male Membership		Males and Females
Replicated Prevailing Social Values Related to Honor-Seeking and Self-Promotion		Subverted Prevailing Social Values Related to Honor-Seeking and Self-Promotion

We can begin with organization and Latin titles. Silvanus cult members divided themselves into at least seven distinct subgroups called *decuriae*. Specific honors in the association included both a formal priesthood, a post of *pater* ("father"), and the office of aedile.

Marcus Alfensus Aspasius, Lucius Volattius Urbanus, and Macius Bictor are identified as priests in the inscriptions. A fellow named Publius Hostilius Philadelphus is called "aedile," a term which is explicitly described as an "honor."

The presence of this now familiar term in a non–elite association should not go unnoticed. We saw "aedile" used as the title of a key office in (1) the senatorial *cursus honorum* at Rome. The word was, in turn, appropriated by elites at Philippi, who used it as a designation for an office in (2) the local decurion *cursus*.

Now we encounter a non-elite proclaiming that he has attained the honor of "aedile" in (3) a voluntary cult association. The trickle-down effect of social value replication—preoccupation with honorific titles and the public display of those titles—could hardly be more transparent.

In the case of our Silvanus aedile, the parallels extend to the man's activities in the cult. Earlier in the chapter we saw a decurion aedile, Lucius Decimius Bassus, spend 30,000 sesterces on a fountain for Philippi's forum. Here in the colony's Silvanus cult, our elite decurion's act of benefaction is replicated in miniature, as Publius Hostilius Philadelphus, the association's aedile, finances a pair of inscriptions and a stairway adjacent to the god's temple.[15]

The inscription that mentions the stairway also enumerates the names of seven other cult members who contributed significantly toward the construction of the temple:

Publius Hostilius Philadelphus, on account of the honor (given to him) of being aedile, furnished this inscription at his own expense and inscribed the names of those members who contributed work:

Domitius Primigenius, a bronze statue of Silvanus with a temple.

Gaius Horatius Sabinus, 400 roof tiles for the covering of the temple.

Nutrius Valens, two marble statuettes, Hercules and Mercury.

Paccius Mercuriales, 250 denarii for concrete in front of the temple, and Olympus on a painted table for 15 denarii.

Publicius Laetus 50 denarii for the temple building.

Paccius Mercuriales, also, along with his sons and one of his

---

15. Pilhofer, *Philippi, Band 2*, pp. 170–71: 163/L002, lines 1–2; 164/001, lines 1–2, 24–25.

freedmen, 50 denarii for the temple building, along with a statuette of Liber made of marble for 25 denarii.

Alfenus Aspasius, the priest, a bronze statue of Silvanus with a base, and he also deposited during his lifetime 50 denarii for his death.

Hostilius Philadelphus had the rock cut, at his own cost, for the stairway up to the sanctuary.[16]

We gain an appreciation for the replication of the elite practice of benefaction among the members of the Silvanus cult by comparing the amounts of money donated by cult members, above, with the 30,000 sesterces it cost Lucius Decimius Bassus to build his fountain in Philippi's forum.

One denarius was worth four sesterces. The elite decurion Lucius's contribution to the fountain project was therefore thirty times as large as the most generous gift towards the Silvanus temple (250 denarii) and 150 times the average gift of 50 denarii.

Here, again, although the social distance between Lucius the decurion and the non-elite Silvanus group is vast, the values and behaviors of the two status groups mirror one another in a remarkable way. In each case we see persons leveraging their respective financial resources to gain honor in a public setting.

Conclusion

When Paul crossed over from Asia into Europe and arrived in Roman Philippi during the middle of the first century A.D., he stepped into a highly stratified relational environment in which elites and non-elites alike competed vigorously with their social peers for offices and other public honors.

The origins of Philippi, as an imperial colony of military veterans, guaranteed that Rome's *cursus honorum*, which for generations had defined the career paths of ambitious and well-positioned

---

16. Ibid., 164/L001, p. 176.

senators in the capital, would reproduce itself among decurions in Philippi. Urban benefaction further provided these local elites with an opportunity to trade wealth for recognition, and inscriptions honoring various donors to public projects proliferated throughout the colony.

Non-elites in Philippi, like the worshippers of Silvanus, above, mimicked the practices of their social betters, as they gathered together in voluntary associations that boasted honorific offices and engaged in benefaction in ways remarkably similar to the activities of the decurion order.

Christians in Philippi were hardly immune to such tendencies. It would have been wholly natural for the church to adopt the social practices of the dominant culture. We should, therefore, expect to find Christians competing for titles and honors in a church hierarchy that replicated the steep verticality of the broader culture.

Inscriptions suggest that by the middle of the second century this was precisely the case. A follower of Jesus named Aurelios Kuriokos, for example, boasted on his gravestone that he was a "teacher" in the church.[17] A woman named Posidonia wanted passers-by to know that she held the honor of "deaconess."[18]

The pressure to conform to the colony's relational norms was surely present when the apostle Paul founded the church a century earlier. Paul, however, would have no part of the pomp and social posturing that characterized life in Philippi, since it threatened to compromise the apostle's radically alternative vision for relational life in the nascent Christian community.

As we will see in the chapters to follow, self-promotion, honor-seeking, and the abuse of authority—then or now— flies in the face of Paul's vision for power relations in the church. This is patently clear in both (a) the other-centered manner in which Paul and Silas leveraged their social capital in their ministry in Philippi (Acts 16) and (b) Paul's portrayal

---

17. Ibid., 071/G437, p. 73.
18. Ibid., 077/G067, p. 77.

of the humiliation and exaltation of Christ in his letter to the Philippians (2:6–11).

Christians in Philippi were to pattern their lives not after the values of Rome, but after a Jewish Messiah who willingly exchanged his immeasurably exalted status for the shame of a crucified slave—all for the benefit of rebellious human beings whom he had created.

Paul intended the example of Jesus to indelibly mark the ways in which power and authority were used in the Christian community at Philippi. The Holy Spirit intends Paul's teachings to transform our understanding of leadership in our churches today. We turn now to the biblical materials, as we seek to recapture Paul's cruciform vision for authentic Christian leadership.

Questions for Reflection

1. What happened to the social hierarchy of a town when it was colonized by the Romans?

2. In what ways were the social values of Philippi like those of Rome itself?

3. Compare the Silvanus cult group with the early Christians. How were they the same? How did they differ?

4. Given what you now know about the social world of Roman Philippi, do you think that local residents—elite or non-elite—would have found Christianity attractive? Why or why not?

5. By the second century, Christians in Philippi were preoccupied with titles and status in a manner similar to the broader culture in the colony. Do you think the church in America today has been influenced in unhealthy ways by the social values of the culture in which we live? If so, in what ways?

PART TWO

Power and Authority in the Early Church

Paul's Cruciform Vision for Authentic Christian Leadership

Challenging the Social Status Quo

Paul, Silas, and the Ministry in Philippi

These men are promoting customs that are not legal for us as Romans to adopt or practice.— Acts 16:21

We are now prepared to read the Bible against the background materials surveyed in the previous chapters. We will follow Paul and Silas through their adventures in Philippi, as narrated in Acts 16, and treat selected passages from Philippians. Chapter 5 then explores in some detail Paul's majestic portrayal of Christ in Philippians 2:6–11.

Luke (Acts) and Paul (Philippians) exhibit a remarkable sensitivity to the preoccupation with status and honor that characterized interpersonal relationships among the residents of Philippi. Both authors were well aware of the distinctly Roman orientation of Philippi, and they were particularly attuned to the cultural values and social codes that determined how people in the colony treated one another.

Paul's take on Roman relational priorities becomes crystal clear both in Acts 16 and in his letter to the Philippians. As we will see, Paul was not at all enamored with the pride of honors that permeated Philippi's relational ethos.

Paul taught and modeled a radically alternative approach to status, privilege, and interpersonal relationships—a way of life based on the cruciform example of Jesus Christ. In both his ministry in Philippi (Acts 16) and his letter to the church in the colony (Philippians), the apostle forcefully challenged what Jon Lendon has called the "ceaseless, restless quest for distinction in the eyes of one's peers" that defined human relations in this markedly Roman settlement.[1]

Paul's goal was to create a very different kind of community among the followers of Jesus in first-century Philippi. The Philippian church was to be a community that discouraged competition for status and privilege, a place where the honor game was off-limits, in summary, a community in which persons with power and authority used their social capital not to further their own personal or familial agendas but, rather, to serve their brothers and sisters in Christ.

Later in the book (chaps. 7–9) we will apply Paul's vision for community to our lives as Christians today. First, however, we must establish a biblical foundation on which to build that practical application. As we dig deep into Paul's community-building strategy in Acts and Philippians (chaps. 4–6), I would encourage you to begin to reflect, even now, on the implications of what you are learning for your own congregation and for your role as a church leader.

Paul's Jesus-like take on status and authority had the potential to utterly transform community life for the better among followers of Jesus in first-century Philippi. The apostle's other-centered approach to power relations offers great promise for generating a healthy context for life and ministry in our churches today, as well.

Acts 16 — Paul's Ministry in Philippi

One day in A.D. 49, Paul and Silas set out on the apostle's second missionary journey (Acts 15:36–41). The two men first

---

1. Lendon, *Empire of Honour,* 35.

visited several cities in the East, where Paul and Barnabas had established Jesus communities on Paul's first journey (16:1–5).

Paul intended to stay in the regions of Asia (modern Turkey) and evangelize the Roman provinces of Asia Minor and Bithynia. The Holy Spirit had other plans. In response to a vision Paul had one night in Troas, the missionaries crossed over from Asia to Europe, finally settling for some time in Philippi, a town Luke identifies as a "Roman colony" (vv. 6–12; see v. 12).

As was his custom, Paul first sought out a local synagogue. What he found instead was a group of women gathered for prayer on the Sabbath outside the city gates. Lydia embraced Paul's message about Jesus, and she served as Paul's patron in the colony, hosting Paul and Silas in her home (vv. 13–15).

Conflict soon erupted between the missionaries and the local residents of Philippi. It began with a power encounter between Paul and "a spirit of prediction." The slave girl who had the spirit "made a large profit for her owners by fortune-telling" (v. 16). Paul ordered the spirit to depart from the girl and, in so doing, put an end to the profit-making venture (v. 19).

The owners did not appreciate Paul's ministry to the young woman. They proceeded to drag Paul and Silas into the crowded marketplace, where they accused the missionaries before the colony's magistrates of "promoting customs that are not legal for us as Romans to adopt or practice" (v. 21). A crowd rose up against Paul and Silas, and the officials had the missionaries beaten and thrown in prison.

As events unfolded, Paul and Silas experienced a delightful reversal of fortunes, and we will pick up the rest of the story below. It will be helpful at this point, however, to pause long enough to appreciate Luke's sensitivity to the social values of the colony.

It is clear at the outset that Luke was self-consciously aware of two key characteristics of Philippi that we encountered earlier: (a) the marked "Romanness" of the settlement, and (b) the colony's preoccupation with honorific titles for public office. Let's consider each in turn.

The "Romanness" of Philippi

Two bits of social realia in Luke's account mark out Philippi as more distinctly Roman than the other towns Paul visited in Acts. First, Luke specifically designated Philippi as "a Roman colony" (16:12). On the surface this is not particularly striking. It was common knowledge, after all, that Philippi was a colony, inhabited by descendants of Roman veterans of the battles of Philippi (43 B.C.) and Actium (30 B.C.).

What makes the designation unique is the fact that Luke used the term only here in the book of Acts. This is striking, to say the least, since Paul's travels, as Luke described them in his lengthy narrative, took the apostle through at least eight other Roman colonies.[2] One of those was Corinth, where Paul remained "a year and six months" (18:11). Not a single one of these colonies—not even Corinth—is explicitly identified by the author as such. Luke reserved the designation "colony" solely for Philippi.

Some think that Luke was simply better informed about Philippi than the other places Paul visited. It is preferable to assume that in describing Philippi as "a Roman colony," Luke here underscored the Romanness of the settlement, in preparation for the charge brought against the missionaries in the verses to follow.

The charge against Paul and Silas also reveals Luke's sensitivity to the Romanness of Philippi. Only in Philippi, among all the places Paul visited in Acts, do Paul's adversaries accuse the missionary band of "promoting customs that are not legal for us as Romans to adopt or practice" (v. 21).

The legitimacy of the accusation is not the issue here. The degree to which Paul's gospel message was anti-Roman will become increasingly clear as we continue our survey of the biblical materials below. For now it is enough to note that the charge brought by the slave girl's owners proved immediately effective in stirring up the colony's residents against Paul and Silas.

---

2. Pilhofer (*Philippi, Band 1,* 159–60) cites Pisidian Antioch (13:14; 14:19–20), Iconium (13:51; 14:1, 19, 21; 16:2), Lystra (14:6, 8, 21; 16:1–2), Alexandria Troas (16:8, 11; 20:5–6), Corinth (18:1; 19:1), Ptolemais (21:7), Syracuse (28:12), and Puteoli (28:13).

The Romans were social conservatives who valued tradition and who generally resisted innovation in their social and religious customs. A familiar Latin expression, *mos maiorum* (loosely translated, "the way of our ancestors"), served as a conceptual rallying point for Romans who sought to articulate their commitment to Rome's ancestral heritage and traditions.

The charge that the missionaries were advocating another, unlawful set of "customs," therefore, pierced deep into the psyche of the Roman citizens present in the Philippian marketplace that day—thus the reaction of the crowd.

It is critical to note, once again, however, that the charge against the missionaries is unique to the Philippian narrative in Acts. But why?

Paul did not change his tactics in Philippi. He preached the same gospel elsewhere, and he performed exorcisms in other towns, as well. At Ephesus, moreover, Paul's activities created an economic dilemma for local craftsmen that was in some ways analogous to the scenario with the owners of the slave girl at Philippi (Acts 19).

To be sure, Paul's message was inimical to Roman social and religious values in a number of ways. But Paul's gospel was no more anti-Roman in Philippi than it was elsewhere the apostle ministered. Only in the colony at Philippi, however, was Paul accused of promulgating anti-Roman customs.

Here again Luke betrayed a particular sensitivity to the Romanness of the locale. It seems, in fact, from (a) the designation of Philippi as a "Roman colony" and (b) the charge against the missionaries—both unique to the Philippian narrative in Acts 16—that Luke wanted his readers to see that Philippi was "Roman" in a way that the other cities Paul visited were not. This impression is decidedly confirmed when we consider the titles Luke used for the various officials in the colony.

Preoccupation with Honors and Titles

Our survey of the inscriptions from Philippi (chap. 3) revealed a population highly concerned to acquire and proclaim titles and honors associated with public office. Luke was not unaware of this cultural dynamic, as evidenced by the way that he described Paul and Silas interacting with various officials during the stay in Philippi.

Five times Luke used the word *stratēgos* ("chief magistrates") as a title for those who administered justice to Paul and Silas (Acts 16:20, 22, 35, 36, 38). We also meet lesser officials called *rhabdouchos* ("the police") (vv. 35, 38). Yet another individual was labeled *desmophylax* ("the jailer"). These Greek terms occur only here in Acts.

Scholars identify the chief magistrates in Acts 16 as the duumviri of the colony. We encountered several of Philippi's duumviri in the inscriptions cited in the previous chapter. They were the senior officials in the colony, two local elites who co-led the municipality's decurion council.

The word translated "police" (*rhabdouchos*) is also a technical Greek term that corresponds to the Latin *lictores*. *Lictores* marched before the chief magistrates, as the latter made their way through the colony. The police carried the fasces, a bundle of rods symbolizing the magistrates' judicial authority.

The choice of words used in Acts 16 to describe local officials turns out, once again, to be exceptional in Luke's narrative. A comparison with Paul's ministry in another municipality proves revealing.

During the first missionary journey Paul and Barnabas ran into official opposition in another Roman colony, Pisidian Antioch. We read that "the Jews incited the prominent women, who worshiped God, and the leading men of the city. They stirred up persecution against Paul and Barnabas and expelled them from their district" (Acts 13:50).

These "leading men," who had the authority to take such action against Paul and Barnabas, held the same posts as the magistrates in the Philippian narrative. They were Pisidian Antioch's duumviri. However, Luke did not designate them as such using *stratēgos*, the technical term he used in the Philippian narrative. Instead, he referred to them generically as *protos* (lit. "first/prominent"), the "leading men" of the city.

The contrast with Acts 16 must not be missed. In the

Philippian narrative, Luke introduced the duumviri with a generic term. The slave girl's owners dragged Paul and Silas into the marketplace before the *archōntos* ("authorities," v. 19). The word could be applied to persons in various positions of authority.

Luke became more precise, though, in the next verse, where he switched to the word *stratēgos* ("magistrates"), a term that specifically designated the colony's duumviri. He then employed *stratēgos* exclusively throughout the rest of the story (vv. 20, 22, 35, 36, 38).

The fivefold repetition of "magistrates," along with the unique expressions translated "police" and "jailer" in Acts 16, strongly suggest that Luke was consciously aware of the centrality of honor, titles, and status among the social priorities of the colony's residents.

The Story Resumes

We now pick up where we left off in the story in Acts 16. While Paul and Silas were in prison, "suddenly there was such a violent earthquake that the foundations of the jail were shaken, and immediately all the doors were opened, and everyone's chains came loose" (v. 26).

As events unfolded, a terrified Philippian jailer and his whole household believed in Paul's God: "Right away he and all his family were baptized" (v. 33).

The following morning, the magistrates, apparently unaware of the tumultuous events of the previous evening, sent for the missionaries to release them from prison. Paul's response was an unexpected one:

> "They beat us in public without a trial, although we are Roman citizens, and threw us in jail. And now are they going to smuggle us out secretly? Certainly not! On the contrary, let them come themselves and escort us out!" (v. 37)

The reaction of the colony's esteemed duumviri to this brazen challenge from a non-elite, itinerant Jewish preacher provides a surprising twist to the ending of the Philippian narrative:

Then the police reported these words to the magistrates. They were afraid when they heard that Paul and Silas were Roman citizens. So they came and apologized to them, and escorting them out, they urged them to leave town. (vv. 38–39)

In a delightful status reversal, Paul and Silas turned the tables and emerged as social victors in their contest with Philippi's elite duumviri.

The story finally draws to a close. We discover that Paul willingly complied with the magistrates' request that he and Silas leave the colony (v. 39)—but only according to a timetable of his own choosing. First the missionaries returned to Lydia's home.

Only after "they came to Lydia's house where they saw and encouraged the brothers" did Paul and Silas finally depart from Philippi (v. 40). The "brothers" Luke mentions became the nucleus of the Jesus community at Philippi to whom Paul would one day write the letter we call Philippians.

Citizenship In Philippi

Our discussion of social stratification and the judicial system (chap. 3) has prepared us well for the reaction of Philippi's duumviri to the disclosure of the missionaries' citizen status.

Citizens and non-citizens were supposed to be treated differently at the court of justice. Peter Garnsey elaborates on the distinction as it might manifest itself in a veteran colony like Philippi: "In a Roman colony it appears that arrest, beating, and imprisonment were normal for aliens, but that it was potentially dangerous to give citizens the same treatment."[3]

The magistrates at Philippi assumed that Paul and Silas were "aliens" and treated them accordingly. When they found out otherwise, the duumviri became "afraid" (v. 38), and understandably

---

3. Peter Garnsey, *Social Status and Legal Privilege in the Roman Empire* (Oxford: Oxford University Press, 1970), 268.

so. Rome had a tradition of prosecuting governors who mistreated its citizens in the provinces.

But this, in turn, raises an obvious and pressing question. *Why did the missionaries not reveal their citizen status to the magistrates at the outset, and save themselves the beatings and imprisonment?* The answer is to be found in the social demographics of Philippi and, especially, in Paul's understanding of the gospel.

When Paul and Silas were in the colony, about 40 percent of the population would have been Roman citizens. Slanted for social accessibility, this means that perhaps one-third of the persons who responded to the gospel in Philippi possessed citizen status.

The legal privilege associated with the franchise was highly valued by Romans who found themselves in the provinces, far away from the capital city of Rome. Cicero explains:

> Poor men of humble birth sail across the seas to shores they have never seen before, where they find themselves among strangers, and cannot always have with them acquaintances to vouch for them. Yet such trust have they in the single fact of their citizenship that they count on being safe, not only where they find our magistrates, who are restrained by the fear of law and public opinion, and not only among their own countrymen, to whom they are bound by the ties of a common language and civic rights and much else besides: no, wherever they find themselves, they feel confident that this one fact [their citizenship] will be their defence. (*2 Verr.* 2.5.167)

Residents of a Roman colony took particular pride in their citizen status. Each colony, when it was founded, was typically identified with one of Rome's citizen tribes. Philippi's tribe was Voltinia. And the Philippians were proud of it.

One-half of all the first- and second-century inscriptions unearthed at Philippi contain the abbreviation VOL (Voltinia), highlighting the person's Roman citizen tribe. Even a two-year-old child had the expression engraved on his tombstone:

Nepos, son of . . . of the tribe Voltinia, (died at) two years of age, lies buried here.[4]

Once again, the social world of Philippi accords remarkably well with the details of the story of Paul's ministry in the colony in Acts 16. It is fair to conclude from the archaeological data that nowhere in the Roman East were the residents of a local municipality more concerned to proclaim their citizen status than in the colony at Philippi. And only at Philippi, among the places Paul visited on his three missionary journeys, does the issue of Roman citizenship surface in Luke's narrative in the book of Acts.

Notice, as well, that only in Philippians does Paul use formal citizenship terminology to talk about Christian behavior and eschatological expectation (1:27; 3:20). The distinction between citizen and non-citizen was apparently a defining one for the relational environment of Roman Philippi.

The preoccupation with citizenship in the colony, in turn, readily explains why Paul and Silas failed to disclose their status when first brought before the magistrates. As Brian Rapske rightly notes,

> [T]he self-defense of an early citizenship claim would probably have been construed by the magistrates and populace as an assertion of commitment to the primacy of Roman, over against Jewish (i.e., Christian), customs. The signals sent would also have put the church at risk of dissolution if the new Philippian converts did not possess the Roman franchise. At the least, there would have been uncertainty surrounding Paul's commitment to his message. Converts might wonder whether only those suitably protected (i.e., by Roman citizenship) should become believers in Christ and they might think it disingenuous for Paul and Silas to ask others to suffer what they themselves were able to avoid.[5]

---

4. Pilhofer, *Philippi, Band 2*, 600/L229, p. 601.
5. Brian Rapske, *The Book of Acts and Paul in Roman Custody*, vol. 3 of *The*

The behavior of Paul and Silas represents an utter inversion of Roman social priorities and common attitudes toward the citizen franchise.

Consider the policies of Claudius, the current emperor—policies that may have fueled preoccupation with Roman citizenship in a colony like Philippi. Although liberal in his efforts to extend citizenship in the provinces, Claudius was adamant about preserving social and legal distinctions between citizen and non-citizen. According to Suetonius, Claudius executed persons "pretending to be Roman citizens" (Suetonius, *Claud.* 25).

The targets of the emperor's policies were non-citizens who masqueraded as citizens to improve their social standing. The missionaries engaged in precisely the opposite behavior. Paul and Silas were Roman citizens who pretended to be non-citizens, and who severely suffered as a result.

The themes of Roman citizenship and public flogging intersect elsewhere in our sources, where it becomes quite apparent that the unjust flogging of a citizen was a direct affront to Roman social sensibilities. Cicero's rhetoric soars, in this regard, when he prosecutes Verres for beating an innocent Roman citizen while serving as governor of Sicily:

> There in the open market-place of Messana a Roman citizen, gentlemen, was beaten with rods; and all the while, amid the crack of the falling blows, no groan was heard from the unhappy man, no words came from his lips in his agony except "I am a Roman citizen." By thus proclaiming this citizenship he had been hoping to avert all those blows and shield his body from torture. (*2 Verr.* 2.5.162)

Read against the background of Roman social values, the failure of Paul and Silas to leverage their citizen status during the events outlined in Acts 16:20–24 proves to be markedly counter-cultural.

Book of Acts in Its First Century Setting (Grand Rapids: Eerdmans, 1994), 134.

When it mattered most, the missionaries disowned the advantages pertaining to the citizen franchise and instead offered their backs to the policemen's rods and their feet to the jailer's stocks—all this in order to guarantee a level playing field for representatives from any social class in Philippi who might respond to the gospel.

A Striking Parallel

Like Jesus, as portrayed in Philippians 2:6–8, Paul and Silas did not consider their status as something to be exploited but, instead, willingly endured suffering for the benefit of others.

The parallels between the narrative of Acts 16 and the story of Jesus in Philippians 2:6–11 are, in fact, quite illuminating. We will treat the great christological passage from Paul's letter in detail in the next chapter. For now simply notice three rather striking similarities between the two accounts:

Paul and Silas (Acts 16)	Messiah Jesus (Philippians 2)
Refused to exploit their Roman citizenship.	Did not regard equality with God as something to be exploited (v. 6).
Willingly suffered the humiliation of flogging and imprisonment at the hands of Roman magistrates (vv. 19–23).	Willingly suffered the humiliation of crucifixion at the hands of a Roman magistrate (v. 8).
Vindicated by a sudden status reversal. Citizen status recognized. Oppressors are put to shame (vv. 35–39).	Vindicated by a sudden status reversal. Divine lordship recognized. Every knee will bow (vv. 9–11).

There is a more subtle parallel not reflected in the chart. Jennifer Glancy has recently elaborated upon the social implications of flogging in a place like Philippi. Our earlier discussion of the public nature of honor in the Roman world has prepared us well for Glancy's first observation: "Citizen or not, free or slave, a beaten body was a dishonored body; any free person who was publicly stripped and battered with rods suffered an effective reduction in social status."[6]

More illuminating, in view of the above comparison of Acts 16 with Philippians 2, is the relationship Glancy proceeds to uncover between flogging and slavery: "whipping, which brings dishonor to the one who is whipped, is suitable only for slaves, so one who is whipped, even if legally free, warrants description as servile."[7]

According to this cultural script, Paul and Silas essentially allowed the magistrates at Philippi to treat them like Greco-Roman slaves. Jesus, we are informed by Paul, similarly "emptied Himself by assuming the form of a slave" (Phil 2:7). The parallels between Acts 16 and Philippians 2:6–11 are intriguing, to say the least.

I have argued elsewhere that Paul's experience in Philippi influenced the way he framed his picture of Jesus in the letter to the church a decade later.[8] The manner in which Paul and Silas responded to the circumstances confronting them in Philippi would certainly have enhanced the credibility of Paul's pointed challenge in Philippians 2. For while they were in the colony, Paul and Silas had faithfully modeled the very christocentric mindset that forms the heart of Paul's exhortation:

> Everyone should look out not only for his own interests, but also for the interests of others. Make your own attitude that of Christ Jesus, who, existing in the form of God, did not consider equality with God as something to be used for His own advantage. (Phil 2:4–6)

For more than two thousand years local church ministers

---

6. Jennifer A. Glancy, "Boasting of Beatings (2 Corinthians 11:23-25)," *JBL* 123.1 (2004): 124.

7. Ibid., 125.

8. See Joseph H. Hellerman, "Vindicating God's Servants in Philippi and in Philippians: The Influence of Paul's Ministry in Philippi upon the Composition of Philippians 2:6-11," *BBR* 20.1 (2010): 85-102.

have looked to the apostle Paul as a paradigm for Christian leadership. Paul's attitude toward his Roman citizen status (Acts 16) forcefully exemplifies the apostle's cruciform vision for authentic Christian leadership. Today, perhaps more than ever, we need pastors in our churches who, like Paul, view their status and authority as a trust to be employed—even set aside, if necessary—in the service of their brothers and sisters in Christ.

Paul's Letter to the Philippians

Paul's relationship with Philippi did not end with the visit to the colony in 49. In his letter to the church he spoke of the Philippians' "partnership in the gospel from the first day until now" (1:5). Paul was referring to the tangible support the Philippians provided him (a) immediately after he left Philippi ("the first day") and, again, (b) while he was in prison years later ("now").

"From the First Day"

When Paul and Silas left Philippi after their release from prison (Acts 16:40), they headed south along the eastern coast of the Grecian peninsula, spending time in Thessalonica (17:1–10), Berea (17:10–15), and Athens (17:16–34). The missionaries finally settled in Corinth, where Paul remained for eighteen months (18:1–17).

Throughout the period the Philippians apparently gave of their resources to support Paul in his evangelistic efforts. He recalled this near the end of his letter:

> And you Philippians know that in the early days of the gospel, when I left Macedonia, no church shared with me in the matter of giving and receiving except you alone. For even in Thessalonica you sent gifts for my need several times. (Phil 4:15–16)

"Until Now"

Some years later, Paul again found himself in prison (Phil 1:7, 14, 17), presumably in Rome, but possibly in Ephesus. Once again, the Philippians took it upon themselves to provide for the practical needs of the apostle. They sent a monetary gift of some sort to Paul via Epaphroditus, a faithful messenger from the church at Philippi.

The gift led Paul to write his letter to the Philippians. Paul warmly responded to the church's most recent expression of generosity:

> I rejoiced in the Lord greatly that once again you renewed your care for me. You were, in fact, concerned about me but lacked the opportunity to show it . . . you did well by sharing with me in my hardship. . . . I have received everything in full, and I have an abundance. I am fully supplied, having received from Epaphroditus what you provided—a fragrant offering, an acceptable sacrifice, pleasing to God. (Phil 4:10, 14, 18)

When Paul finished writing Philippians, he sent the letter back to the colony with Epaphroditus (2:25–29). He hoped to send Timothy shortly (2:19–24), and Paul himself intended to return to Philippi after his anticipated release from prison (1:25–26; 2:24).

Philippians as a Friendship Letter

Paul's relationship with the Christians at Philippi was especially warm and intimate. Near the beginning of the letter, Paul informed his readers, "I deeply miss all of you with the affection of Christ Jesus" (1:8). He later said, "So then, my brothers, you are dearly loved and longed for—my joy and crown. In this manner stand firm in the Lord, dear friends" (4:1).

In both form and content Paul's letter exhibits the characteristics of an epistolary genre from the ancient world known as a "friendship letter." Scholars have identified a formal pattern in the genre which corresponds to several sections of Philippians:

1. The address and greeting [1:1–2]
2. Prayer for the recipients [1:3–11]
3. Reassurance about the sender (= "my affairs") [1:12–26]

4. Request for reassurance about the recipients (= "your affairs") [1:27–2:18; 3:1–4:3]
5. Information about movements of intermediaries [2:19–30]
6. Exchange of greetings with third parties [4:21–22]
7. Closing wish for health [4:23][9]

Friendship was serious business in the ancient world, in ways that are not always easy for us to appreciate. The issue of friendship even served as a topic for philosophical reflection among Greek and Roman writers.

The ancients expected genuine friendship—ideally enjoyed among equals—to be marked by loyalty, a deep sense of mutual affection, the giving and receiving of goods and services, and a degree of social solidarity that even extended to the sharing of common enemies.

Interpersonal exhortation, using moral examples (good and bad), was also common in the context of friendship in the Roman world. Such discourse abounds in Philippians (exhortation: 1:27–2:18 and 3:1–4:3; exemplary paradigms: the Christ story in 2:6–11, and Paul's story in 3:4–14).

It is in the use of moral examples, in particular, that Paul adapted the genre of the friendship letter to the specific needs of the Christians in Philippi, and we will give special attention to the examples of Jesus (2:6–11) and Paul (3:4–14) in the pages to follow.

Taking into consideration both the form and content of the epistle, Gordon Fee appropriately concludes that Philippians was written as a "hortatory letter of friendship."[10]

The Message of Philippians

The heart of Paul's message is twofold: (1) the Philippian

---

9. Gordon D. Fee, *Paul's Letter to the Philippians,* NICNT, ed. Gordon D. Fee (Grand Rapids: Eerdmans, 1995), 3. Fee's discussion of the literary genre of Philippians (pp. 2–14) should be consulted in full.
10. Ibid., 12.

Christians must stay united; and they must do so (2) in the face of opposition from pagan residents of the colony—all for the sake of the gospel.

The two issues—unity within, opposition from without—surface in the first directly hortatory section, which introduces the body of the letter:

> Just one thing: Live your life in a manner worthy of the gospel of Christ. Then, whether I come and see you or am absent, I will hear about you that you are standing firm in one spirit, with one mind, working side by side for the faith that comes from the gospel, not being frightened in any way by your opponents. This is a sign of destruction for them, but of your deliverance—and this is from God. For it has been given to you on Christ's behalf not only to believe in Him, but also to suffer for Him, having the same struggle that you saw I had and now hear that I have. (1:27–30)

Paul had apparently heard from Epaphroditus that the church was experiencing hostility from the non-Christian residents of Philippi. He was concerned about the social solidarity of the community in the face of this opposition.

Paul likened the sufferings of the Philippians to his own struggles—first, when he was in the colony a decade earlier, and "now," as one who had been imprisoned for the gospel (1:30; see also 1:13). In each case, Paul came into serious conflict with Roman imperial values and priorities.

The comparison Paul drew between his own struggles and the sufferings of his readers suggests that the community's "opponents" (1:28) were maltreating the Philippian Christians for promulgating anti-Roman customs, in a manner somehow parallel to the way that local residents harassed Paul and Silas during their visit in Philippi.

Nothing in the letter points, however, to physical persecution, that is, to flogging, imprisonment, or martyrdom for the gospel. The Jesus community in the colony was likely experiencing the profound social ostracism and economic hardship that often troubled minority groups that had been marginalized by representatives of the dominant culture.

In the midst of these challenges Paul urged his readers to maintain a united front, to strive "with one mind," unmoved in the face of opposition (1:27). The theme of unity, in fact, surfaces throughout the letter (2:2; 4:2).

The Challenge of Unity: Then and Now

Unity is difficult to maintain. Any group of persons banding together for a common cause will eventually encounter "people problems" among its members. This was true in first-century Philippi, and it is true in twenty-first-century America today.

Interpersonal discord—like the situation Paul addressed between Euodia and Syntyche (Phil 4:2)—is a transcultural reality. There is nothing culturally unique about two individuals not getting along with one another.

However, in addition to those transcultural people problems that seem to surface wherever two or more are gathered, a Christian community in a highly stratified social environment like ancient Philippi would have faced culturally-specific threats to unity, as well—threats that had the potential seriously to compromise the social ethos of the church as a whole.

It is easy to identify and, at least, attempt to address a generic interpersonal dispute, like the conflict between Euodia and Syntyche. Paul's solution—he appealed to an unnamed "true partner" to mediate (4:3)—constitutes timeless wisdom that could find application in almost any such situation.

It is profoundly more difficult to "stand outside of ourselves," so to speak, in order to identify and resist culturally systemic patterns of thought and behavior that are antithetical to the gospel, since we have been socialized from infancy to view these patterns as normal. Yet, where social status and honor-seeking were concerned, this is precisely what the Philippians had to do, in order to remain united in the face of opposition against them.

Marginalized by the pagan majority, Christians in Philippi would have been almost irresistibly tempted to replicate the ideals and practices of the dominant culture, by generating in the church a hierarchy of honors that would mimic the social contours of the colony at large. As you will recall, the phenomenon of value replication, in this regard, found expression throughout the empire, as voluntary associations reproduced Roman *cursus* ideology and practice at every turn.

Such adaptation to cultural norms, however, would have divided the Jesus community in Philippi along lines of social status. And this, in turn, would have undermined Paul's desire that the church remain united by "thinking the same way, having the same love, sharing the same feelings, focusing on one goal" (2:2). In response to such a threat Paul, in Philippians, pointedly challenged and subverted Roman hierarchical social tendencies.

It is beyond the scope of this project to offer a detailed running commentary on Paul's letter to the Philippians. I will limit my treatment to a handful of passages that particularly underscore the value of our socio-historical background materials (chaps. 1-3) for the interpretation of the biblical text, particularly where issues of church leadership and Christian community are concerned.

We will first look at the opening greeting (1:1) of the letter, and then examine Paul's list of Jewish honors (3:4–6). Chapter 5 then considers the majestic portrayal of Jesus in Philippians 2:6–11.

Each passage finds Paul reconstructing the honor-oriented world of the colony in Philippi, in an attempt to create an alternative social environment marked by the values and behaviors modeled by Jesus of Nazareth—a social environment where power would be used in the service of others.

The Greeting: Philippians 1:1

The opening greeting of Philippians is unique in several ways. A comparison with Paul's other letters to his churches highlights the differences:

Sender(s) and Recipients in Paul's Letters

	Sender(s)	Recipients
Romans (1:1, 7)	Paul, a slave of Christ Jesus, called as an apostle	all who are in Rome, loved by God, called as saints
1 Corinthians (1:1, 2)	Paul, called as an apostle of Christ Jesus by God's will, and Sosthenes our brother	To God's church at Corinth, to those who are sanctified in Christ Jesus and called as saints
2 Corinthians (1:1)	Paul, an apostle of Christ Jesus by God's will, and Timothy our brother	To God's church at Corinth, with all the saints who are throughout Achaia
Galatians (1:1, 2)	Paul, an apostle—not from men or by man, but by Jesus Christ and God the Father who raised Him from the dead—and all the brothers who are with me	To the churches of Galatia
Ephesians (1:1)	Paul, an apostle of Christ Jesus by God's will	To the faithful saints in Christ Jesus at Ephesus
Philippians (1:1)	Paul and Timothy, slaves of Christ Jesus	To all the saints in Christ Jesus who are in Philippi, including the overseers and deacons
Colossians (1:1, 2)	Paul, an apostle of Christ Jesus by God's will, and Timothy our brother	To the saints in Christ at Colossae, who are faithful brothers
1 Thessalonians (1:1)	Paul, Silvanus, and Timothy	To the church of the Thessalonians in God the Father and the Lord Jesus Christ
2 Thessalonians (1:1)	Paul, Silvanus, and Timothy	To the church of the Thessalonians in God our Father and the Lord Jesus Christ

It is easy to identify what is unique about the recipients of the letter. Only in Philippians are the titles of church leaders included in Paul's opening greeting.

The way in which the letter stands out in the "Sender(s)" column is a bit more subtle but equally informing. Paul described himself (and Timothy) as a slave of Christ Jesus, but not as an apostle. In only one other letter (Romans) does Paul refer to himself in his greeting as a slave, and in Romans the term occurs alongside the more familiar title "apostle," a designation that occurs in six of the church letters (Romans, 1–2 Corinthians, Galatians, Ephesians, and Colossians).

Scholars have variously explained the absence of the familiar title "apostle." Some suggest that "apostle" is missing because Paul's authority was not being challenged in Philippi, as it was, for example, in Corinth and in the Galatian churches.[11] This is doubtful, however, since Paul did not hesitate to use "apostle" in his greetings in Romans and Ephesians, where we have no evidence that Paul's authority was in question.

Gordon Fee traces the absence of the term to the genre of the letter, suggesting that the exhortation in Philippians is predicated on a relation of mutual friendship, and no assertion of apostolic authority was necessary.[12] This explanation is an attractive one, especially since Philippians is the only Pauline epistle formally crafted as a friendship letter. The friendship genre, however, lacks the explanatory power to account for the other exceptional aspects of the salutation.

Why, instead of "apostle," did Paul refer to himself and Timothy as *doulos,* the Greek term for a common slave? Only in Philippians does Paul use "slave" as his sole self-designation. Some have taken "slaves of Christ Jesus" in a positive sense. The Hebrew Scriptures use the phrase "servant of the Lord" of persons like Moses or David (Deut 34:5; Ps 18:1), who enjoyed divinely

---

11. O'Brien, *The Epistle to the Philippians*, 45.
12. Fee, *Paul's Letter to the Philippians*, 62.

delegated authority, and who thus occupied honorable positions. It is suggested that the same idea is present in Philippians 1:1.

A better alternative takes "slave" in Paul's greeting in the opposite sense. Given the high population of slaves in the empire, and their location at the bottom of the social pecking order, Fee rightly asserts that "no one would have thought it [*doulos*] to refer other than to those owned by, and subservient to, the master of a household."[13] Here the connotations of "slave" are anything but positive, since *doulos* in the Roman world was associated with the dishonor of humiliation, subjection, and obedience.

Paul's self-reference as *doulos* would have resonated with a great degree of credibility when the letter was first read to the church in the colony. For, as we saw above, Paul and Silas had refused to capitalize upon their Roman citizenship and took a beating worthy of slaves, when the missionaries first visited Philippi some years earlier.

This interpretation of *doulos* as humble "slave" finds further confirmation later in the letter, where the word appears again. In 2:7 Paul refers to Jesus as a "slave" (*doulos*), in a context that can hardly refer to anything but the abject social status of a Greco-Roman slave.

Now, let's consider the recipients of the letter. The mention of "overseers and deacons" has also attracted much scholarly attention, since it is one of our few pieces of hard evidence dealing with leadership in Paul's congregations. Unfortunately, much of the discussion has been energized by preconceived notions of what church organization must have been like in early Christianity. Episcopalians, Presbyterians, Roman Catholics, Baptists, and others all have their interpretations of the passage, often in support of their respective views of church government.

Clouding the issue further is the unfortunate English translation "bishops" in some versions (KJV, NRSV), which implies a church hierarchy of bishops, priests, and others—a hierarchy that

---

13. Ibid., 63.

developed generations after Paul and his contemporaries had left the scene.

The most straightforward way to interpret our New Testament evidence for positions of church leadership takes "overseer" (Greek *episkopos*) as interchangeable with the more familiar "elder" (*presbyteros*), a Greek term for church leaders occurring elsewhere in Acts and the epistles (Acts 14:23; 20:17; Titus 1:5; Jas 5:14; 1 Pet 5:1).

What we have in Philippians 1:1 is a reference to two groups of leaders—overseers and deacons—who provided oversight to local Christian congregations during the formative years of early church history.

We are left, once again, though, with a rather puzzling question. *Why does Paul make reference to these groups of leaders only in Philippians?* The answer: For precisely the same reason that Paul omits "apostle" and refers to himself and Timothy as "slaves"—a reason that arises directly from the social context of the recipients in the town of Philippi and their preoccupation with honorary titles.

Picture the scene when Epaphroditus returned to the colony. The church is abuzz with great anticipation. Epaphroditus has arrived from Rome with a letter from their beloved and esteemed apostle! A solemn hush descends on the community as Epaphroditus stands to read the letter. He begins with the greeting: "Paul and Timothy, slaves of Christ Jesus: To all the saints in Christ Jesus who are in Philippi, including the overseers and deacons."

One can only imagine the cognitive dissonance that these words would have generated in the minds of the letter's audience. The Philippians had been socialized from infancy to publicly promote and proclaim their own honors and titles, in order to position themselves as high as possible along the relational hierarchy, relative to others in their social networks.

Paul did precisely the opposite. He intentionally downplayed his own social status and elevated the status of his recipients. By portraying himself not as God's authoritative apostle but, rather, as Jesus' abject slave, Paul placed himself on the lowest rung of the social ladder. And by explicitly addressing the leaders of the congregation by their titles, he elevated the recipients of the letter above himself and honored them in the greeting.

Thus, Paul began, at the outset of his letter, to challenge the fixation on titles and status that was so prevalent in the colony, by practicing in his greeting the very relational ethos he would enjoin later in the epistle: "in humility consider others as more important than yourselves" (Phil 2:3). And this is only the beginning of Paul's epistolary exercise in social engineering, as he proceeded throughout the letter to subvert the values and behaviors that characterized the status-conscious world of Roman Philippi.

Paul's Jewish Honors Race

Paul had his own set of honors and achievements to flaunt, and they were rather impressive in the circles in which Paul had run before he met Jesus on the Damascus road:

> If anyone else thinks he has grounds for confidence in the flesh, I have more: circumcised the eighth day; of the nation of Israel, of the tribe of Benjamin, a Hebrew born of Hebrews; regarding the law, a Pharisee; regarding zeal, persecuting the church; regarding the righteousness that is in the law, blameless. (Phil 3:4b–6)

Apart from its Jewish content, from a structural perspective Paul's list of honors bears striking resemblance to the honor inscriptions from Philippi surveyed in the previous chapter.

I suggest in what follows that Paul, in Philippians 3:5–6, intentionally outlined his Jewish honors in the form of a Roman *cursus honorum*. The Philippians, in turn, would have heard the passage against this background.

Several aspects of the text indicate that Paul's list of honors would have reminded the Christians in Philippi of the multitude of honor inscriptions scattered throughout the public areas of the colony. Consider, first, the economy of the language. Peter O'Brien refers to the "tight form and terseness" of the structure of Philippians 3:5–6.[14] Paul enumerated his honors as a concise list, avoiding the use of verbs or connecting conjunctions.

The sentence-by-sentence grammatical structure which characterizes the rest of the letter ends abruptly after 3:4 and picks up again with 3:7. The HCSB translation above fairly represents the language of the Greek original. The staccato structure of Paul's list of honors brings to mind the economy of a stone worker, who, for obvious reasons, would chisel into marble as few words as possible in an honorary inscription intended for public display in a municipality like Philippi.

The manner in which Paul outlined his Jewish honors elsewhere in his letters confirms the above analysis. In Galatians Paul related a similar set of achievements:

> For you have heard about my former way of life in Judaism: I persecuted God's church to an extreme degree and tried to destroy it. I advanced in Judaism beyond many contemporaries among my people, because I was extremely zealous for the traditions of my ancestors. (1:13–14)

Notice that, in contrast to the list of honors in Philippians, here in Galatians Paul used complete sentences, which are grammatically integrated into the surrounding context. The content of Galatians 1:13–14 is similar to Philippians 3:5–6. The structure, however, differs markedly.

A second parallel, 2 Corinthians 11:22–29, is a bit closer in form to our passage, but in the Corinthian text Paul continued to employ finite verbs, and the grammar is much more varied than it is in Philippians 3:5–6.

Philippians 3:5–6 looks like a Roman honor inscription in a second significant way. A diagram of the passage will prepare us to compare the text with the inscriptions from Philippi:

---

14. O'Brien, *The Epistle to the Philippians*, 368.

circumcised the eighth day of the nation of Israel of the tribe of Benjamin a Hebrew born of Hebrews	**ASCRIBED HONORS**
regarding the law, a Pharisee regarding zeal, persecuting of the church regarding the righteousness that is in the law, blameless	**ACQUIRED HONORS**

As the diagram indicates, Paul presented his honors in a two-fold manner. The first occurrence of the word "regarding" (repeated three times) signals the beginning of the second of two text segments.

The two blocks of honors correspond, interestingly enough, to a fundamental twofold taxonomy of status utilized by cultural anthropologists in their studies of honor-and-shame societies. Social scientists refer, in this regard, to "ascribed honor" and "acquired honor," respectively.

Ascribed honor describes birth status. Honors that are inherited—one's patriline, ethnicity, citizenship (in the case of Romans), or tribal affiliation (for Jews and Romans)—fall into this category.

Acquired honor, in contrast, refers to status achieved during one's adult lifetime. Among the Romans, the various posts in the *cursus honorum* would be included here, as would any decorations won in the military. Paul's Pharisaic zeal and behavioral achievements "under the law" are examples of acquired honor on the Jewish side.

It is no accident that the order in which Paul portrayed his honors in Philippians 3:5–6 corresponds precisely to the way that the residents of Philippi outlined their honors in the inscriptions in the colony. In both cases, ascribed honor precedes acquired honor, and this, in turn, further suggests that Paul framed his list of honors in Philippians 3 with Roman *cursus* ideology in view.

Like Paul, elites in Philippi proclaimed first their birth status in the inscriptions, followed by the honorific achievements they amassed as adults. Here are just two examples:

For Lucius Decimius, son of Lucius, of the tribe Voltinia,	ASCRIBED HONORS
quaestor, duumvir[15]	ACQUIRED HONORS

Publius Marius Valens, son of Publius, from the tribe Voltinia,	ASCRIBED HONORS
honored with the decorations of a decurion, aedile, also decurion of Philippi, priest of the divine Antoninus Pius, duumvir, sponsor of games[16]	ACQUIRED HONORS

Compare these inscriptions with Paul's autobiographical reflections in Philippians and Galatians. Both Philippians 3:5–6 and the inscriptions in the colony record ascribed honors first, followed by honors gained during the person's lifetime.

In contrast, Paul in Galatians 1:13–14 made no attempt to enumerate his honors according to the twofold taxonomy reflected above (ascribed honor followed by achieved honor). The text in Galatians focuses solely upon Paul's adult achievements, with no reference to birth status at all.

Apparently Paul's strategy in Philippians 3:5–6 was quite intentional. He presented his Jewish honors in Roman *cursus* form. The contents are quintessentially Jewish. The structure is transparently Roman.

There is more. Peter Pilhofer finds direct parallels between

---

15. Pilhofer, *Philippi, Band 2*, 214/L349, p. 231.
16. Ibid., 395/L780, p. 397.

Paul's honors and common expressions used to denote social status in the Roman world:

> toga of manhood—circumcised the eighth day
> Roman citizen—of the nation of Israel
> tribe Voltinia—of the tribe of Benjamin
> son of Gaius—a Hebrew born of Hebrews

The second and third parallels, taken together, are particularly illuminating.

We noted that more than one-half of the inscriptions from Philippi contain a reference to the person's Roman citizen tribe, Voltinia. Paul boasted of his tribal origins only here (Phil 3:5) and in Romans (11:1), another letter addressed to persons living in a social context that was markedly Roman. He made no mention of the tribe of Benjamin in the autobiographical parallels referred to above (Gal 1:13–14; 2 Cor 11:22–29).

Commentators have sought in vain to explain Paul's reference to Benjamin, by attempting to tease some special significance out of the tribe of Benjamin versus the other Israelite tribes. The Hebrew Scriptures offer little encouragement along these lines. Given the debacle with the tribe of Benjamin in Judges 19–21, and the Benjamite origins of King Saul, who proved to be anything but an exemplary monarch, one would be hard-pressed to argue that Paul intended in Philippians 3:5 to somehow favorably situate Benjamin over against the other tribes of Israel.

A comparison with the Philippian inscriptions again proves illuminating. As it turns out, the expression "tribe of Benjamin" was no more intended to highlight the superiority of Benjamin among the tribes of Israel than Voltinia was intended in the Philippian inscriptions to imply a comparison with other Roman citizen tribes.

The point, in both contexts, was simply to proclaim membership in a citizen tribe of one's respective commonwealth. That is, the emphasis was solely upon citizenship, not upon the specifics of tribal affiliation. Once again, Paul had in view the social world of the colony at Philippi.

We come now to a final aspect of the text that marks out Philippians 3:4–6 as unique compared with Paul's other autobiographical statements. The parallels in Galatians 1 and 2 Corinthians 11 are both apologetic in tone. Paul sought in each case to defend his ministry. Our passage lacks this emphasis, and the tone is accordingly quite dissimilar.

Paul's goal in Philippians 3 was paradigmatic, not apologetic. The apostle presented his honors—and his attitude toward them (see below)—as an example for his readers to follow, not as a defense of his life and ministry. In contrast with the autobiographical parallels in Galatians and 2 Corinthians, therefore, here in Philippians "Paul primarily writes about himself in order to give an example of the way he wants the Philippians to live."[17]

In summary, it is quite clear that Paul structured his list of Jewish honors in a manner that would have instantly resonated with the recipients of the letter in Roman Philippi. Philippians 3:5–6 represents Paul's *cursus honorum.*

Christians with some background in Judaism (Lydia, for example), as well as Gentile converts who had later come to appreciate the Jewish origins of their faith in Messiah Jesus, would have been deeply impressed with Paul's honorable pedigree.

Paul's reference to his membership in the "tribe of Benjamin," in particular, would have resonated positively with a minority of persons in the church who were privileged to possess Roman citizenship. And the *cursus* format of Paul's catalogue of honors would have struck the recipients of the letter as immediately familiar, given the hierarchical, honor-oriented social environment in which they spent their daily lives.

Those hearing the text might even have been led favorably to reflect upon their own honors and achievements, whether in

---

17. Peter Oakes, *Philippians: From People to Letter,* SNTSMS 110 (Cambridge: Cambridge University Press, 2001), 103.

the municipality at large or, perhaps, in the more circumscribed confines of the Christian *ekklēsia.*

Suddenly, however, the passage took an unexpected turn, as Paul forcefully and irretrievably subverted the priorities of anyone who would pride himself in honors, Jewish or Roman, ascribed or achieved. For after enumerating his impressive birth honors and personal accomplishments—including that quintessential prize of citizen status, Paul referred to the whole of his Jewish *cursus honorum* as "loss" and, as if that was not enough, as utter "filth" (vv. 7–8).

The latter term is an exceptionally colorful one. Commentators are divided over whether it means "excrement" (KJV, "dung") or, more generally, "filth" (HCSB). Fee's translation, "foul-smelling street garbage,"[18] forcefully underscores the negative connotations of the word.

Paul could hardly have taken a more countercultural approach to the social values and practices that characterized daily life in Roman Philippi.

Conclusion

The contents of both Acts 16 and Paul's letter to the Philippians prove to be a remarkable fit for the social world of Philippi, or, perhaps more accurately, a remarkable "anti-fit," since Paul, both in his ministry and in his letter, intentionally destabilized Roman social codes and cultural values at every turn.

Reading the Bible in context helpfully illuminates the countercultural nature of Paul's perspective on power, authority, and status. Paul's agenda was pointedly and intentionally anti-Roman. The relational environment Paul envisioned among the people of God was to be altogether different from the social world of the dominant culture of Roman Philippi.

Given the realities of human nature, Paul's cruciform attitude towards power, status, and authority will prove to be radically subversive in almost any cultural setting, including our

---

18. Fee, *Paul's Letter to the Philippians,* 319.

churches in America today. Indeed, those of us who, in the name of efficiency or pragmatism, uncritically adopt secular leadership models for local church ministry would do well to consider just how radically subversive the Christian worldview truly is—especially where the use of institutional power and authority are concerned.

The most powerful subversion of secular values, ancient or modern, however, is yet to come. Paul's vision for other-centered Christian community and social solidarity was not his own creation. Paul patterned his life and ministry after the behavior of Jesus, and he charged the Philippians to do the same.

In Philippians 2:6–11, Paul grounded his countercultural challenge to the relational priorities of the Philippians' broader social environment in the attitude and activities of Jesus himself. We turn now to consider the contours of Paul's grand christological masterpiece.

Questions for Reflection

1. How did Luke, in Acts 16, demonstrate that he was well aware of the Romanness of the colony at Philippi?

2. Why didn't Paul and Silas immediately tell the magistrates that they were Roman citizens and thereby avoid the beating and imprisonment (Acts 16:22–24)?

3. How does the way Paul and Silas leveraged their Roman citizenship in Philippi compare with the attitude and behavior of Jesus, as outlined in Philippians 2:6–11?

4. Paul departed from his usual style of greeting in Philippians 1:1. Given what we know about the social values of Philippi, why do you think Paul did this?

5. What did Paul think about Rome's *cursus honorum,* which was replicated in religious groups in local settings like the Silvanus cult in Philippi?

The Humiliation of Christ

An Unexpected Approach to Power and Authority

Romans lionized strength over weakness, victory over defeat, dominion over obedience. —Garrett Fagan[1]

He humbled Himself by becoming obedient to the point of death—even to death on a cross. —Philippians 2:8

My vocational pilgrimage has been delightfully schizo-phrenic. I still can't decide whether I want to be a seminary professor or a pastor when I grow up. I have oscillated between the two jobs now for nearly two decades.

After some fifteen years of church ministry and a bit of ad-junct teaching, I made the transition to academia in an official capacity in the fall of 1994. I took a part-time but permanent position with the New Testament faculty at Talbot School of

---

1. Garrett G. Fagan, *The Lure of the Arena: Social Psychology and the Crowd at the Roman Games* (Cambridge: Cambridge University Press, 2011), 33.

Theology. The plan was to bring me up to full time when I finished my doctoral program a couple of years later.

The two years came and went, and I was itching to get back into full-time church ministry. I told my dean at Talbot to give the job to someone else, and I jumped on board as a team pastor at Oceanside Christian Fellowship in February 1996. I will never forget the reaction of one particular group of students at the seminary.

For a variety of reasons, related to the expansion of Christianity in the Pacific Rim and to our own history as a school of theology, Talbot has had the privilege over the years of training large numbers of pastors for the church in Korea.

These young men and their families make tremendous sacrifices to come to the States, learn a new language and culture, and get a top-rate theological education to take back to their homeland. They are some of our hardest-working students. They have to be.

One day in early 1996 I announced to my classes that this was my last semester as a professor at Talbot. I was going back into full-time church ministry. (Little did I know that I'd be back in the classroom five years later, but that's a story for another time.)

The reaction of my Korean students took me completely by surprise. They suddenly began to act quite uncomfortable around me. As I probed a bit, I discovered that these international students felt sorry for me. They were somehow ashamed for me, as well.

Traditional Asian culture is wedded to honor and shame in much the same way as the ancient Roman culture was. Instead of public offices in a *cursus honorum,* however, today's Koreans regard educational achievements and vocational status as the key criteria for honor in the public sphere.

The same cultural background also encourages our Korean students to view theological education and church ministry in markedly hierarchical terms. At the top of the pecking order is the seminary professor, with his august educational degrees and pedagogical authority. A local church pastor, although still a big fish in a small pond, doesn't even come close.

The Korean brothers who heard my announcement in class that day could not imagine that a seminary professor would willingly trade a position at the top of the spiritual pecking order for the lesser job of a pastor. They could only assume that someone else made that decision for me—against my will.

So these dear Korean students sympathetically shared in the shame they assumed I was experiencing. It was painfully obvious that they did not know quite how to respond to their now former, demoted professor.

The point of the story should be quite obvious. In an honor culture—Korean or Roman—to willingly step down the ladder of public esteem is simply unthinkable. As the Roman senator Pliny pointedly observed, "It is more uglifying to lose, than never to get, praise" (*Ep.* 8.24.9).[2]

This, however, is precisely what God the Son did for you and me. Jesus willingly stepped down the ladder of public esteem, in his incarnation and subsequent death on the cross. And God the Father, in turn, greatly honored Christ for his counterintuitive, culturally anomalous act of self-humiliation. This, in short, is Paul's message in Philippians 2:6-11.

Philippians 2:6–8 — Jesus' Inverted *Cursus*

Philippians 2:6–11 stands out as one of the most celebrated passages in all of Paul's letters. The text is a familiar one to Christians of all backgrounds, and it has played a special role in scholarly debates about the incarnation.

Paul's portrayal of Jesus in Philippians has much to contribute to such discussions. It is not my intention to denigrate a traditional christological approach, which seeks to elicit from the text information about the deity and humanity of Messiah Jesus.

Paul's agenda in Philippians 2, however, was not christological. At least not in the sense of the two-nature Christology associated with later church councils. Rather, Paul's goal in his

---

2. Trans. Lendon, *Empire of Honour*, 193.

story of Jesus was ecclesiological. It was about life together in the community we call the church, the people of God.

Paul outlined the humiliation and exaltation of Christ in order to encourage the Philippians to adopt in their mutual relations the same attitude toward power and social status that Jesus exhibited during the incarnation. Paul's introduction to his sweeping narrative made this immediately clear: "Make your own attitude that of Christ Jesus" (2:5).

We will examine Paul's masterful story of Jesus verse by verse, under the illuminating rubric of Roman *cursus* ideology. Philippians 2:6–8 turns out to be an inverted honors race.

In marked and intentional contrast to the inscriptions at Philippi, which depicted persons amassing increasingly prestigious titles and honors, Paul portrayed Jesus starting at the top of the heap, so to speak, where he enjoyed equal status with God himself, only to descend the social hierarchy—and willingly so— until he finally allowed himself to be publicly humiliated like a crucified slave.

Such behavior would have struck Roman residents of Philippi as abject folly. In a shocking act of status reversal, however, God suddenly and irretrievably subverted the social values of the dominant culture when he unequivocally affirmed Jesus' counterintuitive approach to power and privilege by exalting him to the highest place, thereby assuring that Jesus—not Caesar—would be publicly acknowledged as "Lord" by every living creature (2:9–11).

It is this same "attitude" (2:5)—this radically alternative approach to status and power—that Paul desired to characterize the Jesus community in the colony at Philippi. And this same attitude must serve as our point of departure for a return to other-centered leadership and healthy power relations in our churches in America today.

Paul presented the humiliation of Christ in three stages which, in turn, corresponded to three levels of social status in the world of Paul's readers. Jesus' social descent can be traced through Philippians 2:6–8 as follows. The key terms are highlighted:

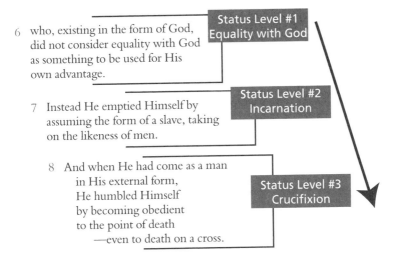

6 who, existing in the form of God, did not consider equality with God as something to be used for His own advantage.

Status Level #1
Equality with God

7 Instead He emptied Himself by assuming the form of a slave, taking on the likeness of men.

Status Level #2
Incarnation

8 And when He had come as a man in His external form, He humbled Himself by becoming obedient to the point of death —even to death on a cross.

Status Level #3
Crucifixion

Residents of Philippi would have been well-acquainted with the various aspects of these three status levels. Roman emperors were often portrayed, on coins and in inscriptions, as possessing divine status, using language strikingly similar to the phrase "equality with God" in verse 6.

Slave status and death by crucifixion were also common social realities for the Philippians. Indeed, the terms "slave" (v. 7) and "cross" (v. 8) would have sharply resonated with the readers' social sensibilities, since the two ideas represented, respectively, (1) the most dishonorable public status and (2) the most dishonorable act of public humiliation imaginable in the Roman world.

Status Level #1 — Equality with God

Christ began his pilgrimage at the very top of the social hierarchy. He existed "in the form of God," and he shared "equality with God" (v. 6). Several expressions in verse 6 work together to underscore the exalted status Christ enjoyed before the incarnation.

"the form of God"

The phrase "the form of God" is a fairly literal translation of the Greek *morphē theou*. The word *morphē* refers most basically to outward appearance and has been traditionally interpreted in the present context in terms of Christ's preexistent glory—the glory which, in the words of the Johannine Jesus, Christ had with the Father "before the world existed" (John 17:5).

O'Brien thus sees in our text a "picture of the preexistent Christ clothed in the garments of divine majesty and splendour."[3] The clothing imagery reminds us of the importance of attire as a public mark of social status in the Roman world (see chap. 1).

Viewing the phrase "form of God" in terms of the visible glory of regal attire finds support elsewhere. O'Brien draws attention, for example, to a parallel from Luke's Gospel, where a nearly identical Greek construction speaks of clothing as a status symbol (Luke 7:25).

In addition, the ideas of "glory" and "clothing" come into contact with one another at several places in biblical literature. Most familiar is a phrase from the Sermon on the Mount: "even Solomon in all his glory was not clothed like one of these" (Matt 6:29 NRSV; see also Luke 12:27; Job 40:10). Clothing and the *morphē*- word group occur together at the transfiguration, as well, where Jesus was "transformed (from *metamorphoō*) in front of them [Peter, James, and John], and His clothes became dazzling—extremely white as no launderer on earth could whiten them" (Mark 9:2-3). Here the three disciples got a glimpse of what Jesus might have looked like before he veiled his glory during the incarnation by taking on the form of a slave (see below, on Phil 2:7).

Finally, there is an analogy on the Roman side. Philo of Alexandria, a Hellenized Jew who was a contemporary of the apostle Paul, used the phrase *theou morphē* (Greek word order, unlike English, is flexible) to describe the emperor Caligula dressed up as a god or goddess (*Leg.* 110).

---

3. O'Brien, *The Epistle to the Philippians*, 209, 211. See also Gerald F. Hawthorne, "In the Form of God and Equal with God (Philippians 2:6)," in *Where Christology Began: Essays on Philippians 2,* ed. Brian J. Dodd and Ralph P. Martin (Louisville: Westminster John Knox, 1998), 101.

The above evidence, along with the Roman social context of the colony at Philippi, leads us to conclude that (a) "the form of God" in Philippians 2:6 refers to Christ clothed in garments of divine glory, and (b) the image functions in our text to underscore the preincarnate Christ's exalted social status.[4]

"equality with God"

Christ's status is picked up and reiterated in a parallel expression later in the verse: "equality with God." Ancient writers described emperors and kings in remarkably similar language.

A second-century Egyptian papyrus reads, "What is a God? Exercising power; What is a king? One who is equal with a God" (*Pap. Heid.* 1716.5). Antiochus IV, a Hellenistic monarch from the second century B.C., promoted himself as a mortal who was "equal to god" (2 Macc 9:12). The historian Appian claimed that the honors Augustus bestowed upon Julius Caesar encouraged later emperors to receive honors "equal to gods" (*BCiv.* 2.148).

In each of these examples the language is nearly identical to the expression "equality with God" in Philippians 2. And in each case the equality in view relates not to ontology—sharing in the divine nature or essence—but to power and status, that is, occupying a godlike position of influence and prestige in the cosmos.

Now one could certainly argue secondarily from Christ's exalted preincarnate status to his divine ontology. The association of Christ Jesus with Yahweh of the Hebrew Scriptures during his exaltation in verses 9–11 is even more transparent in this regard.

But ontology was not Paul's primary agenda in Philippians 2. Relationship was: the relationship between Christ and those he gave his life to save (vv. 6–8), the relationship between Jesus and the Father (vv. 9–11), and relationships between you and I in the family of God (v. 5).

---

4. For a thorough discussion of the meaning of the various terms in Philippians 2:6-8, see Joseph H. Hellerman, "μορφῇ θεοῦ as a Signifier of Social Status in Philippians 2:6." *JETS* 52.4 (2009): 779-97.

To begin properly to grasp this is to begin to appreciate the potential of this magnificent passage to inform our attitudes and behaviors as church leaders today.

"something to be used for His own advantage"

The heart of the verse lies in Christ's attitude toward his divine status: he "did not consider equality with God as something to be used for His own advantage." The phrase in italics, above, translates a single word (*harpagmos*) in the original Greek.

The HCSB differs from some earlier versions. Notice, for example, the NIV's rendering: "did not consider equality with God something to be grasped." The NIV, although not wholly inaccurate here, is potentially misleading in that it leaves open the unlikely possibility that "equality with God" was something Jesus lacked and chose not to grasp.

The HCSB—"something to be used for His own advantage" (see also the NRSV: "something to be exploited")—correctly indicates that Christ in his preincarnate state already possessed "equality with God." The phrase "equality with God" picks up and expands upon "form of God" in the previous clause. Both expressions describe Christ before he became a human being.

It is not Christ's possession (NIV), then, but rather his attitude (HCSB, NRSV) toward his exalted status which is addressed in the verse. And this attitude is quite contrary to the views of status that characterized life in Roman Philippi.

Putting our understanding of *harpagmos* together with *morphē theou,* we might paraphrase Status Level #1 (Phil 2:6) as follows: "who, although he was clothed with the garments of divine glory, did not consider this position of equality with God as something to be used for his own advantage."

Status Level #2 — Incarnation

"He emptied Himself"

The incarnation marks for Jesus the first, deep step down his inverted *cursus honorum.* The reference to Jesus "assuming the form of a slave" is most significant, in this regard, and we will return to the slavery metaphor below.

The dominant image of the incarnation in the verse—"emptied Himself"—has generated an ongoing debate about the nature of the incarnation, a debate that, in the final analysis, has been quite unnecessary. Many have been misled in their understanding of the phrase by assuming that Christ "emptied Himself" of something.

We should question such an assumption on the basis of the passage itself, since Paul further defined the phrase by asserting that something was added—not subtracted—from Christ during the "emptying" process: "he emptied Himself *by assuming the form of a slave.*"

As is now increasingly recognized, the phrase "emptied Himself" should be taken not literally but figuratively. The point is not that Christ "emptied Himself" of something. The point is that he "emptied *Himself,*" or poured himself out. Here the NIV translators are semantically right on target with their figurative rendering of the verb: "he made himself nothing."

The phrase "emptied Himself," then, tells us nothing about the effect of the incarnation upon the divine nature of the Second Person of the Trinity. Again, the issue throughout is that of status—not ontology, or essential nature—as the NIV rightly reflects in verse 7.

"the form of a slave"

The position Jesus assumed, which fills out the idea reflected in the phrase "emptied Himself," was the social status of a Greco-Roman slave. Other options have been suggested for the meaning of *doulos* in Philippians 2:7, but none is as persuasive as a straightforward reading that interprets the word against the background of ancient slavery.

Paul used slave terminology intentionally to elicit a reaction from his audience. The letter's recipients would have been painfully aware of the negative connotations of Jesus as a "slave" in a social setting like that of Roman Philippi.

When grappling with slavery in the New Testament world, it is crucial to distinguish between historical reality, on the one hand, and ideology and rhetoric, on the other. We will begin with the former. In actual experience slavery in antiquity was not a monolithic institution.

Household slaves were at times much better off than the average free peasant laborer. Most slaves, however, lived their lives at the bottom of the social hierarchy, and some suffered in ways almost unimaginable. The following description of a group of rural slaves is probably representative of the institution of slavery in the ancient world:

> Good gods, what scrawny little slaves there were! Their skin was everywhere embroidered with purple welts from their many beatings. Their backs, scarred from floggings, were shaded, as it were, rather than actually covered by their torn patchwork garments. Some wore only flimsy loincloths. All of them, decked out in these rags, carried brands on their foreheads, had their heads half-shaved, and wore chains around their ankles. Their complexions were an ugly yellow; their eyes were so inflamed by the thick dark smoke and the steamy vapor that they could barely see. (Apuleius, *Met.* 9.12)[5]

Slaves in the mines had it even worse:

> But to continue with the mines, the slaves who are engaged in the working of them produce for their masters revenues in sums defying belief, but they themselves wear out their bodies both by day and by night in the diggings under the earth, dying in large numbers because of the exceptional hardships they endure. For no respite or pause is granted them in their labours, but compelled beneath blows of the overseers to endure the severity of their plight, they throw away their lives in this wretched manner, although certain of them who can

---

5. Trans. Shelton, *As the Romans Did*, 176.

endure it, by virtue of their bodily strength and their persevering souls, suffer such hardships over a long period; indeed death in their eyes is more to be desired than life, because of the magnitude of the hardships they must bear. (Diodorus of Sicily 5.38.1)

In contrast, Roman slaves who served in their masters' households sometimes found dignity and respect. Compare Pliny's attitude toward his slaves with the excerpts above about slaves on the farms and in the mines:

I am always ready to grant my slaves their freedom, so I don't feel their death is so untimely when they die free men, and I allow even those who remain slaves to make a sort of will which I treat as legally binding. They set out their instructions and requests as they think fit, and I carry them out as if acting under orders. They can distribute their possessions and make any gifts and bequests they like, within the limits of the household. (*Ep.* 8.16.1–2)

Exceptional, but not wholly unique, was the relationship the Roman statesman Cicero enjoyed with a slave named Tiro. Tiro became Cicero's confidant and literary adviser, and it is quite clear that the two men shared a warm and mutually encouraging relationship. Cicero finally manumitted Tiro, after years of faithful service, in 51 B.C.

Given the variegated nature of slavery in the empire, it would be overly simplistic to group slaves together at the bottom of the social hierarchy in the Roman world. Some slaves had it much better than the mass of poor free persons who constituted the majority of the empire's population. Most had it worse.

So much for historical reality. When we turn to rhetoric and ideology—that is, to slavery as a symbol of all that is shameful and dishonorable—the picture is much more uniform.

A second-century Roman lawyer observed, "The primary distinction in the law of persons is this, that all men are either free or slaves.⁶" This yawning legal chasm generated, in turn, a common, invariably negative attitude toward slavery among elite and non-elite free persons alike. And this outlook prevailed whether the slave in question was rich or poor, powerful or weak.

Even freed slaves retained the social stigma of their birth status. The Stegemanns elaborate:

> [S]ome emancipated slaves held more political influence than many senators. Yet the odium of unfree birth clung to them through their lives and as such was, naturally, not only a problem of their own self-consciousness but also a social factor. For in the mind of the ancient elite, as we have seen, it was origin, first and above all, that determined status.⁷

As a result, in the symbolic universe of Roman social discourse the word *slave* assumed decidedly negative, socially shameful connotations. Dio Chrysostom put it like this:

> Men desire above all things to be free and say that freedom is the greatest of blessings, while slavery is the most shameful and wretched of states. (*Or.* 14.1)

Notice that, for Dio Chrysostom, the problem with slavery is not that it restricts one's personal freedom. That is a modern view of slavery. Romans, like Dio Chrysostom, did not think of slavery primarily in terms of restraint versus freedom.

Rather, the problem with slavery, as Ramsay MacMullen insightfully notes, had to do exclusively with the social shame of

---

6. Gaius, *Institutes* 1.3.9, cited by Susan Treggiari, "Social Status and Social Legislation," in *The Cambridge Ancient History,* ed. Alan K. Bowman et al., vol. 10 (Cambridge: Cambridge University Press, 1996), 873.

7. Ekkehard W. Stegemann and Wolfgang Stegemann, *The Jesus Movement: A Social History of Its First Century,* trans. O. C. Dean Jr. (Minneapolis: Fortress, 1999), 60.

servile status: "That slavery even under a humane master negated pride and self-respect was its only essential evil, in the ancient mind."[8]

To summarize, a household slave with a benign master generally enjoyed a much better standard of living than the typical rural slave. But when it came to ideology and rhetoric, the profound dishonor associated with slave status guaranteed that the term "slave" would serve as a useful symbol for social shame in the Roman world. As Dale Martin observes, "Slave terminology almost always carries negative connotations in Greco-Roman literature."[9]

The distinction between slavery as a variegated historical phenomenon and "slave" as a uniformly negative status symbol helpfully informs our interpretation of Paul's portrayal of Christ in Philippians 2. For when Paul referred to Jesus as a "slave" in verse 7, he had in view not historical reality but, rather, the social shame universally associated with slavery in the Roman world.

We know this to be the case because, according to the unanimous witness of the gospel traditions, Jesus of Nazareth did not, in fact, possess the legal status of a slave. He was a free peasant craftsman.

In what sense, then, did Paul portray Jesus as a "slave"? In a relative sense—relative, that is to Christ's preincarnate status as one clothed in the garments of divine glory (v. 6). It might help to see the main clause of the verse diagrammed with its gerund modifiers:

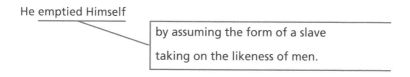

He emptied Himself
by assuming the form of a slave
taking on the likeness of men.

---

8. MacMullen, *Roman Social Relations*, 199 n. 89.
9. Dale B. Martin, *Slavery as Salvation: The Metaphor of Slavery in Pauline Christianity* (New Haven: Yale University Press, 1990), 46.

The first modifier explains how Christ "emptied Himself." He did so "by assuming the form (outward appearance) of a slave." In the last line, Paul explained how Christ took on "the form of a slave," namely, by "taking on the likeness of men."

Paul's point was this: for the preincarnate Christ, who was equal to God, willingly to take on "the likeness of men" was tantamount to a Roman free person (elite or non-elite) willingly exchanging a legal position of honor for the shameful status of a Greco-Roman slave—an utterly unthinkable exercise in self-humiliation:

Preincarnate Christ		Roman Free Person
↓	is like	↓
Taking on Human Nature		Taking on Slave Status

The juxtaposition in our passage of the two parallel expressions "form of God" (v. 6) and "form of a slave" (v. 7) is arresting and clearly intentional. Peter Oakes summarizes: "Between being like God and being like a slave, there is the widest status gap imaginable by Paul's hearers. Paul is saying that for Christ to become human meant that deep a drop in status."[10]

For Christ to do so willingly—he "emptied *Himself*"—would have struck Roman sensibilities as abject foolishness. Yet, as we will discover below, this countercultural, counterintuitive approach to power and status is precisely the behavior that God ultimately honors and affirms (vv. 9–11).

Slaves and the Military

Paul's slavery metaphor would have resonated in a particularly negative way among the residents of a Roman military colony, due to the social stigma of slaves in the Roman army.

Rome's army was a citizen army, and the fact that only Roman citizens could fight in the army further cemented the

---

10. Oakes, *Philippians*, 196.

distinction between free and slave status in the Roman world. So serious were the Romans about this, in fact, that slaves who tried to serve in the army by misrepresenting themselves as free men were put to death (Pliny, *Ep.* 10.29–30).

The practical realities of international relations sometimes compromised social priorities, however, so that Rome was on occasion forced to recruit slaves into the army to defeat an otherwise superior foe. The Romans looked back on these incidents not with gratitude for the help provided by slaves during such pressing circumstances but, rather, with disgust and regret that necessity had forced citizen soldiers to stoop so low as to fight alongside such social rabble.

The Roman moralist Valerius Maximus introduced his treatise titled "Of Necessity" with the following assertion: "The bitter laws and cruel commands of odious necessity have forced our city and foreign nations too to suffer many things grievous not only to understand but even to hear" (7.6.1a). Valerius's first example of things "grievous not only to understand but even to hear" is the inclusion of slaves in the Roman army:

> In the Second Punic War, when Rome's manpower was exhausted by several adverse battles, the senate on the motion of Consul Ti. Gracchus decreed that slaves be purchased publicly for use in war and to repel the onset of the enemy. . . . How great is the violence of sour chance! The community that until then had scorned to have *capite censi* [non-propertied free men] even of free birth as soldiers added bodies drawn from servants' attics and slaves collected from shepherds' huts to its army as special strengthening. So sometimes a noble spirit yields to expediency and bows to the power of Fortune in cases where unless we choose counsels of safety those of handsome show lead to collapse. (7.6.1a)

Perhaps the residents of Philippi would have recalled the more recent enrollment of slaves in the army of Augustus, the colony's patron emperor:

Except as a fire-brigade at Rome, and when there was fear of riots in times of scarcity, he [Augustus] employed freedmen as soldiers only twice: once as a guard for the colonies in the vicinity of Illyricum, and again to defend the bank of the river Rhine; even these he levied, when they were slaves, from men and women of means, and at once gave them freedom; and he kept them under their original standard, not mingling them with the soldiers of free birth or arming them in the same fashion. (Suetonius, *Aug.* 25)

Philippi was founded by army veterans who took great pride in their citizen status, as indicated by the numbers of inscriptions that boast of membership in the Roman tribe Voltinia. The descendants of these veterans who populated the colony during the first century—along with other residents of Philippi influenced by Roman social values—would have been sharply attuned to the dishonorable stigma of slavery.

Our discussion of Roman slavery sheds much light on Paul's strategy in his portrayal of the social pilgrimage of Jesus. Only in Philippians 2:7, among all his letters, does Paul call Jesus a "slave."

It is not hard to see why. Philippi was arguably the most status-conscious municipality east of Rome itself. Nowhere else would the use of slave terminology to describe the deity of a non-elite religious association have so pointedly chafed against the grain of the dominant culture's social sensibilities.

Paul's agenda, moreover, was transparently relational. He began his christological masterpiece by urging the Philippians to have among themselves the same "attitude" as Christ Jesus (v. 5). He then portrayed Jesus "assuming the form of a slave." In this way, Paul challenged his audience to adopt, in their mutual relations, an attitude toward honor and power that was diametrically opposed to the status-conscious value system of the world in which they lived.

Christ veiled his glory and assumed slave status for the readers' salvation. As Peter Oakes observes, "Jesus abandons his privileges for the sake of others."[11] The Philippians had to adopt a similar mind-set in their relations with their brothers and sisters in the Christian *ekklēsia*. And so must we who serve as shepherds in churches in America today.

Status Level #3 — Crucifixion

Jesus then descended to Status Level #3 along his inverted *cursus:* "He humbled Himself by becoming obedient to the point of death—even to death on a cross" (v. 8).

In his "death on a cross" Jesus descended to the lowest rung of the social ladder. Crucifixion was the most utterly humiliating and socially degrading experience imaginable in Greco-Roman antiquity.

The theme of obedience and the "cross" terminology are both important for grasping the depths of Christ's humiliation, and we will consider each in turn.

"obedient to the point of death"

Obedience and slavery were closely associated with each other in the minds of Paul's readers, since slaves were, of course, expected to obey their owners. Outside of slave discourse, however, obedience terminology is quite rare in ancient literature.

In a fascinating study of honor in the Roman world, Jon Lendon draws attention to "the audible quiet of the ancient sources on the subject of aristocrats' obedience."[12] Even where a functional hierarchy existed between two elite males (for example, between an emperor and a consul, or a consul and a quaestor), Romans carefully avoided the use of obedience terminology, due to its association with the stigma of slavery.

Other metaphors were employed instead. A quaestor was expected to respond to a consul like a son to his father (Pliny, *Ep.* 4.15.9; Cicero, *Fam.* 13.10.1.). Even an emperor like Trajan, in

---

11. Ibid., 116.
12. Lendon, *Empire of Honour*, 20.

his correspondence with equestrian officials, avoided all mention of obedience.

Lendon explains the absence of obedience terminology in aristocratic discourse:

> These evasions are symptoms of more than the euphemistic concealment of an ugly reality; they were an attempt to ameliorate the acute discomfort that stark relations of obedience between one aristocrat and another inspired. This was a world where aristocrats, even privately, did not think of themselves primarily as the servants of others.[13]

With the inclusion of the phrase "obedient to the point of death" (Phil 2:8), Paul's picture of Jesus thus continued intentionally to traverse a social trajectory that was decidedly countercultural to Roman sensibilities.

"even to death on a cross"

The HCSB translation, which uses an em dash (—) followed by the phrase "even to death on a cross," reflects the emphatic grammar of the Greek original. And appropriately so, for among the ancients crucifixion was the most publicly dishonorable experience imaginable. As Peter O'Brien categorically asserts, "By first-century standards no experience was more loathsomely degrading than this."[14]

Much is made in popular Christian circles of the physical suffering Jesus endured as he died. The vivid portrayal of the crucifixion in the 2004 blockbuster *The Passion of the Christ* is a case in point.

The New Testament, in contrast, makes almost nothing of Jesus' physical suffering on the cross. This should not surprise us. For to the authors of the Gospels the manner of Jesus' death was hardly unique.

---

13. Ibid., 21.
14. O'Brien, *The Epistle to the Philippians*, 231.

Thousands of persons were crucified in the ancient world, and many suffered physically much more severely than Jesus. Some individuals lingered in agony for days before they died and were finally removed from the cross. Physically, Jesus had it easier than most. The distinctiveness of Jesus' death by crucifixion lies elsewhere.

The biblical materials emphasize two ways in which the crucifixion of Christ was, in fact, unique. First, Jesus in his death bore humanity's sins on the cross, and correspondingly suffered spiritually and emotionally in ways that no other crucified person had ever suffered.

Jesus' agony in Gethsemane, where he wrestled with his destiny (Mark 14:32–36), and the alienation from the Father, which he experienced during the crucifixion (Mark 15:34), both attest to this reality. This aspect of the crucifixion of Jesus is a familiar one, especially among conservative evangelicals who emphasize the propitiatory nature of Jesus' sacrificial death in our preaching and teaching.

Less familiar is a second way in which the New Testament marks out Jesus' crucifixion as unique. Jesus' death was also distinctive in the degree to which Jesus was socially degraded during the crucifixion.

Crucifixion meant social (as well as physical) death for anyone who died on a cross. But for someone who was "in the form of God" and who shared "equality with God," crucifixion entailed a degree of humiliation that was unimaginable in a socially stratified world that was preoccupied at every turn with gaining and retaining public honor. Philippians 2 makes precisely this point about Jesus' crucifixion, in a way unparalleled elsewhere in Scripture.

The Social Stigma of Crucifixion

Hebrews 12:2 refers to the "shame" of the "cross," and Christians were highly sensitive to the anomaly associated with the worship of a crucified deity. One might even say that the very expression "crucified God" was socially oxymoronic.

155

None of this was lost on the pagan populace. According to Justin Martyr, non-Christians "charge us with madness, saying that we give the second place after the unchanging and ever-existing God and begetter of all things to a crucified man" (*First Apology* 13.5).[15] As Martin Hengel notes, Justin's response to the charge "make[s] it clear that the dishonour involved in the death of Jesus by crucifixion was one of the main objections against his being son of God."[16]

Detractors like Celsus, a century later, rejected as utter foolishness the idea of a deity "bound in the most ignominious fashion" and "executed in a shameful way" (Origen, *Contra Celsum* 6.10).[17]

Christian reflection on the social stigma of the humiliation of Christ continued for centuries. Lactantius wondered why God did not choose to have Jesus undergo "an honorable kind of death" instead of an "infamous kind of punishment" (*Institutiones* 4.26.29).[18] The Latin originals of both phrases contain terminology common to the semantic field of honor and shame.

Bishop Melito of Sardis was perplexed by the social dissonance associated with the idea of a crucified Christ, and he shared his thoughts on the subject with his congregation in a sermon one Sunday:

> He who hung the earth [in its place] hangs here, he who fixed the heavens is fixed there, he who made all things fast is made fast upon the tree, the Master has been insulted, God has been murdered, the King of Israel has been slain by an Israelitish hand. O strange murder, strange crime! The Master has been treated in unseemly fashion, his body naked, and not even deemed worthy of a covering, that [his nakedness] might not

15. Trans. Cyril C. Richardson, ed., *Early Christian Fathers* (New York: Macmillan, 1970), 249.

16. Martin Hengel, *Crucifixion In the Ancient World and the Folly of the Message of the Cross,* trans. John Bowden (Philadelphia: Fortress, 1977), 1 n. 1.

17. Trans. Hengel, *Crucifixion,* 7.

18. Trans. Hengel, *Crucifixion,* 7 n. 11.

be seen. Therefore the lights [of heaven] turned away, and the day darkened, that it might hide him who was stripped upon the cross. (*Homily on the Passion* 96–97)[19]

Melito makes no mention of the physical pain Jesus suffered during the crucifixion. What Melito struggles with is the public humiliation Jesus endured.

Another Christian preacher, John Chrysostom, similarly reflected, "Where can anything be found more paradoxical than this? This death was the most shameful of all, the most accursed. . . . This was not an ordinary death" (*Homily on Philippians* 8.2.5–11).[20]

Followers of a Crucified God

The early Christians could not escape the social stigma of Jesus' crucifixion, and detractors were quick to trace a logical line from the cross of Christ to the social status of Jesus' followers. The dishonor associated with crucifixion was widely utilized to shame professing Christians in later anti-Christian polemic.

Caecilius, Minucius Felix's pagan interlocutor, reasons as follows:

> To say that their ceremonies center on a man put to death for his crime and on the fatal wood of the cross . . . is to assign to these abandoned wretches sanctuaries which are appropriate to them . . . and the kind of worship they deserve. (*Octavius* 9.4)[21]

Tacitus capitalized upon the dishonor associated with the crucifixion of Jesus to cast aspersions upon Christians in Rome. "Christus," Tacitus informs us, "the founder of the name, had undergone the death penalty in the reign of Tiberius, by sentence

---

19. Cited by Hengel, *Crucifixion*, 21.
20. Trans. Mark J. Edwards, ed., *Galatians, Ephesians, Philippians*, ACCS New Testament 8 (Downers Grove, IL: InterVarsity Press, 1999), 250.
21. Trans. Hengel, *Crucifixion*, 3.

of the procurator Pontius Pilatus." The resulting "disease" found its way to Rome, "where all things horrible or shameful in the world collect and find a vogue" (*Ann.* 15.44).[22]

Crucifixion and Slavery

The social stigma of the cross was further magnified by its association with slavery. People in the ancient world viewed crucifixion as a punishment particularly fitting for a slave, a connection reflected in both language and practice.

The Latin language had developed a technical expression— "slaves' punishment" (*servile supplicium*)—which numbers of Roman writers used as a circumlocution for death by crucifixion. Valerius Maximus, for example, criticized the fact that a Roman general punished his deserters in the army with crucifixion: "Roman blood should not be insulted by paying the slaves' penalty [*servile supplicium*], however deservedly" (2.7.12).[23]

The Roman statesman Cicero viewed the crucifixion of slaves as a component of the *mos maiorum*, Roman ancestral tradition. During his own generation, some six thousand slaves hung on crosses along the Appian Way after the Romans had suppressed a revolt under Spartacus (Plutarch, *Crass.* 8–11; *Pomp.* 21; Appian, *BCiv.* 1.116–120). Later, Seneca, a contemporary of the apostle Paul's, would claim that slaves who attempted to strike back at their owners "stood under certain threat of crucifixion" (Seneca, *De Clementia* 1.26.1).

The crucifixion of slaves was so widespread that the image could even serve as material for Roman playwrights. The comedies of Plautus are representative. In one play a slave named Sceledrus comments, "I know the cross will be my tomb. There's where my ancestors rest—father, grandfather, great-grandfather, and great-great-grandfather" (*Mil. Glor.* 372).

Another comedy portrays an untrustworthy slave named Chrysalus worrying that his master will discover his deceitful

---

22. See also Hengel, *Crucifixion*, 3 n. 3.
23. Trans. Hengel, *Crucifixion*, 51 n. 1.

behavior: "[My master will] change my name for me the minute he gets back, and transform me from Chrysalus ["gold-bearer"] to Crossalus ["cross-bearer"] on the spot" (*Bacch.* 362).

Cicero has left us the most informative passage in ancient literature detailing the relationship between slavery, crucifixion, and citizen status. Each of these issues is important for the interpretation of Philippians, and they converge in a remarkable way in the trial of a Roman senator named Verres.

Apparently Verres had committed an unthinkable crime, when he flogged and crucified Gavius of Consa, a Roman citizen, while serving as governor of Sicily. Cicero is the prosecuting attorney. We pick up the story just after he has described the flogging of Gavius:

> And so, gentlemen of the jury, in the middle of the forum in Messana, a Roman citizen was flogged. And the whole time, while he suffered, while the whip cracked, no groan, no cry of any kind was heard from the tortured man except "I am a Roman citizen." In reminding Verres of his citizenship, he thought that he would escape the beating, . . . but when he kept crying out and demanding the rights of citizenship, Verres ordered his staff to make for this poor tormented man a cross. That's right, a cross! . . . Gentlemen of the jury, this was the only cross ever set up in the part of Messana that overlooks the straits. Verres chose this spot, with its view of Italy, deliberately so that Gavius, as he died in pain and agony, might recognize that the narrow straits marked the boundary between slavery and freedom, and so that Italy might see her own son hanging there, suffering the most horrible punishment ever inflicted on slaves. To put a Roman citizen in chains is a wrong. To flog him is a crime. To execute him is almost parricide. And what shall I call crucifixion? So abominable a deed can find no word adequate enough to describe it. Yet even a crucifixion did not satisfy Verres. "Let him gaze upon his native land. Let him die within sight of justice and liberty." Oh Verres, it was not Gavius, not some unknown man, whom you tortured and

crucified in that place, but the universally acknowledged correlation between liberty and Roman citizenship. (*2 Verr.* 2 [5] 162, 168–170)[24]

The rhetoric soars. Notice the way Cicero draws together the themes of crucifixion and slavery: the cross is "the most horrible punishment ever inflicted on slaves." The connection was self-evident to the Roman mind, since (a) slavery was the lowest legal class in Rome's highly stratified social world, and (b) crucifixion constituted the most degrading form of public humiliation imaginable.

For Cicero, however, there is more involved in Verres's crime than just the crucifixion of an undeserving individual. For the Romans, crucifying slaves had become another way of reinforcing in the public arena a social hierarchy that served the interests of the dominant culture.

By crucifying a Roman citizen, Verres had seriously compromised these values. Verres did not simply torture and crucify an individual. As Cicero's rhetoric emphasizes, in his treatment of Gavius, Verres had tortured and crucified "the universally acknowledged correlation between liberty and Roman citizenship" (*2 Verr.* 2[5] 170).

Finally, note the pointed contrast Cicero draws between slave status and crucifixion, on the one hand, and citizen status and freedom, on the other. The themes were polar opposites in Cicero's worldview.

They were also polar opposites in the social world of Roman Philippi. It is hardly accidental, in this regard, that Paul chose to portray Jesus as a crucified slave before a Philippian audience that lived in a municipality where slaves were the dregs of society and where Roman citizen status was such a highly valued social commodity.

Christ's descent down his inverted *cursus* was complete. In "assuming the form of a slave" at the incarnation, Christ took to

---

24. Trans. Shelton, *As the Romans Did*, 287.

himself the most dishonorable legal status in the Roman Empire. And then, by becoming "obedient to the point of death—even to death on a cross," Jesus reached the utter depths of public humiliation.

Clearly, as Paul informed us earlier in the passage, Christ did not regard his exalted preincarnate status as something to be exploited for his own advantage. He relinquished it for the benefit of others.

As the Roman senator Pliny observed, "It is more uglifying to lose, than never to get, praise" (*Ep.* 8.24.9).[25] Christ lost praise, and he did so willingly.

Such an approach to power and prestige constituted a direct inversion of Roman social norms and expectations. Had Paul's story of Jesus ended at verse 8, there would have been little to encourage the status-conscious residents of Philippi to confess Jesus as Lord and join the marginalized Christian community in the colony.

The end of the story, however, was still to be told. And as we discover in the verses to follow, it was precisely Jesus' counter-cultural use of power and status—for others, not for himself—that God unequivocally affirmed, when he exalted Jesus to the highest place and granted him "the name that is above every name."

Philippians 2:9–11 — A Stunning Status Reversal

Philippians 2:9 marks the crucial transition in Paul's story about Jesus. In a shocking and surprising inversion of Roman social values, it turns out that Jesus is greatly honored for his selfless use of divine status:

> Therefore God also highly exalted him and gave him the name that is above every name, so that at the name of Jesus every knee should bend, in heaven and on earth and under the earth, and every tongue should confess that Jesus Christ is Lord, to the glory of God the Father. (vv. 9–11 NRSV)

---

25. Trans. Lendon, *Empire of Honour*, 193.

The grammatical subject has suddenly changed. Throughout verses 6–8 Christ was the main actor in the drama. In verse 9, "God" became the subject of Paul's statements, as God responded to Jesus' counterintuitive approach to power and prestige.

The conjunction "Therefore" (NRSV; "For this reason," HCSB) should also not be missed. Commentators talk about the inference here being "self-evident."[26] Yet the exaltation of a crucified slave would have been anything but "self-evident" to persons steeped in the social values of Roman Philippi. The irony would have rendered Paul's rhetoric all the more arresting for the first-century recipients of the letter.

The Philippians could rest assured, however, that Jesus would truly be honored for his social pilgrimage. For as Paul asserted, the only One in the universe with the indisputable authority to do so had completely redefined what counted for honor in the grand scheme of things.

A Key Cultural Script

The exaltation of Christ in Philippians 2:9–11 plays upon a cultural script that would have been immediately familiar to Paul's audience. Grants of honor in the Roman world trickled down—not up—the social hierarchy. That is, an aristocrat could grant an honor to someone who occupied a lower position in the social hierarchy, but not vice versa.

A characteristic dynamic came into play in such situations, moreover, which related directly to the social status of the benefactor. Jon Lendon summarizes: "To be praised by any given aristocrat added to one's own prestige *in proportion to that aristocrat's prestige*."[27]

The qualification in italics is an important one. The higher a man's social status, (a) the more honor he could bestow on

---

26. O'Brien, *The Epistle to the Philippians*, 233; Fee, *Paul's Letter to the Philippians*, 220 n. 10. See also Frederick W. Danker, ed. *A Greek-English Lexicon of the New Testament and other Early Christian Literature,* 3rd ed. (Chicago: University of Chicago Press, 2000), 198.
27. Lendon, *Empire of Honour*, 48, my italics.

another, and (b) the more certain it would be that the grant would be publicly acknowledged by others.

Symmachus, a distinguished fourth-century aristocrat, wrote,

> My testimony can make no addition to your honour. For the old saying runs "to be praised by a praiséd man," and my humbleness cannot much help the brilliance of your reputation. (Symmachus, *Ep.* 9)

Symmachus is self-effacing here, but the point remains clear. Symmachus assumes that the social status of an aristocrat who grants an honor determines just how much prestige the recipient will enjoy.

The same cultural script played itself out in ancient Philippi, where several inscriptions boast of honors given by the emperor himself. Tiberius Claudius Maximus, for example, wanted passers-by to know that he was decorated by none other than Domitian and Trajan.[28]

The brother of a newly-minted senator set up an inscription in Philippi's forum broadcasting the fact that his brother, Gaius Julius Maximus Mucianus, owed his senatorial status directly to a grant from the emperor Antoninus Pius:

> For Gaius Julius Maximus Mucianus, the son of Gaius of the tribe Voltinia, *a vir clarissimus*, honored with the *latus clavus* by the divine (Antoninus) Pius.[29]

The emperor stood at the apex of Rome's social hierarchy, of course, and the honors he assigned were magnified accordingly. In fact, the emperor was the only person in the whole empire who could unilaterally grant senatorial status to a person of a lesser rank. The higher a person's social status, the greater the honor he could give to another.

---

28. Pilhofer, *Philippi, Band 2*, 522/L210, p. 506.
29. Ibid., 240/L465, p. 256.

Paul drew directly upon this cultural reality in Philippians 2:9–11. In the worldview of Paul and his readers, of course, God far exceeded the Roman emperor in rank and authority. Accordingly, God was in a position to grant to Jesus the highest status imaginable.

The switch of subjects from "Christ" to "God" in verse 9 is thus quite intentional. For who better than God to bestow upon Jesus "the name that is above every name"?

However, an aristocrat's social status not only determined the degree of honor he could bestow upon a person of lower status but also determined the efficacy of that grant—that is, whether or not the recipient's newly acquired status would be affirmed by the broader populace.

These are really two sides of the same coin, for, as we saw in chapter 2, a person's honor, to be at all legitimate, had to be publicly acknowledged. Conversely, "to claim honor that the community does not recognize is to play the fool."[30]

Here, again, the social status of the one bestowing the honor comes into play. Lendon helpfully explains:

> When one man honoured another in the Roman world, he granted him a quantum of honour, which, provided that the bestower was sufficiently distinguished himself, the aristocratic community at large then accepted that the recipient possessed; *a man's ability to mobilize aristocratic opinion in favour of another man was proportional to his own honour.*[31]

Notice how this ancient social code illuminates Paul's strategy in Philippians 2. Given the cultural script summarized in the above quotation—that "a man's ability to mobilize aristocratic opinion in favour of another man was proportional to his own honour"—the position of God at the very top of the social hierarchy of the universe becomes highly significant. God's social status virtually

---

30. Malina and Rohrbaugh, *Social Science Commentary*, 371.
31. Lendon, *Empire of Honour*, 48, my italics.

guarantees that every created being—"in heaven and on earth and under the earth"—will publicly acknowledge God's counterintuitive, markedly anomalous gift of exalted status to a crucified slave.

"the name of Jesus"

The threefold repetition of the term "name" in verses 9–10 is also highly informative. There is some debate in the literature about just what "name" Paul had in view in the expression "the name of Jesus" (v. 10).

Some take the phrase to mean "the name which is Jesus." The Greek will also allow the interpretation "the name which belongs to Jesus," however, and this has led others to identify the name as "Lord," found later in verse 11.

The debate may be wholly unnecessary, however, since Paul most likely did not have a specific name in view at all. The Greek word translated "name" (*onoma*) was commonly used in the semantic field of honor discourse, where *onoma* meant "fame" or "reputation."

Accordingly, Paul's point in the passage was not that Jesus received a new name—certainly not the name "Jesus," for he received the name "Jesus" at the incarnation, not at his exaltation. Nor was "Lord" a new name for Jesus. It had been his all along. Paul, in fact, cited in verses 10–11 a passage from the Hebrew Scriptures that implied as much (Isa 45:23).

Also absent from the passage is the idea that Christ is about to occupy a position of power and authority that he did not possess before the incarnation.

What is new for Jesus is the certainty that one day his identity as eternal Yahweh—as "Lord"—will be publicly acknowledged by every living creature. It is the public affirmation of Jesus' exalted status, then, that serves as Jesus' reward for his humiliating social pilgrimage down the inverted *cursus*.[32] We can fairly translate the passage as follows:

---

32. For this reading of the passage, see Hellerman, "Vindicating God's Servants."

Therefore God also highly exalted him and gave him the fame (status) that is above every fame, so that at the fame of Jesus every knee should bend, in heaven and on earth and under the earth, and every tongue should confess that Jesus Christ is Lord, to the glory of God the Father.

This understanding of the passage makes good sense of the language, and it accords perfectly with the social setting of Paul's readers, who were immersed in a status-conscious culture where a person's "name," that is, his "public fame," counted for so very much.

"Jesus Christ is Lord"

Finally, it is not insignificant that Paul presented Jesus being publicly proclaimed as "Lord" in an imperial setting where the Roman emperor typically received such honors. The word *Lord* (*kyrios*) is found fifteen times in Philippians. As Mikael Tellbe notes, *kyrios* "permeates the letter."[33]

"Lord" had a twofold resonance in Paul's vocabulary, related to Paul's Jewish background and the Roman imperial context in which he ministered. The Hebrew YHWH (Yahweh) was generally translated "Lord" (*kyrios*) in the Greek Old Testament, and Jesus was identified with Yahweh and called "Lord" by Aramaic-speaking Christians in the East early in New Testament history.

Given this data, and the Old Testament passage Paul cited in verses 10–11 (Isa 45:23), we may safely assume that Paul in Philippians 2 was intentionally connecting the confession of Jesus as "Lord" (*kyrios*) with the Old Testament name of God, "Yahweh."[34]

One wonders, however, just how much Old Testament

---

33. Mikael Tellbe, *Paul Between Synagogue and State: Christians, Jews, and Civic Authorities in 1 Thessalonians, Romans, and Philippians* (Stockholm: Almqvist & Wiksell International, 2001), 250.

34. Larry W. Hurtado, "Lord," in *Dictionary of Paul and His Letters,* ed. Gerald F. Hawthorne et al. (Downers Grove, IL: InterVarsity Press, 1993), 560–69; Fee, *Paul's Letter to the Philippians,* 225.

background the Christians in Philippi possessed. Much closer to home conceptually for the Philippians was the association of *kyrios* terminology with the Roman emperor. As N. T. Wright has recently noted, "In the Mediterranean world where Paul exercised his vocation as the apostle to the Gentiles, the pagans, the fastest growing religion was the Imperial cult, the worship of Caesar."[35]

The word *Lord* (*kyrios*) was used of the Roman emperor as early as A.D. 49 in Egypt, where Claudius is identified in a papyrus fragment as "Lord Caesar" (*P. Oxy.* 1.37.5–6). Later, during the reign of Nero (when Paul wrote Philippians), the appropriation of "Lord" as a title for the emperor became more widespread.

An inscription from Corinth (A.D. 67), for example, extols Nero as the "greatest ruler of the whole cosmos" and "Lord" (*SIG* 2.814.30–31, 55). When used of the Roman ruler, moreover, the term "Lord" has both political and religious connotations. As Tellbe maintains, to declare that "the emperor is Lord" is similar to confessing that "the emperor is god."[36]

One could hardly imagine a greater chasm in the social hierarchy than that between the emperor of Rome and a crucified slave. Yet in God's social economy it is Jesus—not Caesar—who will one day be rightly and finally acknowledged as "Lord" of the cosmos by every living creature.

An Anti-Imperial Paul?

American evangelicals have generally failed to appreciate Paul's subversive, anti-imperial rhetoric in passages like Philippians 2:6–11. Our familiar emphasis on Jesus as a personal savior, along with the separation of church and state in America, have led us to privatize and spiritualize much of what was public and political in Paul's letters.

Recent New Testament scholarship has reacted sharply to this blind spot. Numbers of critical scholars now see Paul challenging Roman imperialism at every turn, and they leverage the apostle's

---

35. N. T. Wright, "A Fresh Perspective on Paul?" *BJRL* 83.1 (2001): 22.
36. Tellbe, *Paul Between Synagogue and State*, 252.

anti-Roman rhetoric to prophetically confront perceived imperial excesses of American public policy and practices today.

Conservative and critical scholars alike miss Paul's point where Rome is concerned. Paul's agenda was not to influence the political process of Rome. Nor, at the other end of the spectrum, did Paul intend to dichotomize between personal faith in Jesus and public imperial politics in such a way as to wholly affirm both as separate, equally legitimate spheres of authority.

Trendy academic portraits of an anti-imperial Paul typically reveal more about the strident political sensibilities of their authors than about the strategy of the apostle himself. And although problems certainly exist, on any fair analysis, the United States of America has not been as unredeemably self-centered and imperialistic as some critical Pauline scholars would have us believe.

The comparison is anachronistic to begin with, at any rate, since Paul could not have altered the political contours of the dominant culture if he had wanted to. Unlike American citizens today, Paul had no access to Rome's political process.

So much for adopting Paul as the poster child for everything anti-Roman and, by extension, anti-American.

The conservative evangelical approach, however, also fails to do justice to Paul. It will not do to relegate the lordship of Christ, as Paul expresses it in Philippians 2:11, to the privatized, subjective world of me and my personal relationship to Jesus. There is an "us" that needs to be considered, as well.

We cannot ignore the social implications of Paul's gospel. The residents of Philippi grasped this right away. They charged Paul and Silas with "promoting customs that are not legal for us as Romans to adopt or practice" (Acts 16:21). There was something anti-Roman about Paul and his gospel, and that "something" was about more than personal faith in Jesus.

The key here is to recognize that, in Paul's view, Jesus (like Caesar) was Lord of a group, a people, a social collective. And Paul intended Jesus' group—the church in Philippi—to be radically different from the surrounding culture in its social priorities and relational ethos. In this sense, Paul's gospel was anti-Roman to the core.

Rome would remain in power. That was a given. And followers of Jesus would have to accommodate themselves to that reality (Rom 13:1–5; 1 Tim 2:1-2). Roman social practices would find no place, however, in Paul's vision for Christian community. For that community was to be a cross-shaped community, patterned after the example of Jesus (Phil 2:5–11).

Conclusion

Jesus began his social pilgrimage at the top of the pecking order, clothed in garments of divine glory, sharing equality with God himself. For Jesus, however, status and power were not social commodities to be exploited for personal or familial gain (v. 6).

In a move that can only be viewed as radically subversive and countercultural, Jesus willingly surrendered his divine status, choosing, instead, to embrace the abject position of a crucified slave (vv. 7–8). In so doing, Jesus leveraged his considerable social capital in a manner diametrically opposed to the ways in which power and position were exploited both by the emperor at Rome and by the local aristocracy in Philippi.

Then, in a sudden and shocking status reversal, Jesus—not Caesar—received the honor of being publicly proclaimed "Lord" at the hands of the only One whose status accorded him the right to bestow such an honor—namely, God himself (vv. 9–11).

Paul's image of Jesus using his authority in the service of others flew in the face of the cultural values and social codes of first-century Philippi. Persons socialized to embrace the status-conscious relational values of first-century Philippi could hardly have missed the point.

Paul's culture-shattering project in social engineering, however, was not complete. The apostle recognized that it would be challenging for the Philippians to embrace Jesus' ideal of other-centered, servant leadership. The example of Jesus, as crucial as it was, was apparently not enough.

What was needed to guarantee that Jesus' example would

became a reality among the Philippians was a social context—a way of doing church—that encouraged a Jesus-like use of authority on the part of leaders and others with status in the Philippian church. We turn now to examine Paul's vision for the church in Philippi to function as a surrogate family led by a plurality of pastors.

Questions for Reflection

1. Pretend for a moment that you have forgotten everything you know about Jesus. What would we know about Christ, if all we had to go on was Philippians 2:6–11? Make a list of attributes and character qualities of Jesus solely from Philippians 2.

2. What did Paul mean when he claimed that Christ existed "in the form of God," or that he possessed "equality with God"?

3. Describe the institution of slavery in the ancient world. What was so bad about being a slave in the eyes of the Romans? Why did Paul refer to Jesus as a "slave" only here (Phil 2:7) in his letters?

4. Discuss the relationship between crucifixion and social status. Using a concordance, search the New Testament for the word *cross* and for forms of the verb "crucify." Do you find any other passages where the social stigma of crucifixion is in view?

5. Hellerman describes the exaltation of Jesus in Philippians 2:9–11 as "shocking and surprising." Why would God the Father's response to Jesus' behavior, as illustrated in verses 9–11, have caught Roman readers off guard?

When Jesus Is Not Enough

Creating a Context for Other-Centered Leadership

> *Honor is always presumed to exist within one's own family of blood.*—Bruce Malina[1]

> *Show family affection to one another with brotherly love. Outdo one another in showing honor.*—Romans 12:9-10

The other-centered approach to power and authority illustrated in the humiliation and exaltation of Christ—and exemplified in the behavior of Paul and Silas in their ministry in Philippi—comes to life anew when viewed against the background of Roman social values and practices. There is something to be said for reading the Bible in its historical and cultural context.

Yet the basic contours of Jesus as the ideal servant leader are readily transparent even to readers of the Bible who lack awareness

---

1. Bruce J. Malina, *The New Testament World: Insights from Cultural Anthropology* (Louisville: Westminster John Knox, 2001), 38.

of the honor-seeking and social posturing that characterized the ancient world. Servant leadership is all over the pages of the New Testament.

This, in turn, generates a glaring *non sequitur:* Why don't we use our authority like Jesus used his? Why, instead, do even the brightest among us so often leverage our positions of power to promote our own agendas, to the relational detriment of the very people we claim to serve?

If anyone ought to know better, it should be a seminary professor who has been saturated with the New Testament ideal of other-centered leadership. Dr. Jeffrey Richmond's pilgrimage with Christ Community Church, however, clearly demonstrates that long-term exposure to the biblical paradigm is not enough, in and of itself, to guarantee the healthy exercise of pastoral authority.

He Should Have Known Better

Dr. Richmond was Shawn's mentor in his doctoral program at a large evangelical seminary. Shawn, a young man in his early thirties, was serving at the time in a struggling church that fiercely resisted renewal. Dr. Richmond was commuting across town to preach on Sundays to another congregation.

Shawn counseled with his professor about the challenges he faced in his current ministry. He mentioned that he planned to look for another pastorate. Shortly thereafter, Dr. Richmond invited Shawn to come on board with him at Christ Community Church.

The professor pitched the arrangement as follows. Dr. Richmond would continue to drive in and minister part-time at the church. Shawn would be the full-time, on-site pastor. They would share leadership responsibilities, along with the Sunday preaching.

Shawn was humbled and greatly encouraged that his professor held him in such high esteem. The position sounded ideal. Shawn and his family soon relocated across town and joined the leadership team at Christ Community Church.

Shawn encountered a rather different church from the one he had anticipated. From day one, he found himself caught in the middle of an adversarial relationship between the staff and the congregation.

As it turned out, trust between pastor and people had broken down before Shawn arrived on the scene, and Dr. Richmond had brought Shawn in to do his housecleaning. Shawn recalls:

> The deck was stacked against me before I even arrived. Because of negative feelings people had toward Dr. Richmond, it seemed that from the start, people were unwilling to even give me a chance. I was hurt that a portion of the congregation would not engage in any way with me, because they saw me as Dr. Richmond's "heavy." They viewed him as the part-time pastor from afar and me as simply "his" man on the scene.

Shawn had been wholly unaware of these dynamics before he took the job.

Shawn's relationship—or, rather, lack thereof—with the church board did little to help the already unhealthy situation. Shawn was not invited to the leadership meetings. His marching orders came directly from Dr. Richmond, with the backing (his mentor assured him) of the elders.

Shawn willingly tackled his assignments, however, both because he had Dr. Richmond's support and because he felt that the tasks genuinely needed to be done, in order to move the church in a positive direction.

The congregation's reaction only became more and more negative. Early in his eighteen-month tenure at Christ Community Church, Shawn notes, "[T]he youth pastor and an influential member embarked upon a vicious and long-running campaign to discredit me, impugn my character, and have me removed from my position."

Meanwhile, Dr. Richmond began to portray the relationship between pastors (Shawn and his professor) and elders in similarly pessimistic terms. The elders "just don't get it." Or so Shawn's mentor maintained.

Excluded from meetings between Dr. Richmond and the board, Shawn could only assume the veracity of the information his mentor shared with him. He had no reason to do otherwise. This would prove highly problematic in the weeks ahead.

Dr. Richmond finally told Shawn that the only chance the church had to succeed was to make some big changes. The professor made a pitch to the board about his vision to close down the church, sell the property, and use the money to launch a new church a few miles away. Shawn began to do the leg work of looking into potential places to meet and collecting data from other church planters.

A few months later Dr. Richmond informed Shawn that the elders were about to decide whether or not to go ahead with the plan. If they rejected the vision, then Dr. Richmond was going to look for another job. He encouraged Shawn to do likewise.

The elders responded with a compromise arrangement. They were willing to close down the church for a few months, and then restart under a new name in the present facility. The leaders were not ready, however, to sell the property and completely start over.

Dr. Richmond was not satisfied. He advised Shawn to put out feelers for a new position. The elders were never going to let the two of them do what needed to be done to move Christ Community Church forward. Shawn assumed, of course, that his professor would seek employment elsewhere, as well.

A short time later, the truth came out, when one of the elders took Shawn out to lunch. This well-meaning church leader had intended to offer Shawn some words of support and encouragement. What happened was precisely the opposite:

> Shawn, I want to know if there's anything I can do that would help you do your job better. I know Dr. Richmond is letting you go for performance issues, but I'm wondering if we can do something to help you perform better.

Shawn felt like he had been punched in the stomach. He had

heard nothing whatsoever about either his termination or his allegedly poor performance.

Shawn had not had a performance review in the eighteen months he had been at Christ Community Church. Everything he did was at Dr. Richmond's request. And Shawn's mentor had never found cause to criticize Shawn's work ethic.

Quite the contrary. Dr. Richmond had assured Shawn all along the way that he was doing a fine job with his responsibilities.

Shawn shared all this with the well-intentioned elder over lunch that day. By the time the two men concluded their conversation, Dr. Richmond's duplicity had become painfully clear—to Shawn, at any rate.

The elders invited Shawn, for the first time, to their meeting the following evening. Shawn's presence in the room caught his mentor completely by surprise.

In the course of the discussion, a board member pointedly asked Dr. Richmond (1) if he had fired Shawn and (2) if he had told Shawn that he was fired. The esteemed professor, of course, had done neither. Instead, he had privately informed Shawn that they both ought to look for new jobs, because the church was going nowhere.

Dr. Richmond, however, was unwilling to admit as much. He talked in circles, never directly answering the elder's questions.

As the meeting progressed, the board failed to press the issue, so Shawn felt compelled to narrate his own version of the events. His story elicited little response. Shawn then asked to be excused and left Dr. Richmond and the elders to deal with the fallout.

The next day Shawn received an e-mail from his mentor calling him to a meeting in the professor's office at the seminary. Shawn anticipated an apology. Instead, he got an earful from Dr. Richmond, who told him that he had everything all worked out, but that Shawn had messed it up.

Now, at last, the true explanation for the recent course of events became transparently clear. The "everything" that Dr. Richmond had "all worked out" was a way to get rid of Shawn, so he could preserve his own job during a financially challenging time at the church.

And it would have all worked out quite fine—for Dr. Richmond, that is—if Shawn had kept his mouth shut and taken to heart his mentor's advice to leave Christ Community Church for another ministry.

Several days later Shawn e-mailed Dr. Richmond, in order to continue the dialogue. He received no response. The meeting in the office was the last time Shawn's mentor made any effort to communicate with him.

Shawn soon resigned from Christ Community Church. He also requested (and received) from the dean of the seminary a new mentor for his doctoral program.

Shawn has since embarked upon a new ministry, in a church where things look a whole lot more promising. As he expressed it in a recent note, "What a blessing it is now to be able to serve in a healthy place!"

Dr. Richmond was ultimately relieved of his position at Christ Community Church, but not because of duplicity and the abuse of pastoral authority. Ironically, even with Shawn off the payroll, the church ran out of money and could no longer afford to pay Dr. Richmond.

The Social Context of Ministry

What went wrong at Christ Community Church? Dr. Richmond was a leader who should have known better, a highly trained theologian who knew his Bible—and knew the biblical paradigm of servant leadership—backwards and forwards.

As we will discover in the pages to follow, good theology alone is no panacea for authority abuse. Other factors play into a situation like the one described above.

Perhaps most important is the social context of ministry. By this I mean the organizational structures of our churches, and the ways that these frameworks either encourage or discourage healthy relations among leaders and transparency between pastors and their people.

Again, this is not to minimize personal responsibility. Dr. Jeffrey Richmond must answer to God for the way he handled his relationship with Shawn.

As events unfolded at Christ Community Church, however, systemic structural and relational issues—such as the exclusion of Shawn from the elder meetings, and the adversarial relationship between the congregation and its pastors—opened the door to Dr. Richmond's dark side. Unencumbered by the kinds of checks and balances that a healthier church might have had in place, Dr. Richmond's felt need for self-preservation trumped years of exposure to biblical truth.

The sad result was that this esteemed seminary professor—who should have known better—blatantly misused his authority in his relationship with Shawn and the church.

This brings us to the main point of the chapter and to the heart of the book itself. It is a simple but incontrovertible fact that certain ways of doing church naturally lend themselves to a Jesus-like use of authority on the part of the leaders. Others do not. This is true for us today, and it was the case among followers of Jesus in ancient Philippi, as well.

The Philippians, like Dr. Richmond, certainly had plenty of exposure to the model of Jesus as a servant leader. The biblical ideal was readily at hand, both in Paul's letter itself (2:6-11) and in the vivid memory of the personal examples of Paul and Silas during their first visit to the colony a decade earlier (Acts 16).

Like us, however, Christians in Philippi surely struggled to embrace God's countercultural approach to leadership. These young believers had been socialized from infancy to pursue their own status-driven agendas. It would have been quite natural for the Philippians to replicate the honor-seeking values of the culture at large in the church, just as the members of the Silvanus cult in the colony had done, for example (chap. 3).

Judging from the way he crafted his letter to the Philippians, Paul wisely anticipated these intense social pressures. The example of Jesus would not be enough to guarantee that Paul's readers would use their positions of relative power and influence to serve one another.

As is the case with church leaders today, the Philippians needed more than an ideal pattern for other-centered living. They needed a social context—a practical framework for Christian community and leadership—that would provide the kinds of checks and balances necessary to ensure that authority would be used "for building up and not for tearing down," as Paul expressed it elsewhere (2 Cor 13:10).

Paul's strategy, in this regard, involved two fundamental components of church life, both markedly relational in nature: (1) the Philippians were to see themselves as members of a new family, where the honor game was now off-limits, and (2) their leaders were to serve in community with others who held positions of authority in the congregation.

This twofold approach to church life and ministry would go a long way toward ensuring that the Philippians would resist the values of the dominant culture and use their social capital in a Jesus-like manner, as they related to one another in their local church fellowship.

The Church as a Family

Anthropologists who study societies like ancient Rome include in their descriptions of honor cultures three key characteristics that helpfully illuminate Paul's strategy for creating community and encouraging servant leadership in his letter to the Philippians:

1. Honor is a group value
2. Families compete for honor with outsiders
3. The honor game is off-limits within the family

We will consider each of these three ancient social realities in turn.

Honor Is a Group Value

We have already come to appreciate the primacy of honor

as a social value in the ancient world. As Philip Esler notes, Mediterranean culture was a "fiercely competitive" environment in which

> virtually any social interchange, such as business affairs, politics, sport, literary contests, dinner invitations or even arranging a marriage, constitutes an arena in which people strive to enhance their honour at someone else's expense.[2]

The pursuit of honor, however, was not an individual endeavor in the New Testament world. Mediterranean antiquity evidences characteristics of what anthropologists call strong-group culture—a social environment in which the good of the group takes priority over individual goals and happiness. We see this most clearly in the practice of arranged marriages, which were contracted not primarily to satisfy the relational needs of a bride and groom but, rather, to enhance the honor and future viability of their extended families.

Cultural values and social codes related to honor and shame inevitably intersected the strong group orientation of ancient society in some decisive ways, with the result that (a) social groups served as key repositories of honor and (b) the family—the most important group of all—took pride of place, in this regard. Bruce Malina elaborates:

> Honor is always presumed to exist within one's own family of blood, that is, among all those one has as blood relatives. . . . Outside that circle, all people are presumed to be dishonorable, guilty, if you will, unless proved otherwise. It is with all these others that one must play the game, engage in the contest, put one's honor and one's own family honor on the line.[3]

---

2. Philip F. Esler, "Family Imagery and Christian Identity in Gal 5:13 to 6:10," in *Constructing Early Christian Families: Family as Social Reality and Metaphor*, ed. Halvor Moxnes (London: Routledge, 1997), 123–24.

3. Malina, *The New Testament World*, 38.

In a social context like this, persons vigorously compete for honor not only (or even primarily) as individuals but, rather, as representatives of families, seeking to defend and augment the honor of their extended kinship groups.

Families Compete for Honor with Outsiders

The cultural script outlined above was actively in play when Paul established the church in Philippi. Colonists labored zealously to acquire honor and to publicly proclaim the achievements of family members. The great majority of more than seven hundred inscriptions unearthed in the region portray one family member honoring another and thereby securing public recognition for the broader kinship unit.

The burial inscriptions are a case in point. Family members who paid for these monuments were not content to identify the deceased by name, as is generally the case on grave markers in America today. Persons in Philippi sought to honor themselves and their relatives by listing the various official titles acquired during the subject's lifetime.

From the colony's western cemetery, for example, comes the following inscription:

> Marcus Antonius Macer, son of Marcus, of the tribe Voltinia, honored with the decorations of a decurion, quaestor, has for himself and for his daughter, Cassia Valentia, (set up this inscription).[4]

Here a local elite identifies himself as a Roman citizen ("tribe Voltinia"), underscores his connection with the colony's governing body ("decorations of a decurion"), and boasts an important honorific title ("quaestor")—all within the context of a family burial monument.

The same location produced an inscription in which a wife honored her husband by listing his numerous titles:

---

4. Pilhofer, *Philippi, Band 2*, 396/L781, p. 397.

For Lucius Salvius Secundinus, son of Secundus, of the tribe
Quirina, quaestor urbanus, adlecto inter aedilcios by Imperator
Antoninus Augustus, praetor urbanus, legatus pro praetore of
the province of Asia, Petrusidia Augurina, his wife, set up (this
inscription).[5]

We won't pause to consider in detail the technical terms used
to describe Lucius's accomplishments. It is sufficient to note (a)
the concern for family honor reflected in the inscription—a husband, his father, and his wife are included—and (b) the preoccupation with honorific titles, a phenomenon that surfaces in
inscription after inscription in the colony.

On another tombstone a son lists the achievements of his deceased father and adds his own honors, as well:

For Titus Flavius Alexander, the son of Titus, from the tribe
Voltinia, decurion of Philippi, fifty-eight years old, his de-
serving father, and for himself, (has) Titus Flavius Macedonicus,
son of Titus, from the tribe Voltinia, honored with the decorations of a decurion, (set up this inscription) during his lifetime.[6]

We move now from the cemetery to Philippi's forum, the
center of town, where urban benefaction provided aristocratic
families with further opportunity to flaunt their honors and to
compete with other noble families within the confines of the
same public space. We examined several of these inscriptions earlier, noting, in particular, the lists of honorific titles they contain.
Here I wish to focus, instead, on the dynamics of family honor.

Consider the fountain inscription we encountered in chapter
3:

Lucius Decimius Bassus, the son of Lucius, from the tribe
Voltinia, aedile of Philippi, has, on the basis of his will, ordered

---

5. Ibid., 386a/L839, p. 386.
6. Ibid., 502/L247, p. 482.

(this fountain) to be made for himself and for Lucius Decimius, the son of Lucius, from the tribe Voltinia, the quaestor and duumvir of Philippi, his father, and for Gaius Decimius Maxsimus, the son of Lucius, out of the tribe Voltinia, his brother, at a cost of 30,000 sesterces.[7]

The location in the forum, at the heart of public life in the colony, served as a fitting place to honor several of the Decimii family, and the original benefactor (Lucius Decimius Bassus), as well as his father (Lucius) and brother (Gaius), all listed above, are each featured in other inscriptions placed near the fountain.

A similar pair of inscriptions, found in proximity to those honoring the Decimii family, proclaim the status of another elite kinship group. Both monuments were erected by Gaius Mucius Scaeva, who honors his father and his uncle, respectively:

For Gaius Mucius Scaeva, son of Quintus, from the tribe Fabia, the first centurion of the Sixth legion, Ferrata, prefect of the cohort, on the basis of his own will, Gaius Mucius Scaeva, son of Gaius, has set up (this inscription).[8]

For Publius Mucius, son of Quintius of the tribe Voltinia, centurion of the Sixth Legion Ferrata, duumvir iure dicundo in Philippi, Gaius Mucius Scaeva, the son of Gaius, has set up (this inscription) on the basis of the will of Gaius Mucius Scaeva, son of Quintus, of the tribe Fabia.[9]

The proximity in the Philippian forum of the Decimii inscriptions to those honoring members of the Mucii family speaks volumes about the way in which elite families competed for honor in the public arena of this status-conscious Roman colony.

Non-elites got on the family honor bandwagon, as well. Freed

---

7. Ibid., 213/L347, p. 230.
8. Ibid., 218/L352, p. 234.
9. Ibid., 219/L353, p. 235.

slaves from Philippi, for example, who were granted the honor of participating as priests in the imperial cult, sought, like their social betters, to publicize their status in family honor inscriptions. In one monument a wife honors her deceased husband, whom she describes as an "Augustale," a post specifically reserved for freedmen serving in the worship of Augustus.[10]

We conclude our survey of family honor with an example illustrating how brothers and sisters honored one another in the colony. Gaius Julius Maximus sought to impress persons frequenting Philippi's busy forum with his brother's imposing catalogue of honors and titles, and he added a few of his own, as well:

> For Gaius Iulius Maximus Mucianus, the son of Gaius, of the tribe Voltinia, a *vir clarissimus*, honored with the *latus clavus* by the divine (Antoninus) Pius, quaestor pro praetore of Pontus and Bithynia, aedile of the grain supply, designated praetor, also decurion of Philippi and in the province of Thracia, (for) his brother Gaius Iulius Teres, the Thracharch, father of senators, (has set up this inscription) in the place determined by a decree of the decurions.[11]

As we saw in chapter 3, the phrase *vir clarissimus* identifies Gaius as a Roman senator. The *latus clavus* is the broad purple stripe that only senators could wear on their citizen togas. Gaius had brought great honor to his extended family. His brother wanted to inform the rest of Philippi about his family's social status.

Archaeological data from the colony thus accords quite nicely with the anthropological model of family honor outlined earlier. Kinship group members honored one another, and individual families appear to have competed with other families for status in the public arena. We are now prepared to consider the third and final aspect of the model.

---

10. Ibid., 037/L037, p. 40.
11. Ibid., 240/L465, p. 256.

The Honor Game Is Off-Limits Within the Family

Concern for family honor generated a set of corresponding boundaries that defined the appropriate social contexts for honor exchanges between individuals in the ancient world, and it is this aspect of the model that offers the most payoff for our interpretation of Paul's strategy for community formation in the church.

Specifically, persons were expected to compete for personal and familial honor only with outsiders. Within the family another ethos prevailed entirely. Here the honor game was off-limits.

It was considered highly dishonorable, for example, for one brother to contend with another for individual honor. Instead, members of a Mediterranean family were expected to defer to one another in honor, to use their social capital to serve—not compete with—their siblings, in order to present a united front to the outside world.

This reality sheds much light on Paul's concept of the church as a family, as we will see below. For in the Jesus community at Philippi, individuals who were formerly fierce competitors for honor in the colony at large now found themselves to be brothers and sisters in Christ.

An Ancient Witness

Plutarch has left us our only surviving treatise on brotherhood from the ancient world. He identifies the honor game as singularly inappropriate among siblings.

Plutarch is a realist who recognizes that one brother will often be more naturally gifted than a sibling for engaging in honorable public endeavors. In such cases, Plutarch insists, the superior brother should defer to the inferior.

The truly virtuous stronger sibling "permits his brother to be left out of no task that is worthy of notice and would bring honour, but makes him a sharer in all honourable enterprises" (*On Brotherly Love*, 485C). Plutarch elaborates:

> One would therefore advise a brother, in the first place, to make his brothers partners in those respects in which he is

considered to be superior, adorning them with a portion of his repute and adopting them into his friendships, and if he is a cleverer speaker than they, to make his eloquence available for their use as though it were no less theirs than his; in the next place, to make manifest to them neither haughtiness nor disdain, but rather, by deferring to them and conforming his character to theirs, to make his superiority secure from envy and to equalize, so far as this is attainable, the disparity of his fortune by his moderation of spirit. (484D)

Later in the treatise Plutarch decries a "contentious and ambitious spirit" among siblings (487F). Ideally, brothers should envy no one. But "if this is impossible, they should turn their malignancy outwards and drain it off on those not of their blood . . . by nature suitable objects for envy and jealousy" (485E).

Plutarch's convictions align perfectly with our anthropological model, and they are colorfully reflected in the colony at Philippi, where we see persons (a) vigorously competing for family honor against representatives of other families by (b) boasting in public inscriptions about the achievements of their own family members.

Hellerman Family Solidarity

Much of the above is common sense contextualized in a culture much different than our own. Although it manifests itself in different ways among different people groups, interfamily solidarity is a transcultural value that remains desirable even in our families today.

As family therapists will tell us, parents do their children a great disservice by comparing them with one another, pitting them against each another, and thereby promoting sibling competition for parental affection and affirmation in the home. The psychological damage done in such an environment often reaches far into adulthood.

Healthy families encourage siblings, instead, to rejoice in one another's victories and to grieve together when a brother or sister struggles, or somehow suffers the sting of defeat, in public, outside the home.

The Hellermans warmly recall our youngest's (Rachel's) remarkable victory at an art show, when she was in grammar school. Rachel had been drawing cartoon animal characters since she was old enough to pick up a pencil. She had become quite good at it. We encouraged her to submit an entry to a local student art competition.

Rachel drew a detailed picture just for the event, and we were confident that she would win at least a second- or third-place ribbon among her third-grade peers. The day of the show arrived, and we were initially disappointed to find Rachel's drawing displayed nowhere among the winners at her grade level.

We asked one of the docents where we might find Rachel's entry, assuming that a group of runners-up was displayed elsewhere in the room. The woman warmly smiled and exclaimed, "Oh, you're Rachel Hellerman?!" She then took us to the other end of the room, where we discovered that Rachel's piece had won "Best of the Show," triumphing over the entries of all the students, from the first through the eighth grade!

If the Hellermans lived in first-century Philippi, I would have hired a stoneworker to chisel out an honor inscription. Then I would have set up the monument right in the center of town, where everyone could have seen it:

Rachel Hellerman, sister of Rebekah Hellerman, daughter of Joe and Joann Hellerman, "Best of the Show," Hermosa Beach Annual Student Art Show. Her father set up this inscription.

The point here is a simple one. Family members honor other family members when they accomplish something significant in their lives. And healthy families also typically band together in our antipathy toward outsiders who hurt one of our own.

Rachel is now in college, living on campus at Biola University, an hour or so from home. She was so busy in the spring of 2010 that she insisted she didn't have time to come home for Mother's

Day. Then, on the Saturday of Mother's Day weekend, Rachel discovered that the fellow she thought was her boyfriend was, in fact, dating someone else.

Rachel's world momentarily fell apart and, suddenly, she found plenty of time to come home for Mother's Day, where mom, dad, and sister commiserated with her in our collective indignation toward the behavior of her now former boyfriend.

Those of us fortunate enough to grow up in relatively healthy home environments are familiar with the kind of interfamily solidarity illustrated in stories like these. Interfamily solidarity was important to the Romans, as well, but, as we have seen above, it was accompanied by a forceful, overtly public competitive ethos vis-à-vis representatives of other families that is quite foreign to our experience in the West today.

Returning to Philippi

To summarize, persons in ancient Philippi (a) vigorously competed for honor with outsiders, (b) granted honor to family insiders, and (c) publicized family achievements on inscriptions erected throughout the colony.

But what happens in Philippi when an outsider, someone from another family who is my adversary in the quest for honor, suddenly becomes a member of my family? Now the honor game—the practice of leveraging my power and authority against this individual to further my own agenda and that of my blood family—is off-limits.

This is precisely what happened when residents of Philippi became Christians and joined the local Jesus community. Former adversaries in the public court of honor now belonged to the same spiritual family. As a result, according to their own cultural values and social codes, the Philippian Christians were now expected to use their status and social capital selflessly, in the service of others in the church community.

In his letter to the Philippians, a key part of Paul's strategy for encouraging the proper use of power and authority in the church was to remind his readers that they were now family. The honor game was no longer an option. Their social context had been radically transformed. The Philippians were now brothers and sisters in Christ.[12]

The Church as a Family in Philippi

For Paul the church was a family. The metaphor occurs throughout Paul's writings, and we find it in Philippians, as well. Paul employed the Greek term *adelphos* ("brother") to refer to his fellow Christians nine times in the letter.

In six instances, *adelphoi* (the vocative of *adelphos*), translated "beloved/brothers and sisters" (NRSV), was used to directly address Paul's readers (1:12; 3:1, 13, 17; 4:1, 8). Elsewhere, other forms of *adelphos* designated the Christians who were with the apostle in Rome (1:14; 4:21), and described Epaphroditus (2:25), who had brought the Philippians' gift to Paul while he was in prison.

Paul also used family language when he referred to God as "Father" (1:2; 2:11; 4:20), and when he characterized the Philippians as "children of God" (*tekna theou*, 2:15). Paul clearly conceived of the Jesus community in Philippi as a surrogate family.

The sibling terminology, in particular, would have forcefully resonated with Paul's readers. Due to the patrilineal orientation of extended family systems in the ancient world, brothers and sisters (who came from the same bloodline) generally exhibited a higher degree of social solidarity than any other same-generation relationship, even including spouses, who did not come from the same bloodline. We saw this concern for sibling solidarity reflected in the excerpts from Plutarch, cited above.[13]

---

12. For a more detailed discussion see Joseph H. Hellerman, "Brothers and Friends in Philippi: Family Honor in the Roman World and in Paul's Letter to the Philippians," *BTB* 39:1 (2009): 15–25.

13. For an extended treatment of the church as a surrogate family, see Joseph H. Hellerman, *The Ancient Church as Family* (Minneapolis: Fortress, 2001) and (for a more popular audience) Hellerman, *When the Church Was a Family: Recapturing Jesus' Vision for Authentic Christian Community* (Nashville: Broadman & Holman, 2009).

Paul's strategy was brilliantly conceived. By positioning the Christian community as a surrogate family, Paul profoundly subverted the honor culture that determined the contours of social relations in Philippi. There would be no adversarial competition for honor among Christians in the church in the colony, for they were now brothers and sisters in the family of God.

Instead of honor-seeking, Paul challenged the Philippians, as family, to grant honor to one another, or, as he put it in the letter, "Do nothing out of rivalry or conceit, but in humility consider others as more important than yourselves" (2:3).

Additionally, Paul redefined the criteria for granting and receiving honor in the Christian community, compared with the dominant culture. Romans gained honor for acts of courage on the battlefield and for offices they won in the political arena. Philippian Christians would be esteemed, instead, for acting like Jesus, that is, for using status and authority in the service of others.

Paul modeled these values and practices in his own missionary work (see chap. 4, on the ministry in Philippi), and they surface, again, in the way Paul commended Epaphroditus to the Philippians.

Epaphroditus had brought a gift to Paul from the Philippians. Paul sent Epaphroditus back to Philippi with the following personal note:

> But I considered it necessary to send you Epaphroditus—my brother, coworker, and fellow soldier, as well as your messenger and minister to my need—since he has been longing for all of you and was distressed because you heard that he was sick. Indeed, he was so sick that he nearly died. However, God had mercy on him, and not only on him but also on me, so that I would not have one grief on top of another. For this reason, I am very eager to send him so that you may rejoice when you see him again and I may be less anxious. Therefore, welcome him in the Lord with all joy and hold men like him in honor, because he came close to death for the work of Christ, risking his life to make up what was lacking in your ministry to me. (2:25-30)

We saw in a previous chapter that the residents of Philippi were highly preoccupied with honorific titles, more so than persons elsewhere along Paul's journeys. Notice that Paul began his commendation by honoring Epaphroditus with a series of five titles: "brother . . . coworker . . . fellow soldier . . . messenger . . . minister" (v. 25).

Nowhere else in Paul's letters did he string together more than two such titles to describe a coworker. This is hardly a coincidence. Paul had the social context of Philippi directly in view.

First and foremost, Epaphroditus belonged to God's family ("brother," v. 25). Paul exhorted the Philippians to "hold men like him in honor" (v. 29). Paul did not single out Epaphroditus for honor, however, for feats of bravery on the battlefield, or because he held a public post in the colony. Instead, the Philippians were to honor Epaphroditus "because he came close to death for the work of Christ" (v. 30).

In summary, by identifying the church as a family, Paul sought to establish a relational context in which the honor game was no longer acceptable for those who claimed to be followers of Jesus. Instead of competing with each other and grasping for honor, Christians in the colony were to relate like siblings, that is, they were to "outdo one another in showing honor," as Paul instructed another congregation situated in a decidedly Roman social setting (Rom 12:10).

Such a conception of Christian community, if embraced and put into practice, would have gone a long way toward (a) encouraging community members to interact with one another after the example of Jesus in Philippians 2:6–8 and (b) protecting the Philippians from authority abuse at the hands of persons in the congregation who might have been tempted to use relative degrees of status to promote their personal or familial agendas.

A Community of Leaders

The second aspect of Paul's strategy for community formation concerned church oversight. Paul's philosophy of leadership was markedly relational in nature.

From what we can tell, for example, none of Paul's congregations had a solitary (or "senior") pastor figure. All were led by a plurality of overseers. And Paul modeled team leadership in his own life and ministry, as well, partnering with Timothy, Silas, and others to spread the gospel throughout the Roman Empire.

Plurality Leadership in Paul's Churches

We saw that Paul addressed church leaders by title in his greeting in the letter to the Philippians. If there was a sole pastor figure in charge of the church at Philippi when Paul wrote, then it is highly anomalous that Paul failed to address him as such, referring, instead, in the plural to groups he called "overseers and deacons" (1:1).

The same is the case elsewhere Paul ministered. After establishing congregations in Lystra, Iconium, and Pisidian Antioch, for example, Paul and Barnabas "appointed elders in every church" (Acts 14:23). Paul similarly referred in the plural to leaders at Thessalonica: "those who labor among you and lead you in the Lord" (1 Thess 5:12).

The church in Corinth, as well, apparently had no sole pastor figure. For the community was still led by "elders" when the church at Rome wrote a letter to the Corinthians (often referred to as *1 Clement*), more than a generation removed from Paul (1:3). See, too, Titus 1:5, where Paul instructed Titus on the island of Crete to "to appoint elders in every town."

Finally, consider the Ephesian church. According to the chronology of Acts, Paul ministered in Ephesus longer than anywhere else, approximately three years. Surely the apostle's ideals for leadership structure would manifest themselves there, if anywhere, among Paul's congregations.

In Acts 20, Paul gave his final charge to the leaders at Ephesus, in a highly charged, deeply passionate encounter. Again, plural titles were used. Those in view are alternatively described as "elders" and "overseers" (20:17, 28; the terms are interchangeable in the New Testament, referring to the same group of leaders).

I find it inconceivable that the senior pastor of the church at

Ephesus would have been absent from this important meeting, if, indeed, such a position existed. Clearly it did not. The Ephesian Christians were led by a plurality of pastor-elders.

It is interesting to note, in light of Paul's conviction that the church is a family, that the apostle's model of plurality leadership was culturally anomalous, to say the least. Families in the ancient world universally functioned under the aegis of strong one-man leadership, in the person of a family patriarch.

It would have been quite natural, therefore, for Paul to appoint a single man to serve as the overseer of each local church family. The members of Paul's churches would have felt right at home, so to speak, since the natural families to which they belonged were each led by a single male figure. Instead, Paul appointed a group of elders to lead each of his communities.

Perhaps Paul's convictions regarding plurality leadership in the family of God go back to Jesus, who is remembered to have said, "do not call anyone on earth your father, because you have one Father, who is in heaven" (Matt 23:9). At any rate, Paul was certainly not alone in advocating team leadership. The same model surfaces elsewhere in the New Testament (Jas 5:14; 1 Pet 5:1-4; Heb 13:17).

Some, of course, will take issue here, offering as counter-evidence the role of James in the Jerusalem church (Acts 15), or, perhaps, that of Timothy at Ephesus (1 Tim). Others suggest that the household model of early Christianity necessitates that a single patron figure, a household head, would have functioned as a leader in each of Paul's communities.

I find none of these arguments persuasive, for reasons that would take us far afield from the issue at hand. At any rate, it is not my agenda to argue for plurality leadership as the one biblical model for church government, though I believe this to be the case. I am more interested here in function than structure.

What I want us to consider in the pages to follow is the practical value of shared leadership, the benefits of the model for leaders and church members alike, particularly where the exercise of pastoral authority is concerned.

Most instances of authority abuse in our congregations today are perpetrated by senior pastors who answer to no one for the decisions they make about church vision and staffing. Perhaps even more troubling (but hardly surprising), almost without exception these men have no genuine brothers in their congregations, that is, no other men who function as their close, relational peers.

The New Testament pattern of plurality leadership would go a long way toward (a) protecting our churches from the harmful activities of these dysfunctional, isolated leaders and (b) encouraging the healthy exercise of pastoral authority.

Team Ministry in Paul's Mission to the Gentiles

Paul modeled the team approach in his own life and ministry. Paul's authority as an apostle was much greater, of course, than the authority of those who ministered alongside him. We do not expect to find the playing field completely level where Paul and his missionary coworkers are concerned. This, however, makes the degree to which Paul partnered with others all the more remarkable.

Most readers are familiar with the fact that Paul traveled and ministered with others on his journeys, as recorded in Acts. Barnabas accompanied Paul on his first journey (13:2). Silas and Timothy were with the apostle on the second journey (15:40; 16:3), as, apparently, were Luke (see 16:10, where the author switched from "they" to "we") and later Priscilla and Aquila (18:18). We also find Paul in the company of a band of coworkers on the third journey (19:22, 29; 20:4).

When we turn to Paul's letters, we discover that "coworker" (Greek *synergos*) was, in fact, Paul's favorite word to describe those with whom he served. He used the term twelve times to identify, among others, Priscilla and Aquila (Rom 16:3), Urbanus (Rom 16:9), Timothy (Rom 16:21; 1 Thess 3:2), Titus (2 Cor 8:23), Epaphroditus (Phil 2:25), Clement (Phil 4:3), Justus (Col 4:11), Philemon (Phlm 1), and Mark, Aristarchus, Demas, and Luke (Phlm 24).

In spite of the relative position of formal authority the apostle occupied compared to his fellow missionaries, moreover, Paul's relationship with his coworkers does not seem to have been one of structure and hierarchy. One senses, rather, that Paul shared deep relational bonds with these folks.

Paul called Timothy, for example, "my dearly loved and faithful son in the Lord" (1 Cor 4:17). And the mutual affection that existed between Paul and the leaders of the church at Ephesus is readily apparent in Acts 20, where Luke described Paul's final meeting with the Ephesian elders:

> After he said this, he knelt down and prayed with all of them. There was a great deal of weeping by everyone. They embraced Paul and kissed him, grieving most of all over his statement that they would never see his face again. (vv. 36–38)

Not only did Paul open himself up to coworkers and church leaders, he also exhibited a remarkable degree of transparency and vulnerability before persons in his congregations—even those who failed to reciprocate. Paul wrote to the Corinthians,

> We have spoken openly to you, Corinthians; our heart has been opened wide. You are not limited by us, but you are limited by your own affections. I speak as to my children. As a proper response, you should also be open to us. (2 Cor 6:11–13)

Paul Barnett rightly views this passage as a window into Paul's philosophy of ministry:

> Here [in 2 Cor 6] we hear Paul in his most human self-disclosure. The apostolic office, which is to a significant degree a model for subsequent pastoral and missionary ministry, is a human ministry; it can never be a mere institution.[14]

---

14. Paul Barnett, *The Second Epistle to the Corinthians*, NICNT, ed. Gordon D. Fee (Grand Rapids: Eerdmans, 1997), 335.

Don't miss Barnett's final assertion: for Paul, ministry "can never be a mere institution."

The damage that institutionalism has done to people in our churches will become painfully evident in the chapters to follow. Paul's antidote, it seems, was a decidedly relational approach to ministry. Paul conceived of the local church as a surrogate family, led by a plurality of pastor-elders, who open their lives up to each other and to the people in their congregation.

Conclusion

Social context is everything to healthy pastoral ministry. Well, not quite everything. We need a model. We need an archetype. We need the example of Jesus to inspire us with God's vision for servant leadership in our churches. That is a given.

The example of Jesus, however, is not enough. It was not enough for the Philippians, and it has proven insufficient to generate other-centered leadership in numbers of our churches today.

Paul responded to his own cultural challenges by crafting a social context for ministry that would encourage Jesus-like leadership on the part of persons with power and authority in the Christian community.

Paul's strategy, in this regard, was twofold. First, he reminded the Philippians that they now belonged to a new family. God was their Father. They were brothers and sisters in Christ. According to the Philippians' own cultural values, this meant that the honor game was off-limits among those who sought to follow Jesus.

No longer would Christians in Philippi compete with fellow believers for the honor of their respective blood families, as they had done in the colony before they were saved. They would now defer in honor to their Christian siblings. And this honor would be granted to those who used their social capital in the service of others, after the example of Jesus, as portrayed in Philippians 2:6–11.

Second, Paul addressed the critical matter of church leadership. Paul's approach here, as it turns out, was also distinctly relational. We find no evidence of one-person rule anywhere in the churches Paul established. A plurality of elders provided oversight to each local congregation. And as we have seen, Paul modeled team ministry in his own missionary journeys, as well, traveling with bands of like-minded persons throughout the eastern Roman Empire.

We gather from his letters, moreover, that Paul's understanding of team leadership had little to do with organization and structure, and everything to do with relational mutuality. Paul would not be satisfied merely to have a set of church by-laws requiring a plurality of pastors. He would insist that such a team develop intimate relational bonds, as its members partnered together to do the work of the ministry, whatever the formal structure of the church might happen to be.

Paul's strategy was truly brilliant. He recognized that only in the social context of a healthy surrogate family—led by a plurality of individuals who related to each other as siblings, and who lead in community together—could Jesus's ideal of servant leadership triumph over the social values of the dominant culture and become a reality among the Philippian Christians.

I will maintain, in the pages to follow, that the same is the case for many of our churches in America today.

Let's return, as we wrap up the chapter, to Christ Community Church, in order to imagine what might have been, in the case of Shawn and his mentor, Dr. Jeffrey Richmond, had the apostle Paul had his way with the congregation.

Imagine Christ Community Church as a healthy surrogate family. The church would have brought Shawn on staff not as a hireling to do Dr. Richmond's housecleaning but, rather, as a brother in Christ, where the first priority would have been to cultivate meaningful sibling relationships between a young, new pastor and those he came to serve.

Imagine the pastors and elders of Christ Community Church as a united, mutually encouraging team of peer shepherds. Shawn would have spent his first year at the church gathering together weekly with Dr. Richmond and the elders of Christ Community Church, not to do any vision-casting or decision-making, but solely to speak into each other's lives, to pray for the church, and to pray for each other and for the families represented around the table. Imagine the kind of trust and transparency such gatherings might have generated among church leaders.

Now, finally, imagine the kind of church ministry that could have naturally arisen at Christ Community Church from such a healthy relational environment.

There are, of course, no guarantees of church health in the broken world in which we live. Doing family at church will prove as challenging as doing family at home. Deeply wounded, dysfunctional leaders will find ways to circumvent even the most carefully crafted sets of checks and balances. We will continue to stumble along, even in the best of circumstances, in our efforts to pattern our lives and ministries after Jesus.

The wisdom of Paul's twofold strategy for leadership and community formation, however, becomes crystal clear in the reimagined scenario outlined above. I have little doubt that a very different story would have played itself out during Shawn's tenure, had Christ Community Church embraced Paul's vision for the church as a family, led by a plurality of relationally connected leaders.

Questions for Reflection

1. Why do you think that some leaders in our churches fail to use their positions of power like Jesus does in Philippians 2:6-8?

2. How would the family metaphor—we are "brothers and sisters" in Christ—have changed relationships among followers of Jesus in Philippi, compared with the way those relationships would have functioned in the dominant culture?

3. The Roman Empire had a single leader at the top. The Roman household had an authoritative father figure at the top. Yet Paul never appoints a senior pastor to lead his churches. Why not? Why do you think we have departed from the common New Testament model of a plurality of pastors?

4. What are the benefits of the team approach to church ministry? Of the senior pastor model? What are the pitfalls of each approach?

5. Review the story about Dr. Richmond and his associate Shawn at the beginning of the chapter. How might things have turned out differently if the church had adopted Paul's twofold approach to ministry and leadership?

PART THREE

Power and Authority in the Church Today

Cultivating a Social Context for Servant Leadership

Stepping Over the Line

The Abuse of Authority in the Evangelical Church

> *Those who go beneath the surface do so at their peril.*
> —Oscar Wilde[1]

I developed a great deal of trust in authority figures during my childhood. It started at home. My father acted as a benevolent, loving patriarch toward the rest of the family. I learned early on that the things Dad said and did around the house were seldom self-serving, but were intended instead for the benefit of others in the family.

Even as my father was failing physically during an eight-year battle with emphysema, he would curl his arm, show us his biceps, and assure us that he still had "one last punch." This display of paternal power always made the rest of the family happy. We knew that Dad's "one last punch" was not for us. It was for anyone who would dare break into our home. I felt safe and secure in my father's presence.

School was much the same. Our teachers all seemed to use

---

1. Oscar Wilde, *The Picture of Dorian Gray* (New York: Modern Library, 1998), xii.

their authority in ways that enhanced classroom learning and encouraged relational integrity. When a teacher sent me to the principal's office—not an uncommon occurrence—somehow I just knew that the teacher was right and I was wrong. I truly admired most of my grade school teachers and willingly respected the rest.

That goes for my Sunday school teachers, as well. My parents, neither of whom were church attenders, nevertheless figured that little Joey needed some religious training. For seven years they dropped me off at a Southern Baptist church for Sunday school. When I turned twelve I was off the hook, and more than a decade passed before I returned to church as a young adult.

What little I remember about those early years in Sunday school is all positive where church authority figures are concerned. I still warmly recall the kind woman who tried to teach us the Bible stories, perhaps because I had a crush on her daughter, who was also in the class. When I came back to church as a newly converted twenty-three-year-old in 1975, I had every reason to believe that the Baptist church that welcomed me into its fold was a healthy, nurturing institution led by leaders with personal integrity.

National leaders? My formative years in the public schools taught me to view major political figures through the lens of the likes of George Washington, Thomas Jefferson, Abraham Lincoln, and Franklin D. Roosevelt—all of whom were consistently portrayed as noble servants of the common good. My positive view of the presidency was further reinforced during my fifth-grade year, when John F. Kennedy was assassinated and then memorialized in glowing terms during the ensuing weeks of national mourning.

Kennedy had already found a special place in my world. To this day, I vividly recall being hoisted up on my mother's shoulders to see Kennedy in person, when he made an appearance at a Los Angeles area shopping center during the summer of 1960. I campaigned up and down the street for JFK the following November with all the enthusiasm that a nine-year-old could muster. My joy over Kennedy's victory in the presidential election was only slightly tempered by the revelation of the unthinkable in the Hellerman home: Grandma had voted for Richard Nixon.

I still remember JFK's most memorable quote: "Ask not what your country can do for you—ask what you can do for your country." As a kid I figured that Kennedy and other national leaders maximized their positions of power in public office to do exactly that.

Convinced Otherwise

All that changed somewhere along the way. I cannot quite pinpoint when or where. Today, however, this otherwise upbeat and optimistic husband, father, pastor, and scholar tends to distrust persons—especially males—who occupy positions of authority in large institutional contexts.

One Sunday I informed my congregation that I would not make a very good Democrat because I do not trust big government. Then I remarked that I would not make a very good Republican because I do not trust big business. Finally, I said that I probably do not make a very good pastor—according to current criteria for pastoral success among American evangelicals—because I do not trust big-church religion. In each case my hermeneutic of suspicion targets the persons who wield authority in these large and imposing institutions.

Some of this is my own stuff. I was an only child, a natural leader, and never a joiner. If I cannot be the one in charge, I tend to question the wisdom of those who are. This is a character flaw that I continue to work on to this day.

I am also a product of the 1960s, when I enthusiastically embraced all the disdain for traditional values that came with those tumultuous years in American social history. I spent much of the following decade of my young adult life smoking pot and playing in a rock band—not a rich soil for cultivating respect for leaders and other persons in positions of authority in the culture at large.

The problem I have with authority, however, is not just about me. Not by a long shot.

My distrust of big government, big business, and big church is firmly rooted in the reality of what all of us have observed—and many have personally experienced—in recent decades, in settings both national and local, in contexts political, corporate, and ecclesiastical.

The picture is not a pretty one. We have been betrayed by our leaders on every front. Watergate, Enron, Bernie Madoff, Jim Bakker—the list could go on and on. We have good reason to be at least somewhat leery of power and authority.

Our focus here, however, is not with political or corporate ethics. Nor will we concern ourselves with larger-than-life religious celebrities of national prominence who have betrayed the trust of their followers.

This is a book about the local church. Accordingly, we will wrestle, in our final three chapters together, with the problem of authority abuse in the contemporary evangelical church. Sadly, we have more than enough material to occupy our attention.

A Biting Critique

I am hardly alone in my reservations about the ways that some of our leaders are using their authority. Voices from the movement broadly known as the emerging church almost universally express concern about ministerial power in the church in the West today. The dismantling of hierarchies and the decentralization of pastoral authority are at the heart of emerging Christianity's agenda for church renewal.

Sally Morgenthaler's barbs at the senior pastor, CEO model of local church leadership have been as pointed as any. Her sentiments, while stridently polemical, nevertheless represent the convictions of a significant cross-section of younger evangelicals and deserve extended citation.

For Morgenthaler, the business model of ministry generates a social context that is all about

> one leader's vision; one take on what God is up to in the community, the nation, and the world; one single, often blurry, and out-of-context frame in this speeding movie we call life.[2]

---

2. Sally Morgenthaler, "Leadership in a Flattened World: Grassroots Culture

The CEO pastor operates as

a "my-way-or-the-highway" autocrat—a top-down aficio-
nado whose ecclesiastical machine whirs only to the sound of
his own voice and functions tightly within the parameters of his
own limited vision.[3]

A single dominating take on God's will for the community
excludes all other voices and ultimately undermines that community itself:

With luxurious facilities bordering on the obscene, organizational hierarchies designed to feed pastoral ego, and constituencies of the robotically religious (who else would tolerate
living in a machine?), it's not hard to figure out that one's story,
creativity, and opinions aren't welcome. Newsflash: the "Forty
Days of Honest Dialogue" campaign is *not* coming to your
local suburban church-plex anytime soon.[4]

And if anyone objects to the institutional status quo?

Pity the member who questions the machine and develops any
significant influence. Sooner or later that member will be disposed of—shunned, silenced, and quietly removed from any
position of authority on staff, boards, worship teams, or within
the most lowly of programs.[5]

Don't be put off by Morgenthaler's over-the-top rhetoric.
Yes, it is decidedly unfair indiscriminately to categorize all mega-
churches as "constituencies of the robotically religious." And
the swipe at Rick Warren and Saddleback Community Church

---

and the Demise of the CEO Model," in *An Emergent Manifesto of Hope*, ed.
Doug Pagitt and Tony Jones, 175–88 (Grand Rapids: Baker, 2007), 182.
3. Ibid., 181.
4. Ibid., 182.
5. Ibid., 181.

("Forty Days of Honest Dialogue") is clever but hardly sourced in the Spirit.

It would be easy to continue to deconstruct the overstatement and caricature that comprise the bulk of Morgenthaler's assertions. I want us to move beyond the rhetoric, however, to hear the personal hurt that likely generated the callous tone of this sharp critique.

Comments like Morgenthaler's generally don't come from the antiseptic pen of an ivory tower biblical scholar who is attempting, at least, to be fair to the evidence at hand. They come from a person who has been on the receiving end of the very practices that Morgenthaler so harshly rejects.

As we will see below, numbers of creative and gifted persons in our churches have experienced at the hands of church leaders precisely what Sally Morgenthaler describes in the last paragraph cited above. They have been "disposed of—shunned, silenced, and quietly removed from any position of authority" by senior pastors who have abused their God-given authority as shepherds of their congregations.

Timothy's Story

Our first story comes from a seminary student who spent his whole life in the same church in the western United States. Timothy's family was one of the first to join Chinese Christian Fellowship. Timothy was the first baby in the church's nursery nearly three decades ago.

Timothy's church consists of two distinct people groups: a Cantonese congregation and a church of English-speaking Chinese Americans. A senior pastor oversees the Cantonese church. Several associate pastors have shepherded the English congregation over the years. A single church board governs both language groups. Timothy was involved in the English-speaking church.

As a result of events outlined below, in 2010 Timothy left the only church he had ever known, and justifiably so. The story is a sad one, however, because, as Timothy related to me, "I loved the church and was hoping to return to it after graduating from seminary and spend the rest of my life serving there."

Mid-2009 had, in fact, looked quite promising for Timothy's church. In the summer of 2007, an associate pastor who led the English congregation resigned, after serving the church for years. For the next year-and-a-half the congregation relied on guest preachers and a couple of interim pastors.

The English congregation flourished during the period without a paid pastor. The church was united, the teaching was rich, and many people stepped up to serve in various ministries.

In the spring of 2009, the church hired a new associate pastor. Timothy describes Ralph as "intelligent, articulate, winsome, and humble."

Pastor Ralph and his wife proved to be a natural fit for Timothy's congregation. People in the church responded enthusiastically to the new man's teaching and to his example of "humble, gospel-centered living," as Timothy expressed it. In Timothy's own words,

> All the good things that preceded the associate pastor's arrival were quickened in these months. In addition, our regular attendance was growing. In all my time at the church, this was the most exciting and hopeful.

The senior pastor, Lew, however, apparently felt threatened by the successes of his new associate.

Pastor Lew's insecurities were framed, initially, as "concerns" about the associate pastor's eschatology. There were, in fact, some significant differences. They were on the table during the hiring process, however, and Ralph graciously refrained from teaching his eschatological views in any context in the church, out of respect for his senior pastor.

Pastor Lew was not satisfied, but insisted that the pastor of the English congregation must embrace his point of view. After Ralph had studied the issue in some detail, he responded that he could not, in good conscience, adopt the senior pastor's eschatology.

The doctrinal smokescreen then cleared, and the attacks

turned personal. The senior pastor presented the following list of grievances to the governing board:

- Ralph was late to every single meeting.

- Ralph was disrespectful to the senior pastor because he ate while talking to him.

- Ralph was not on the church premises enough.

- Ralph did not wear a tie when speaking.

- Ralph took off his dress shirt after service while still on church property.

- Ralph did not study the doctrinal issues enough.

- Ralph did not fill the pulpit for the senior pastor when asked.

- Ralph received his theological training at the wrong seminary.

Some of the items were pure fabrication. Those that were not were inconsequential or exaggerated.

Lew had shared none of these grievances with Ralph before the meeting. Nor was Ralph present to respond to the allegations. The whole scenario caught him completely by surprise.

A series of board meetings ensued at which Pastor Lew engaged in a campaign to force Ralph out of the church. The senior pastor instructed the board members that God was testing them. If they voted against Lew's wishes, they would fail the test and go against God's will.

An initial vote chose to retain the associate pastor. The senior pastor responded with an e-mail to the board informing them that they had compromised the truth and disregarded doctrinal purity. A questionable appeal to procedural issues outlined in the church by-laws voided the favorable vote.

The campaign continued in several meetings for three months. Ralph was finally forced to resign.

My student, Timothy, along with most of the English congregation and the board, had finally had enough. Timothy recalls the exodus:

> Those of us who were leaving the church tried our best to leave gracefully, expressing our support for those who would stay behind. However, the pastor, his family, and his main ally (a female board member with whom Lew had earlier had an affair—see below) mounted a campaign against us as we made plans to exit. They sent e-mails and had conversations with people telling them that we were being deceived, and insinuating that we were wolves in sheep's clothing—emergent, undiscerning, compromisers, and apostate.

The reprehensible behaviors reflected in the above narrative were hardly unique during Pastor Lew's years of ministry at Chinese Christian Fellowship. Timothy recalls,

> Over the years, I had heard rumors of his method of running things in church, but I always gave him the benefit of the doubt and chalked up internal conflicts to bad communication and the cultural gap between the Chinese and English congregations.

Unhealthy patterns now began to surface, however, as former staff and departing board members, who had kept silent for years, began to compare notes.

As it turned out, two previous English-speaking pastors had become similarly entangled with Pastor Lew and his insecurities. The first was on staff for a couple of years in the early 1990s. One day he received his pink slip without warning.

As he would later do with Pastor Ralph, Pastor Lew read a laundry list of grievances to the board, which he did not discuss beforehand with his associate pastor. Several board members resisted Lew's agenda. The senior pastor gave an ultimatum: either fire the associate pastor or Lew would resign. The board backed down, and the associate pastor's fate was sealed.

Shortly thereafter, associate pastor #2—we will call him Rich—came on board in 1996 and served the church for eleven years. Like Ralph who would follow him, Rich was warmly received and quite successful with the English congregation.

The English church began to grow under Rich's leadership. Lew clearly felt threatened. When attendance in Rich's church surpassed that of the Cantonese congregation, the senior pastor ordered the attendance board in the back of the auditorium to be taken down. The weekly attendance report disappeared from the church bulletin, as well.

And then there was Pastor Lew's affair with the church board member. During Pastor Rich's tenure, a member of Chinese Christian Fellowship ran into his senior pastor in Las Vegas. Lew was holding hands with a woman who was not his wife.

The pastor claimed he was there to help with a church plant. He said he just happened to run into the woman while in Las Vegas.

Lew had previously told the church, however, that he was headed to Southern California for a conference that weekend. The surprised board member decided to take Pastor Lew at his word and not pursue the matter.

He should have inquired further. Several years later, the same woman was going through a divorce. Lew held "counseling sessions" with the woman in their cars at night, in empty parking lots. Her husband became suspicious and hid a voice recorder in the woman's car.

The husband presented the evidence to the church governing board. An investigation was launched. The senior pastor admitted to the affair, but claimed it was over. Lew agreed to accountability meetings with two deacons on the board.

The meetings turned into discussions about church ministry. Little attention was paid to the pastor and his problematic issues. One of the two deacons became so troubled by Lew's cavalier attitude toward his sin that he left the church.

The board sought to bring the matter to the denomination

for disciplinary measures. Again, Lew threatened to resign. And once again, the board backed down.

Board members who caved in later remarked that they were torn by the decision. They ultimately voted to put the issue to rest, they claimed, because they did not want to cause strife in the church.

Lew then turned his animosity toward the associate pastor, who had been involved in the investigation. The pettiness would be almost silly, if it had not finally cost Pastor Rich his ministry.

Along the way, Pastor Lew initially refused to baptize Rich's children, though he ultimately assented and allowed Rich to baptize them. Lew's wife would not allow Rich's kids to sing in the children's choir. Rich finally resigned from his position as associate pastor at Chinese Christian Fellowship.

Timothy notes, in retrospect, that Pastor Lew never had a mentor or any type of accountability in place. Timothy remarks,

> We learned that he had a history of alienating other area pastors. They were not to be associated with because their churches were "theologically liberal," meaning they read Rick Warren books and weren't Calvinists. In our denominational conference, I watched [Pastor Lew] sit alone during the sessions and leave immediately after they were over.

As Timothy sat in my office relating the sad history of his church family, I, like Timothy, could not help but deeply grieve over what could have been. God had so clearly tried, again and again, to bring quality leadership to the English congregation of Chinese Christian Fellowship—a group of believers who were ready to learn, serve, love one another, and reach their community for Christ. Sadly, Pastor Lew's emotional insecurities and destructive behavioral patterns subverted the work of God at every turn.

It is rather sobering to consider how much damage a single church leader can do. Most telling, in this regard, are Timothy's comments, in the quotation above, about his pastor's anti-social tendencies.

Lew's fears and insecurities—along with a weak, compliant church board—left this senior pastor alone in the world and alone in his church. The results continue to be tragic both for Pastor Lew and for Chinese Christian Fellowship.

Timothy, however, has learned something that he will take with him through many years of fruitful ministry:

> This entire episode has been a great lesson for me on the dangers of isolation and the need for accountability in a minister's life. I know the same sinfulness in this man lurks in my own heart, and I need to be vigilant in keeping it in check.

Yes, Timothy, we all do.

Andrew's Story

Andrew's pilgrimage in local church ministry hit rock bottom on the day after Easter 2007. In his own words,

> What just happened here? Am I really here? These were some of my thoughts as I lay in an emergency room hospital bed. It was around 4:30 A.M., and my wife had just left to get ready for work. She had lain with me in the hospital bed for as long as she could. I knew she had to leave, but I didn't want her to. I couldn't stand to be alone at that point in time. Just a week ago everything seemed different. I was working in the College Ministry of our church, my wife and I had community, and we had friends. Now I was lying in a hospital bed under suicide watch. No friends. No community.

A few days earlier Andrew had been fired from his staff position as the Young Adults Pastor in his church.

Andrew's background helps to explain the overwhelming sense of grief and heartache he experienced, when he suddenly lost his job and his church family. Andrew spent his teenage years involved in gang activity. During most of his sophomore year in high school, he was incarcerated in a juvenile facility.

It was in juvenile hall that Andrew first heard the gospel. He attended church services in the detention center, and he read the gospel tracts he found scattered throughout his unit. "They got me curious to learn more."

When he was released, Andrew initially returned to his previous lifestyle, but apparently God would not let him go:

> By the time I was about to turn twenty-one, something happened. I wanted to learn more about Jesus. I also wanted to be born again, though I didn't quite know what that meant at the time. So in February of 2001, I was baptized and began going to church. It was great, and I slowly began to grow in Christ.

A change to a new church in 2003 ignited Andrew's faith. Andrew met the young woman who would become his wife, and he began actively to serve as a volunteer in various areas of ministry. He became, as he puts it, "part of a community where I finally felt I was accepted."

Andrew found his work with college students to be particularly fulfilling. Consider the profound sense of meaning and purpose that ministry brought into Andrew's life:

> I was ecstatic! Growing up, I never thought I would amount to anything. I had many people tell me that I would end up in prison. Now God had given me a purpose, a destiny in Him that I could not wait to fulfill. I wanted nothing else but to go into full-time ministry.

It didn't take long for Andrew's dream to become a reality. Church leaders recognized his gifts and calling, and after several years of growth and training, Andrew was formally installed as his church's Young Adults Pastor in 2007.

Andrew's ministry was thriving. He enjoyed a camaraderie among staff members that included regular lunches and fellowship together. A church secretary adopted Andrew as her "little brother." The future looked bright, indeed.

I first met Andrew as a student in a beginning Greek course at Biola University in the fall of 2003. Andrew's background was unlike that of his fellow students, many of whom had been raised in Christian homes, sheltered from the hard knocks Andrew had experienced.

God is no respecter of persons, however, and, perhaps because of my own conversion out of the drug culture as a young adult, I felt particularly drawn to Andrew. I considered myself privileged to play a small part in this young man's education, and it was a joy to witness, firsthand, the wonderfully redemptive story that was unfolding in Andrew's life.

"Then," Andrew relates, "almost a year later, it all came crashing down."

One day the senior pastor and another associate called Andrew to a private meeting. Someone had accused Andrew of speaking inappropriately to a female employee of the church.

Andrew was not told whether the complaint came from the woman herself or from a third party who heard the alleged conversation. He denied the charge. The hour-long discussion that followed appeared to convince the two pastors that it was all a misunderstanding. "They believed me," Andrew recalls, "when I said it wasn't true."

Andrew wanted to clear the air. He requested that all parties meet together, so that he could apologize, if, indeed, he had unknowingly said something to offend the woman.

The pastors resisted the suggestion. They told Andrew to "let it go," and they asked him to take some time off from his ministry.

Andrew had previously scheduled dinner that evening with a church elder and his wife. During their conversation Andrew shared the day's events. The couple assured Andrew that everything would be okay.

Andrew spent the next ten days away from the church. He began to wonder whether he should resign his position. His wife was close to him during the whole process, ready to support him in any decision he might make.

Andrew shared his thoughts with some of the leaders in the church. They strongly discouraged him from stepping down, claiming, in Andrew's words, "It would be the worst thing I could do."

When Andrew returned to work, it was as if nothing had happened. At the next pastor's meeting, "I was assured that I was loved and that everything was all right." They instructed Andrew, however, to stay away from the female staff member involved in the incident.

Andrew responded by pressing, once again, for a face-to-face meeting, so he could get some closure and put the incident behind him. Leadership refused to budge.

One evening, several days later, an elder informed Andrew that a decision had been made about him. He was to meet with the senior pastor first thing in the morning. The next morning found Andrew in the pastor's office, along with the associate pastor.

Andrew broke the initial silence by apologizing, again, for anything he might have said or done that offended anyone. The senior pastor responded as follows:

> I think you are being deceitful right now, Andrew. You are a deceiver and a liar. We are letting you go for two reasons. One, you are not our type of guy, and, two, you have feelings for [the female staff person].

Throughout the confrontation, the other pastor, who had previously claimed to believe Andrew and who had been his mentor at the church, "looked at the floor, at the ceiling, at his shoes—everywhere but at me."

Andrew told his boss that he could not, in good conscience, admit to actions that he didn't do. "The senior pastor continued ripping me to shreds," Andrew recalls.

Midway through the meeting, in walked the elder who had assured Andrew over dinner two weeks before that everything would be all right. Neither he nor Andrew's mentor offered anything in Andrew's defense.

Again, Andrew was told, "You are not our type of guy." His teachings were not "in line" with the pastor's vision for the church. The pastor told Andrew to clean out his office, leave the premises, and say goodbye to no one.

The following Monday found Andrew under suicide watch in the emergency room of a local hospital. His world had utterly fallen apart. His wife had come home to find him with a phone in one hand, talking to a suicide counselor, and a kitchen knife in the other.

Andrew describes the emotional and spiritual heartache that gripped his life during the next several months:

> I was released from the hospital and began a time of wondering, sadness, depression, anger, rage, and healing. For the next six months I was numb. I questioned my heart for the Lord's work. I questioned my faith. My wife was my rock and spiritual leader during this time. My family and my nephews, along with my wife, saved my life and my faith.

Andrew's church family had dropped out of the picture: "My wife and I did not receive one phone call from anyone at the church during this time."

More than a year later, in the fall of 2009, Andrew and his wife received a call from a neighbor who had some important information for Andrew about developments at the church. The senior pastor had informed a board member that the young woman who had made the charge against Andrew was no longer at the church and that Andrew was innocent of the original allegations.

Andrew observes, "I started to cry like a baby when I got off the phone with our neighbor." Sadly, to date no one in leadership at the church has made any effort to apologize to Andrew or to restore the church's relationship with him.

It is tempting to chalk up the whole unfortunate story of Andrew's pilgrimage with the leadership of his church to one big misunderstanding—a "he-said, she-said" scenario gone terribly awry.

Andrew's treatment at the hands of his senior pastor, however, was hardly an anomaly. As it turns out, Andrew's experience was but one in a series of such instances, which, taken together, reveal a systemic problem with authority in the church and in the denomination at large.

Andrew was not the first church employee to find himself on the receiving end of the unfair exercise of pastoral authority. A maintenance man—a friend of the senior pastor for fifteen years and a ten-year church employee—was fired for not "agreeing with the church's vision."

A year before Andrew's termination, the senior pastor fired a high school pastor for "a different philosophy of ministry that was not according to the vision of the church." Some years before that, another pastor had been dismissed for similar reasons.

Even more problematic, some of the men who were fired were ostracized from the church community. Their reputations were publicly compromised, "their names smeared to the congregation," Andrew recalls.

When the high school pastor was terminated, for example, the senior pastor instructed other church employees, including Andrew, to ignore the man if they encountered him in public. Perhaps this is why Andrew and his wife received no contacts from the church after Andrew's departure.

The abuse of authority in Andrew's church can be traced to both institutional and personal dysfunction. Institutionally, the church operates under the rubric of a distorted ecclesiology, which views the senior pastor as "God's anointed," whose decisions are never to be questioned. In retrospect, Andrew observes,

> We followed a model where the senior pastor is accountable to no one but God. It is God that gives the senior pastor a vision for the church, and if someone does not agree with the senior pastor's vision, they are disagreeing with God's vision for the church.

This was particularly the case where staff members were concerned:

It was as if the senior pastor was a master of puppets, and we were all on strings. If someone questioned his authority, then the next move was simple: cut the strings and replace them with another puppet, another "yes man."

A congregation that places this much authority in the hands of a senior pastor is a set-up for spiritual abuse, particularly if the pastor—like Andrew's boss—struggles with emotional insecurities and the narcissistic need to always be right and always be in control.

Andrew's boss, at is turns out, was particularly threatened by the fact that Andrew was attending Biola University, instead of the denomination's Bible school. Andrew recalls being constantly questioned about his teaching at the church, because he failed to consult and parrot the interpretations of the denomination's "all-star pastors."

The church is part of a denomination that insists that its pastors teach the party line, which generally consists of interpretations of Scripture taught by the movement's founder. Andrew describes his former congregation as "extremely rigid in their teachings, especially in nonessentials."

Andrew's less-than-sensitive rebuttals to questions about his education didn't do much to help his cause: "I remember saying that I chose to go to Biola because I wanted to learn *how* to think instead of *what* to think." Such comments are not likely to set well with an autocratic, insecure leader.

In retrospect, it appears that false allegations of impropriety proved to be a convenient excuse for Andrew's senior pastor to fire him for reasons quite unrelated to the issue at hand.

It is not unreasonable to seek unanimity among a local church's teachers, where doctrine and Bible interpretation are concerned. Perhaps Andrew was, in fact, no longer a fit for a denomination like the one he found himself in. In that case, however, Andrew's senior pastor had a wonderful opportunity to mentor this promising young minister, rather than to marginalize him as he did.

The pastor could have gently and lovingly helped Andrew to

appreciate the importance of the church's theological distinctives. And he could have made a meaningful effort to assist Andrew in finding a ministry in another congregation that might have been a better fit for his convictions and his teaching style.

Instead, Andrew's pastor was quick to leverage what turned out to be an unchristian act of slander, in order to force Andrew out of his ministry, away from his church family, simply because, as he said to Andrew, "You are not our type of guy."

Andrew is on the mend, but the road has been a rocky one. It was months after the incident before Andrew could read anything related to the Bible or theological studies. More recently Andrew wrote,

> I now know that it was for the best interest of my walk with the Lord that all this happened. I am a broken man, and I think I am right where God wants me to be. I now know grace and humility in a way that I have never known before. But it has taken its toll, and at times I feel like I am only a shell of what I used to be. When you lose your job, friends, community, sense of worth, sense of value, honor, and integrity all in the same day, it does things to you. Especially when it didn't have to happen in the first place.

> People in leadership who abuse their power hurt real people, and they destroy real lives. I pray that all those who have been mistreated can find hope again in Jesus and find a community to fellowship at, despite their pain and distrust of the church. As for me, I am still sad, and I am still angry. I pray that I can deal in a healthy way with my issues and be used for good by God again one day. I just need a little help sometimes.

In the spring of 2010, Andrew was back at Biola in one of my New Testament Greek courses. Several of us on faculty continue to teach and encourage this promising young man, because we truly believe in Andrew and the gifts God has given him.

Andrew, however, still has a good bit of healing ahead of

him—healing that would have been unnecessary if Andrew's senior pastor had exercised his authority in a healthy, nurturing way.

Janelle's Story

I met Janelle in June 2011, as a Doctor of Ministry student in an ecclesiology course I taught in a seminary in the Pacific Northwest. A young mom with two children, Janelle describes herself as "highly creative and very energetic."

Janelle was raised as a pastor's kid and has clearly inherited her parents' love for Jesus and their commitment to the local church. Janelle sensed a call to ministry as a teenager, and she has been pursuing her vocation ever since.

During her early twenties, Janelle spent four fruitful years serving at a Southern California megachurch with a multi-staffed children's ministry. She recalls: "I loved my job and had developed some great relationships with many of the staff members—especially a couple of them within the children's ministry team."

This set of meaningful peer relationships—found, ironically, in the context of what would prove to be a highly institutional environment—would ultimately prove to be the occasion for Janelle's termination.

Janelle worked closely at Central Church with Rachel and Steven. Rachel was a young mom at the same life stage as Janelle. She was hired about two years after Janelle. The two women soon discovered that they had much in common. Janelle recalls:

> I instantly knew Rachel was a kindred spirit to me. We spent most of our lunches together, shared similar interests, we both were married with children, and almost always knew what the other was thinking.

Rachel soon became one of Janelle's "best friends."

Steven, a young married pastor, had already served at Central Church for several years when Janelle joined the team. Janelle describes him as "highly intelligent, charismatic, loved by people at the church, and amazing at his job." Yet he also struck Janelle as "somewhat entitled, egocentric"—a "favored son who typically got want he wanted." A rising star at the church, Steven was currently on the inside track for a promotion that would accord him a new title and a salary increase.

As the peer employees in their department, Janelle, Rachel, and Steven were drawn to one another: "We were the youngest ones in the children's ministry, so we naturally hung out together and, above all, we shared a passion for kids." As time passed, however, Janelle began to sense something unhealthy in the way Steven and Rachel interacted:

> The relationship between Steven and Rachel had grown too close for comfort. At lunches, they insisted on sitting next to each other. And then there was that stare that was always a few seconds too long to be the friendly type.

Janelle initially gave her coworkers the benefit of the doubt and kept quiet. The relationship between Steven and Rachel, however, became increasingly affectionate.

Things began to unravel quickly when Rachel opened up to Janelle. Janelle recalls, "Finally, over a five-dollar meal at a local restaurant, Rachel confessed to me. She was ready to drop everything for Steven—including her husband."

Janelle did not know quite what to do: "Was I supposed to tell someone? Or should I keep what I know to myself?"

She decided first to continue to counsel with Rachel. "Bad idea! The relationship soon grew out of my control or wisdom." Janelle then confronted Steven:

> One day after class, I shared with Steven that I felt his relationship with Rachel was inappropriate and that he needed to be careful. Steven never admitted to anything but his face grew white and I knew from his body language that he was uncomfortable with the conversation.

Janelle assumed that the confrontation would be enough to

motivate Steven to sever the relationship. That would be the end of it all. Instead, the following Monday Janelle lost her job:

> I had just finished my daily shot of caffeine, when I was called into a surprise meeting at work. Walking into the small, dimly-lit room, around a cherry wood table sat the senior pastor, executive pastor, children's pastor, and one of my coworkers. All of them looked grim and subdued. After a quick interrogation and a short prayer, I was fired.

What had happened was unfortunate but not surprising. In her well-meaning attempts to challenge Steven and Rachel to end an unhealthy relationship, Janelle had unknowingly isolated herself. After being confronted by Janelle that day, Steven, fearing for his job, went to his superiors claiming that Janelle had fabricated the whole scenario. Rachel, too, opted for a strategy of self-protection: "when being questioned, she denied everything in fear of losing not only her job but her marriage and family."

The result? Janelle had no one to confirm her story, and the church leaders terminated her immediately. Three months later Steven was promoted to his new position at Central Church.

The situation was undoubtedly a messy one. I could not help but grieve for Janelle as I read her first-person account of her pilgrimage. But I also found myself empathizing with the church leaders who had to sort all of this out.

Janelle was clearly the innocent party. It is hard to see, however, how her supervisors could have figured that out, given Steven and Rachel's unwillingness to acknowledge their affection for one another. The pastoral leaders clearly lacked the information they needed to fairly address this thorny interpersonal dilemma. It was a dilemma, however, that the church could probably have prevented to begin with.

Most problematic was the fact that Central Church apparently left three young, relatively immature Christian workers to do ministry together without any meaningful relationships with their superiors. A sensitive mentor might have noticed the warning signs that Janelle saw with Steven and Rachel. An older, more mature shepherd would have been in a better position to confront the issue than Janelle was.

Additionally, a mentor who shared a close relationship with Janelle would surely have been much less quick to dismiss Janelle's story as a fabrication. After all, Janelle had served at the church for four years. Yet apparently her supervisors did not know her well enough to assign even a degree of credibility to what she had to say. One suspects an acute lack of meaningful relationships across the church's institutional hierarchy.

And then there was the suddenness of Janelle's termination. Mentor or no mentor, shouldn't Janelle's supervisors have taken a bit more time to pray through the issues and try to sort things out?

At the risk of Monday-morning-quarterbacking, yes, I think that the pastors should have given more time and care to a decision as important as the termination of an effective church employee. The way the termination was handled, moreover, speaks volumes about the unhealthy relational dynamics of the institutional church. And it is here where an unbiblical, utilitarian approach to people— so common to corporate Christianity—clearly manifests itself.

In addition to losing her job, Janelle experienced the same kind of intentional marginalization and isolation from her church family that Andrew had encountered after his termination. I'll let Janelle tell what happened immediately after she was fired:

> While I walked across the campus, I noticed many of the church kids playing in the gym. I waved to one of the little girls, and the executive pastor said that I was not allowed to talk with anyone, including my coworkers. I was being treated like a criminal. All that were missing were the handcuffs and a prison sentence.

The following day was equally painful. Janelle found her nameplate removed from the door of her office. Another staff member was already moving in. Janelle's office couch—a personal belonging, not church property—had been placed outside and was sitting in the rain.

Particularly heartbreaking for Janelle was the sense of betrayal she felt by persons she had grown close to during her time at Central Church:

> I felt as though I had been erased from these past four years in a matter of minutes. Where was their loyalty? How could someone be treated like this? I had both of my children during that time, went on retreats with staff, and even went shopping for clothes with my boss. My best friend denied the truth and left me in the lions' den to be devoured. I felt like I had just lost my family in that church. The family I shared all these years with threw me out like a bag of old clothes. It was as if I had been dumped from a relationship. The only thing missing was the common phrase, "Can we just be friends?"

That "common phrase" was missing because even friendship was off-limits. Janelle received no contacts at all from her coworkers at the church. After some time had passed, she found out why: "One of the pastors from that church shared with me that they had been told not to have any contact with me because the relationship had been severed."

The ensuing years saw Janelle take a break from seminary and avoid church ministry for a season. "What they did to me ultimately crucified my innocence and destroyed my reputation, along with passion for ministry."

After some time had passed, a bit of gentle exhortation from an elder in Janelle's new church renewed her commitment to vocational Christian service: "You know, Janelle, you can't run from God forever," he remarked. "Don't you think it's time to get back into the game?"

The timely words of this godly man led Janelle to do some much needed soul searching:

> I knew that I hadn't turned my back on God, but I was still so angry. And it was my anger that was keeping me from doing what God had called me to do. It was in my hurt and recovery

that I realized that even if it was painful, God had a purpose for my life that I was to respond to and not ignore.

Janelle is now back on track, up to her ears again in church ministry, and her story ends on a positive note. Here Janelle narrates a recent encounter with her new supervisor—an encounter that contrasts sharply with the way she was treated at Central Church:

> A couple of years after I was hired on at my current church, I was called in to an impromptu meeting with the senior pastor. My boss said, "I need to talk with you about something." "What had I done?" I thought. "If I was fired at my last job for something I didn't do, then anything could happen for no reason." Right away, the pastor noticed that I was uneasy. But because he had taken the time to get to know me over the years, he said, "Just because I want to talk with you, Janelle, doesn't mean I'm going to fire you. If there is something that I am seeing in you that I am concerned about, we will work through it. I won't just throw something at you without warning, even if it were something really bad and ugly. You are family. This is your family."

The contrast with the leadership at Janelle's previous church could hardly be more arresting. Central Church had treated Janelle like an expendable institutional employee. Her new pastor treats her like family.

Perhaps the most revealing statement in the above quotation is Janelle's observation that her current pastor "had taken the time to get to know me over the years." That was the very thing that Janelle's supervisors at Central Church had apparently never taken the time to do.

Conclusion

When it comes to the use of power and authority in the local church, some of us are not getting it. The contrast between the exercise of pastoral authority in the stories above and the example of Jesus in Philippians 2 is painfully evident at every turn.

The rest of this book seeks to explain why. It is not enough to have an ideal for servant leadership in the example of Jesus. Like Paul (chap. 6), we need to give some serious thought to the social context of ministry, that is, to the ways that we structure and organize our churches.

The next chapter grapples with several systemic problems in our churches that particularly lend themselves to the abuse of pastoral authority. A concluding chapter then outlines a constructive alternative to church as we know it—a relational approach to congregational life and ministry that offers a hopeful way back to Paul's cruciform vision for authentic Christian leadership.

Questions for Reflection

1. Our culture is currently characterized by a hermeneutic of suspicion toward authority figures. Do you think this is justified? Why or why not?

2. People like Sally Morgenthaler (see the quotations near the beginning of the chapter) have become embittered toward institutional Christianity. If Sally was your friend, how would you respond to her attitude toward the church?

3. Review "Timothy's Story." At what points in the narrative could the church board have intervened to move events in a more positive direction?

4. What was missing in Andrew's church that allowed his pastor to abuse his authority the way he did?

5. How might Janelle have handled things differently, when she sensed that Steven and Rachel were becoming too close? What could the church have done to prevent Janelle's termination to begin with?

The Challenge of Social Context

Systemic Pitfalls of Corporate Christianity

> *So long as men worship the Caesars and Napoleons, Caesars and Napoleons will duly rise and make them miserable.*—
> Aldous Huxley[1]

Several years ago Oceanside Christian Fellowship terminated Bill, one of our paid pastors. Bill's poor use of time and his lack of productivity had generated not a little frustration among others at the church, who were carrying more than their weight in their respective areas of ministry.

A move to a new facility—which called for sacrifice and a servant's attitude on everyone's part—sharply accentuated the latent resentment that had been building among the staff. We knew that something was seriously wrong when Ellen, one of our most

---

1. Aldous Huxley, *Ends and Means: An Inquiry into the Nature of Ideals and into the Methods Employed for Their Realization* (San Francisco: Harper and Brothers, 1937), 99.

productive and effective ministers, began to explore the secular job market.

The elders had made an attempt to address the issue along the way but, frankly, we did not take the initiative we should have earlier, so that the situation had deteriorated unnecessarily by the time we set up a meeting with Bill and the rest of the pastor-elders.

I was part-time at the church and had little firsthand exposure to the dysfunction in the office, though I do recall being quite annoyed when Bill showed up late, week after week, to our Wednesday elder meetings.

Joann and I are very close to Ellen, however, and I became extremely troubled when I found out that her frustration with Bill had led Ellen to start looking for another job. I came to the meeting with guns loaded, determined to be an advocate for Ellen and for the rest of the church staff.

For several hours we went back and forth with Bill. There was next to no ownership on his part. Here were six of Bill's fellow elders raising serious concerns about his work as a pastor and church employee. He responded by rationalizing his behavior and telling us that we had it wrong on every count.

Bill pretty much determined his own future at OCF when he maintained, "I take a long time to make a decision, but when I do decide, I am almost always right."

A series of follow-up meetings led to Bill's termination, and we have since hired a new pastor to take his place. The atmosphere around the office has changed dramatically for the better.

I had said some very pointed things to Bill in the course of that initial meeting. All of my statements were objectively true. In the heat of the discussion, however, I did not share my convictions in a loving way.

After Bill left the room, as we sat around planning our next steps, several of my fellow pastor-elders told me, in no uncertain terms, that I had been hurtful in my comments. They insisted that I owed Bill an apology.

The rebuke was hard to hear. It caught me completely off guard.

Our natural tendency in a situation like this is to retreat into a defensive posture. I was tempted to rebuff the critique and to go back over the things I had said in the meeting, one by one, demonstrating that each point I made was true. After all, it didn't seem like the two remaining elders had a problem with how I handled myself.

What kept me from defending my behavior, however, was the relationship I had with the men who challenged me about the tone of my comments that day.

As OCF's pastor-elders, we met every week, early on Wednesday morning, to pray for one another, for our families, and for the people in our church. We had been doing so for years.

I knew these men well enough to trust them with my life. They knew me, too. They appreciated my strengths. And they were quite aware of my weaknesses. I recognized that these guys would only rebuke me with my best interests—and the best interests of the church—in view.

So we set up a meeting, and I humbly apologized to Bill for the hurtful manner in which I had framed my words. I assured Bill that I stood by the content of what I had said. But I told him that I deeply regretted the way in which I communicated it to him. I asked Bill for his forgiveness, and he graciously responded in turn.

That Would Never Happen in My Church

Just last month, one of my Korean students, Jonathan, asked to conduct a short interview with me during office hours. Jonathan had received an assignment in another course that required him to interact with several pastors about their approach to ministry. I was happy to oblige.

One question on the survey asked, *What does a leader need in order to be successful?* I replied that a pastor needs (among other things) three kinds of relationships to succeed long-term in local church ministry: (1) mentors to guide him, (2) peers to serve alongside him, and (3) younger disciples to raise up as future leaders.

Jonathan and I proceeded to discuss each of these relationships. He was particularly intrigued by category #2, since Korean pastors generally lack peer relationships in their congregations. To illustrate the importance of a community of leaders, I told Jonathan the story about the hard experience I went through during the painful process of Bill's termination.

Jonathan's response was revealing. When I finished sharing how I had been rebuked by my fellow elders, and how I, in turn, apologized to Bill, Jonathan immediately asserted, "That would never happen in a Korean church."

It is not hard to see why. Pastors in traditional Asian congregations do not have the kind of peer relationships that characterize OCF's board of pastor-elders. The pronounced social hierarchy and relational expectations of an honor culture guarantee that no one would ever rebuke the behavior of a preaching pastor in the presence of other men in the church.

Nor would a Korean pastor entertain the prospect of "losing face" by apologizing to another person in the congregation for the way that he had handled himself in a meeting. The social context of ministry in traditional Asian culture does not allow for such a scenario.

The result, of course, is that a pastor in a Korean church like Jonathan's has much more latitude, behavior-wise, than any Christian ever ought to have. Here, I suggest, the cultural values and social codes of a traditional honor culture have decidedly compromised the relational contours of the gospel.

Things are hardly different, however, in many of our corporate-style Anglo churches in America. In my experience it is a rare event for a senior pastor to get called on the carpet for anything short of blatant sexual immorality or, perhaps, an equally serious moral compromise, such as embezzlement of church funds.

Hurtful treatment of associate staff? Subtle manipulation of the truth in the service of slick and effective ministry? As we saw in chapter 7, in many congregations that's just the price of doing business. As long as the pews are full of people and the offering basket is full of money, the pastor is doing just fine, thank you.

The Social Context of Ministry

These stories raise a most pressing issue where the contextualization of Paul's cruciform vision for authentic Christian leadership is concerned. The socio-cultural context of ministry has tremendous ramifications for the ways in which leaders leverage their power and authority in the local church.

It is a simple fact that some ways of doing church encourage the healthy exercise of ministerial authority. Others do not. Many instances of authority abuse in our churches can be traced directly to systemic cultural values—and resulting social contexts—which obstruct, rather than facilitate, healthy, other-centered leadership.

This remains the case whether those values arise from a traditional cultural matrix (Jonathan's), or from a western corporate mentality. I am most familiar with pitfalls related to the latter approach to ministry, so we will consider the problems associated with the American institutional model of church organization and leadership in the paragraphs to follow.

Church as a Business

Several aspects of the corporate model of ministry tend to work in conjunction with one another potentially to compromise the kind of servant leadership modeled by Jesus in Philippians 2:6–11. Perhaps most problematic is the widespread conviction that the church should be led by a single pastor-leader.

No individual has a corner on the truth. We all know this in theory. Yet the way we implement the senior pastor model too often results in one person's vision and teaching style determining the practical realities of day-to-day ministry in the local church.

The model works marginally well, if the pastor happens to be an emotionally healthy person who opens up his life to a handful of other persons in the congregation. Unfortunately, this kind of relational maturity is less and less common among young seminarians preparing for the ministry.

Aspiring pastors, like people in our culture at large, increasingly come from broken or dysfunctional family units. As a result, numbers of our students have not learned to relate in healthy ways to others. Nor have they had the opportunity to see authority exercised in positive, nurturing ways. This becomes particularly problematic in the case of male seminary students raised by abusive or absentee fathers.

Give to an emotionally needy individual (a) a respected seminary education, (b) some secular leadership principles about motivating others to catch his vision, and (c) unilateral power as the senior pastor of a local church—well, I trust you can see how such a scenario provides virtually the ideal context for the unhealthy exercise of ministerial authority.

Further contributing to the potential for power abuse are the businesslike relationships that too often exist between a pastor and his congregation's board of elders or deacons, on the one hand, and between a senior minister and his associate staff, on the other.

In most churches the pastor is not a formal member of the governing board. Almost never does a minister enjoy intimate, surrogate sibling relations with persons on the board, as they lead the church together in genuine community. A more common arrangement finds a board of well-intentioned lay leaders either supporting or obstructing the paid pastor in his vision for the church.

The same utilitarian strategies generally characterize pastor-staff relations in multi-staffed churches, where senior ministers supervise associate staff in a hierarchical context that does little to facilitate the kind of trust and social bonding experienced among persons like Paul and his coworkers, for example, in the early church.

A Road Map for What Follows

We will consider the issues outlined above under two headings: (1) Structural Dynamics and (2) Relational Dynamics. Structural concerns include the corporate-like makeup of numbers of our congregations, along with the questionable measures for success that generally accompany such an approach to ministry. On the relational side, we will wrestle with the counterintuitive but all too common phenomenon of compliant congregations and church boards continuing—often for years—to tolerate the abusive behaviors of emotionally needy, narcissistic senior pastors.

Structural Dynamics

The Pastor as Leader: The Buck Stops Here

When I decided to make a move from academia back into full-time ministry in 1996, I put out feelers through various pastoral employment services. I had ministered in a Conservative Baptist Association church for nearly twenty years, and the denomination had an effective support network in place for connecting prospective candidates with churches in need of pastors. I put my name in the hopper.

As it turned out, I ended up serving in a different denomination, one with almost identical doctrinal convictions. I took a position as a co-pastor in an Evangelical Free congregation that a friend had planted a decade earlier just four miles from my home.

After I had sealed the deal with my new church, I received a call from the area director of the Conservative Baptist Association in Northern California. He had a position in a church in his area that he felt would be a great fit for me.

I thanked him but replied that I had already found a pastorate. And then I innocently added something to the effect of, "I'm particularly excited because my new church has a biblical view of plurality leadership."

Boy, did I ever push a button on that one! The warm demeanor of this denominational leader immediately vanished, and for the next five minutes I listened to an uninterrupted, polemical rant about the *truly* biblical model of leadership: the solo/senior pastor.

After extolling the virtues of one Old Testament prophet and king after another, my "conversation" partner concluded his harangue by forcefully asserting, "I'm sure glad God didn't send a committee to save *me*!"

My ears were burning, but I held my tongue. I cordially thanked the brother for the job offer, hung up the phone, and thought to myself, "Hmm, maybe I ought to buy that fellow a New Testament."

The denominational leader, of course, has a New Testament. And he likely knows it as well as I know mine. Somehow, however, the numerous passages in Acts and the Epistles that illustrate plurality leadership in local congregations did not even appear on the man's radar screen as potentially informative for church leadership under the new covenant. I should have anticipated as much, because I had run into the same convictions in the denomination several years before.

A Deeply Ingrained Tradition

Back in 1985, Richard, our much beloved pastor of Community Baptist Church, retired after more than three decades of fruitful ministry. We had an interim pastor commuting in and preaching on Sunday mornings. I was Pastor of College and Singles at the time, and I did some of the teaching on Sunday evenings while we were between senior ministers.

I particularly enjoyed teaching a series on ecclesiology, which included a look at plurality leadership in the New Testament churches. The reaction was telling. Long-time Baptists in the church liked the messages, but they chalked up "all this silly talk about team leadership" to a young man who had been in seminary too long.

"Not how we do things."

"Impractical."

The most revealing and emphatic response came indirectly, from the retired pastor. Pastor Richard had left the area. Someone, however, was apparently keeping him apprised about activities in his former congregation.

John, another associate pastor on our staff, ran into Pastor Richard at a Conservative Baptist conference. Richard pulled him aside and asked, "What's this I hear about Joe Hellerman teaching on plurality leadership?"

My fellow staffer happened to share my convictions. He replied, "Well, Richard, it *is* biblical."

Richard's reaction said it all: "But, John, it's not Baptistic!"

For a variety of reasons, historical and cultural, the model of one-man leadership in the local church is now a given in the minds of most Christians. The efforts that some go to in order to frame the model in biblical terms are informative.

David McKenna claims, for example, that the pastor is "the cerebellum, the center for communicating messages, coordinating functions, and conducting responses between the head and the body." He is the *"authoritative communicator of the truth* from the Head to the Body" and *"the accurate communicator of the needs* from the Body to the Head."[2] We find no hint of any of this in the New Testament metaphor of the church as the body of Christ.

New Covenant Priorities

Others seem to recognize the lack of New Testament support for the senior pastor model, so they draw their examples from the Old Testament, instead. Consider the motto of Focus on the Family's Pastoral Ministries support website: "Every Moses Needs an Aaron."[3] In their 2012 Clergy Appreciation Month brochure, the motto is accompanied by a graphic that depicts Aaron and Hur holding up Moses's arms while the Israelites fought the Amalekites in the wilderness (Exod 17:12).[4]

The assumption seems to be that the pastors who comprise Focus on the Family's target audience are all solitary leaders, standing, like Moses, between God and his people. Do these pastors need persons to come alongside to help and encourage them?

---

2. David L. McKenna, "The Ministry's Gordian Knot," *Leadership* 1:1 (1980): 50-51.

3. "About Us," Focus on the Family: Thriving PASTOR, accessed April 3, 2013, http://www.thrivingpastor.org/info/aboutus.cfm

4. "Clergy Appreciation Month," p. 2, Focus on the Family: Thriving PASTOR, accessed April 3, 2013, http://www.thrivingpastor.org/images/pdf/CAM%20Guide_2012.pdf

Yes. And Focus on the Family and H. B. London do a highly commendable job of supporting local church ministers.

Do these pastors have persons who serve alongside them as genuine peers in their churches? No. Most of them apparently go it alone. Just like Moses. And we continue uncritically to assume that going it alone is both biblical and proper.

The recourse to Old Testament paradigms is revealing. Few leadership books seriously consider the implications of the transition to a new covenant for church structure and organization.

Stacy Rinehart's *Upside Down: The Paradox of Servant Leadership* is a refreshing exception. Rinehart underscores the innovative relational orientation of New Testament leadership throughout this fine book, specifically contrasting old and new covenant approaches to leading the people of God:

> Leadership patterned after New Testament models does not rely on one central authority figure (as in the days of Moses and David) because Christ provided for us a new basis for relationships, a new source of power, and a new means of growth.
>
> Christ's disciples didn't see themselves as "junior Nehemiahs" charged with the task of discerning God's mind for His people and then instructing everyone accordingly. Jesus instituted a different order based on the mutuality and interdependence typified in the "one another" commands.[5]

This is why the New Testament churches—unlike the people of Israel in the Old Testament—were each led by a plurality of elders.

Unfortunately, most Christian leaders, unaware of these realities, continue to assume that one-man leadership is the biblical norm. This is particularly true of church board members, many of whom come to their leadership roles in the family of God deeply marked by their daily experiences in the business world.

---

5. Stacy T. Rinehart, *Upside Down: The Paradox of Servant Leadership* (Colorado Springs: NavPress, 1998), 103-4.

A Wall Street Mentality

With few exceptions, the local church elders and deacons whom I have known have been godly, well-intentioned servants of the Lord. However, where leadership and church management are concerned, most of them are influenced more by the *Wall Street Journal* than the letters of Paul.

We considered what Paul and the other New Testament writers had to say about plurality leadership in an earlier chapter. The model surfaces throughout the New Testament.

Why, then, are the overwhelming majority of Christians—including the men and women who sit on our churches' governing boards—wholly unaware of the fact that virtually every church mentioned in Acts and the Epistles was governed by a plurality of leaders?

I was oblivious to this reality for my first five years as a Christian. Before I began seminary, I had already enthusiastically devoured my Bible, and I had read through the New Testament several times. Yet the incongruity between (a) plurality leadership in the early church and (b) the senior pastor model of my own congregation had somehow escaped me.

I'll never forget the "aha moment." It happened in a theology course, when we engaged in a simple descriptive survey of the leadership structure of the New Testament congregations.

I was astounded: "elders" in the churches on Paul's first journey (Acts 14:23); "elders" in the church at Ephesus (Acts 20:17); "overseers and deacons" in the church at Philippi (Phil 1:1); "elders" in the churches on Crete (Tit 1:5); "elders" in the churches in Pontus, Galatia, Cappadocia, Asia, and Bithynia (1 Pet 5:1; see 1:1); "elders" in the Jewish churches of the Diaspora (Jas 5:14; see 1:1).

Not a senior pastor in sight.[6] *How could I have missed all this? How could we have missed all this?*

---

6. There is a senior pastor in the New Testament. The closest word we have in Greek to "senior pastor," is *archipoimēn*, which literally means "chief shepherd." ("Pastor" comes from the Greek word *poimēn*, meaning "shepherd.") The word appears only once in the New Testament, and it is not used of the pastor of a local church. It is used of Jesus (1 Pet 5:4).

Quite easily. It is a truism that apart from intentional objectivity, we almost invariably read our Bibles through the perspectives of our own cultural matrices and day-to-day experiences. As a result, we often overlook or miss the implications of those portions of Scripture that do not accord with life as we know it.

That was certainly the case for me. The only church I had known for my first five years as a Christian was led by a senior pastor. All of my seminary buddies belonged to similarly structured congregations. I assumed that this was how they did it in the Bible. And I read the Scriptures with that assumption deeply ingrained in my thinking.

I imagine, in fact, that I could have read through my Bible ten more times and, apart from the guidance of a theology professor that semester, I would have continued to miss the near unanimous verdict of the New Testament about plurality leadership in the local church.

Little wonder that the elders and deacons in our churches don't see it. These dear folks spend forty, fifty, sometimes sixty or more hours each week in a corporate environment, where efficiency and productivity are the name of the game, where the boss is the boss, and where you do what the boss says. It is only natural for these church leaders to default to the same model and to delegate sole authority to the senior pastor who, in their view, ought to function as the "boss" of the local church.

The degree to which corporate thinking has influenced the mentality of our people in this regard is rather profound. I have been in a team-led church for fifteen years. We consistently communicate to the congregation the biblical evidence and pragmatic benefits of plurality leadership.

Our people hear about team leadership in our sermons. They see it modeled from the pulpit as we share the preaching ministry. They get it in our membership class. The topic arises over and over in informal conversations. And we bring up the theme again in meetings involving our various ministry teams. For the most part, our people seem very much to like the idea of a plurality of pastors.

When finances get tight, however, or another serious crisis confronts the church, a handful of our brightest and most capable businessmen—men who have been taught otherwise for years—begin to suggest that maybe Oceanside Christian Fellowship needs a senior pastor, a "buck-stops-here" guy, like the other churches in our area.

I am reminded of Israel asking God for a king, so that they can be just like the rest of the nations.

Vision-Casting and Goal-Setting: How Do We Define Success?

For several decades now, values and practices from corporate America have markedly influenced our views about leadership and church government in the evangelical community. Results have been mixed, at best.

One of the more regrettable outcomes is an unbiblical set of convictions about what counts for success in the ministry. It is here, especially, that a corporate, institutional approach to ministry directly undercuts the organic, relational priorities of New Testament ecclesiology and opens the door to the abuse of pastoral authority.

It has been my experience that deacons and elders are generally quite satisfied to see their churches (a) growing numerically and (b) solvent financially. If attendance is increasing and giving is up, it is assumed that the pastor is doing a good job, and there is little concern, for example, for the health of staff relations, or even, in some cases, for the quality of relationships among people in the congregation at large. David Platt's clever alliteration drives the point right home:

> One of the unintended consequences of contemporary church strategies that revolve around performances, places, programs, and professionals is that somewhere along the way people get left out of the picture.[7]

---

7. David Platt, *Radical: Taking Back Your Faith from the American Dream* (Colorado Springs: Multnomah, 2010), 90.

To be sure, numbers of church boards give small group programs a degree of emphasis in their ministries. Seldom, however, do such leaders rate small group involvement as high on their priority list for their people as they rate Sunday attendance or financial generosity.

Even more rare is the board that includes—as a key benchmark of a thriving church—healthy relationships among its staff. And that, for my money, ought to be an absolutely non-negotiable measure of effective Christian ministry.

Why? Because the church is first and foremost a *relational* community. So if we cannot make relationships work in the church office, among our leaders, something has gone seriously awry.

As Brad Harper and Paul Louis Metzger insightfully observe:

[T]he church exists to love God, its own, the world, and the whole creation because it is loved in covenantal communion with God. This relational orientation signifies that the church is being-driven. A church that begins with a missional purpose before it begins with its identity as communal reality in relation to God is problematic. This orientation is very American but is not biblical.[8]

Stop and think about just how counterintuitive it is, biblically, to prioritize institutional values like Sunday attendance and finances over healthy relationships among a pastor and his staff. A corporate mentality has all but completely hijacked God's relational designs for his people.

Jesus said that the world will know we are his disciples by our love for one another (John 13:35). If we are not successful relationally—at the top, in the church office—then we might as well close up shop, send away our Sunday crowds, and refund their generous offerings.

---

8. Brad Harper and Paul Louis Metzger, *Exploring Ecclesiology: An Evangelical and Ecumenical Introduction* (Grand Rapids: Brazos, 2009), 20.

Randy's Story

A year or so ago I had lunch with an associate staff person at a large church in Southern California. I had preached a guest sermon the week before. My topic was the church as a family, and the message had stirred up some issues for this young man.

Randy's story was not wholly an unhappy one. He loved his work in the trenches with the people in his church. Staff relations, however, were another story entirely.

Poor staff management by a highly gifted but insecure senior pastor had generated such an unhealthy work environment that Randy and his wife were unwilling to make close friends in the church for fear that Randy might lose his job, if word got back to the senior pastor that he was not 100 percent supportive of everything his boss said and did.

The atmosphere around the church office had been much the same as Randy found it for nearly two decades. The church had grown, however, and finances had been generally robust, so the elder board had done next to nothing to challenge the relational incompetence of the congregation's senior pastor.

Unfortunately, this kind of neglect is not uncommon with church boards. Such leaders, socialized to buy into corporate models of pastoral ministry, prioritize the institutional over the relational to the detriment of both relationships in the church and the health of the institution itself.

Things in Randy's church have gone from bad to worse. In recent years, the church has enforced a non-disclosure policy, whereby terminated staff are persuaded to sign a form agreeing to say nothing about activities in the church office in trade for a generous severance package.

God forbid that those Sunday attenders and generous givers might find out what transpires behind the scenes among staff relationships in the church office!

Concerns of an Emerging Generation

Thankfully, many of the young people I work with in the church and in the academy see all of this quite clearly. Numbers of my students have experienced firsthand the systemic problems associated with the institutional church model. Most of them are pretty much done with church as a business.

Younger evangelicals are not enamored with our slick Sunday spectacles, and they are suspicious of institutional hierarchy. Consequently, they are highly sensitive to the need for an alternative social context in which to do ministry.

A respondent whom Robert Webber interviewed in a book on the topic expressed serious reservations—characteristic of his generation—about his boomer pastor's preoccupation with "church growth, platform personality and program development.[9]" Younger evangelicals are ready to exchange the CEO/senior pastor model of leadership for "a circle of equals," "team ministry," or "consensus."[10]

The convictions of this new generation reflect a similar paradigm shift in the business community. Ironically, the traditional corporate model of leadership, which continues to generate so much dysfunction in our churches, is now quite out of fashion in the secular workplace.

As Eddie Gibbs notes, "the leadership literature of the 1980s . . . focused on high-powered, entrepreneurial leadership exercised by larger-than-life 'charismatic' personalities."[11] Several decades later, the model has not delivered what it had promised:

> There is increasing evidence demonstrating that such high-profile, charismatic leadership is not sustainable in the long term and ultimately has a debilitating effect on the entire organization over which it has been imposed.[12]

Instead, current thinking prefers leaders who no longer

---

9. Robert E. Webber, *The Younger Evangelicals: Facing the Challenges of the New World* (Grand Rapids: Baker, 2002), 149.
10. Ibid., 153.
11. Eddie Gibbs, *LeadershipNext: Changing Leaders in a Changing Culture* (Downers Grove, IL: InterVarsity Press, 2005), 25.
12. Gibbs, *LeadershipNext*, 23-24.

control others, but who cultivate those under their charge. The shift in leadership theory parallels a corresponding change in organizational structures in the corporate world—"from hierarchies to networks," as Gibbs puts it.[13]

Consultants in the business community see in the church a need for the same paradigm shift. Management guru Ken Blanchard, the author of *The One Minute Manager,* warned church leaders more than a decade ago that "the popular model of pastor as CEO is brain dead. . . . This philosophy will only hurt the church in the long run."[14] Webber's critique is even more direct: "the business model of the church is out of step with two thousand years of history."[15]

All of this strongly resonates with younger Christians, whose views of pastoral leadership and church organization have changed accordingly. Jim Kitchens, for example, finds young people quite averse to viewing a local church leader as a religious professional:

[Postmoderns] don't want their pastor (or anyone else) to be the community's "professional Christian." Their experience tells them that experts have led them more often into danger than into enlightenment. They quickly transfer their wariness about government leaders, corporate executives, leading scientists, and university administrators directly onto clergy.[16]

Skepticism about the wisdom of investing trust in a single, professional expert generates corresponding convictions about the proper social context for Christian ministry:

[Postmodern Christians] are leery of hierarchical organization charts in which those at the top of the pyramid are the predominant wielders of power. Instead, they value human

---

13. Ibid., 62–63.
14. Webber, *The Younger Evangelicals*, 149.
15. Ibid., 147.
16. Jim Kitchens, *The Postmodern Parish: New Ministry for a New Era* (Herndon, VA: Alban Institute, 2003), 92.

communities with "flat" organizational structures in which many get to speak and in which many voices are considered for their wisdom.[17]

Younger Christians, in summary, "have a deep desire to belong to a *community* rather than an *organization*."[18]

Thank God that someone is getting it. For all the philosophical and theological problems associated with certain expressions of emerging Christianity, on this point our postmodern brothers and sisters have gotten it absolutely right.

The structural dynamics associated with the corporate church model have proven themselves to be utterly inimical to the basic relational contours of the very gospel we preach. We need desperately to return to Paul's cruciform vision for authentic Christian leadership—a vision that calls us to lead together, not alone, with biblical, not corporate, metrics for success in church ministry. The health of our congregations depends on it. And so does the health of our pastors.

Relational Dynamics

Wounded Leaders

An acquaintance of mine served as the chairman of a deacon board in a situation much like the one in Randy's church. Steve is a godly man with a great family, who is a stellar public servant in his community. A natural leader, Steve rose to a key managerial position in his vocation in law enforcement in a local municipality. He is highly respected by both his peers at work and his brothers at church.

Steve would be the first to tell you, however, that his primary role model as a leader did not come from the Bible. Not Jesus but, rather, Captain Kirk of *Star Trek*, has served as Steve's leadership icon since he was a kid.

---

17. Ibid., 99.
18. Ibid.

And why not? Captain Kirk is the epitome of an invariably wise and courageous leader, who has the unquestioned confidence and obedience of his crew at every turn.

As a police officer, moreover, Steve worked in a vocational setting that necessitated a top-down, hierarchical command structure. Officers obeyed their superiors on the force without question, on the field and at the station. This, of course, only served to reinforce Steve's *Star Trek* view of leadership and authority.

Unfortunately, Steve, like many church board members, imported his secular leadership values into the Christian community, thinking it proper to treat his senior pastor, Karl, like his watch commander—or, perhaps, like Lieutenant Uhura treats Captain Kirk.

Unquestioned obedience. Total support.

A leadership philosophy like Steve's often finds subtle theological justification, moreover, in the misdirected view of a church pastor as the unassailable "Lord's anointed." Suddenly, the door is left wide open to the abuse of spiritual authority. And this is precisely what occurred in Steve's church.

I first gathered that Steve was having second thoughts about his philosophy of leadership from a phone conversation we shared several years ago. I had not heard from Steve for years. His call was occasioned by some pressing problems that had arisen in the church.

Pastor Karl had forced the resignation of one of the most beloved and respected associate pastors in Steve's church. The pattern had become a familiar one, and it was clear to many in the congregation that the senior pastor was doing a poor job relating to his fellow staffers. There was a bit of an uprising in the church, and Steve, as chairman of the board, was caught in the middle.

Here was a classic example of (a) an emotionally scarred senior pastor, who lacked the relational straw to make bricks, so to speak, but (b) who was nevertheless given total authority to do as he pleased among his staff and the rest of the congregation, by (c) a board chairman who had been socialized to run a church like a police department or, perhaps, like the starship *Enterprise.* It would be almost comical if the results had not been so tragic.

In the midst of the crisis, Steve called me, an outsider, for some objective advice. He asked, "Joe, should I *ever* question Pastor Karl's authority?"

I replied, "Steve, Karl is not Captain Kirk. You should question the authority of any church leader who cannot get along with his peers, and who marginalizes the kind of top-rate ministers of the gospel who have been forced to resign from Bethany Church during Karl's decade-long tenure."

Steve no longer serves on the board of Bethany Church. Pastor Karl remains securely in control, and associate staff continue to come and go as the senior pastor sees fit.

No Captain Kirks

Star Trek's Captain Kirk is, of course, a creation of modern media. In the real world there are no Captain Kirks. There are no perfect leaders.

What we have, instead, are persons with leadership gifts who are variously equipped emotionally to exercise those gifts in healthy ways with others. Sadly, some of our leaders are hardly equipped at all.

Manfred F. R. Kets de Vries notes, "Leadership is the exercise of power, and the quality of leadership—good, ineffective, or destructive—depends on an individual's ability to exercise power."[19] Kets de Vries ought to know. His background has prepared him in a remarkable way to ferret out and identify the unhealthy exercise of power and authority.

After taking a doctorate in economics from the University of Amsterdam, Kets de Vries earned an MBA and a DBA from Harvard Business School. He then received extensive training in psychoanalysis and was later certified to practice psychoanalysis by the Canadian Psychoanalytic Society and the International

---

19. Manfred F. R. Kets de Vries, *Leaders, Fools, and Impostors: Essays on the Psychology of Leadership* (San Francisco: Jossey-Bass, 1993), 22.

Psychoanalytic Association. Kets de Vries's research has centered around the relationship between emotional deprivation in childhood and narcissistic leadership in the corporate sector later in adult life.

His description of emotionally needy, narcissistic leaders mirrors, to a great degree, much of what we have seen in the stories of pastoral authority abuse outlined in the earlier pages of this book:

> One of a leader's most important roles is to be aware of and to accommodate the emotional needs of subordinates. Leaders driven by excessive narcissism typically disregard their subordinates' legitimate needs and take advantage of their loyalty. This type of leader is exploitative, callous, and overcompetitive, and frequently resorts to excessive use of depreciation. This behavior fosters submissiveness and passive dependency, stifling the critical function of subordinates.[20]

It is not hard to see Randy's senior pastor, or Steve's, reflected in this quotation.

As it happens, I just spent some time last week with Kyle, another staff person from Randy's church. Their boss is convinced that he has assembled an outstanding group of associate staffers. He is right. They are quality guys.

What Randy's and Kyle's senior pastor does not know, however, is that almost to a man these gifted ministers are ready to jump ship at the first opportunity—precisely because of the kind of "exploitative, callous" narcissism described by Kets de Vries.

Not all pastors are narcissistic power abusers. Many come from healthy childhood environments that have equipped them well emotionally to wield the power they have acquired in their churches.

The breakdown of the family in America, however, guarantees that more and more persons will enter into vocational

---

20. Ibid., 35.

Christian ministry with serious unresolved issues, where emotional stability and personal identity are concerned.

The connection Kets de Vries makes between childhood deprivation and the unhealthy use of authority later in life deserves extended citation:

> The degree of encouragement and frustration children experience as they grow up and begin to measure the boundaries of their personalities has a lasting influence on their perception of themselves and others and the relationships they form throughout their lives. Any imbalance between their feelings of helplessness and the degree of protective nurturing they receive from their parents will be felt as a psychological injury. An inappropriate level of frustration, arising from their environment, handling, or ability to cope with discipline, will feed their natural sense of impotence, and they will commonly respond with feelings of rage, a desire for vengeance, a hunger for personal power, and compensatory fantasies of omnipotence. This dynamic continues throughout life, and if it is not adequately resolved within individuals as they grow up, it is likely to be reactivated with devastating effect when they reach leadership positions and learn to play the game of power.[21]

Persons who exhibit "a hunger for personal power, and compensatory fantasies of omnipotence" are as old as Christianity itself: "Diotrephes, who loves to have first place among them, does not receive us" (3 John 9).

It is likely the case, moreover, that the proportion of narcissistic persons in leadership in our churches is greater than it is among the Christian population in general. This is because narcissism and public leadership prove to be mutually attractive. As Kets de Vries asserts, "[I]t is only to be expected that many narcissistic people, with their need for power, prestige, and glamour, eventually end up in leadership positions.[22]

---

21. Ibid., 23.
22. Ibid., 33.

These tendencies would seem to call for some checks and balances in our churches so that we can help our leaders use their power in appropriately selfless, nurturing ways. Unfortunately, the businesslike approach to ministry described earlier in the chapter has virtually nothing to offer to the church in this regard.

The opposite is the case. As it turns out, a hierarchical model of ministry—where the pastor functions as a CEO, supported by a theologically unsophisticated corporate board of directors (elders or deacons), who are more interested in numerical growth and financial solvency than healthy staff relations—proves to be a breeding ground for precisely the kind of unhealthy, narcissistic leadership that Kets de Vries describes.

The issues goes deeper, however, than the unhealthy emotional orientation of numbers of our church leaders, and institutional contexts which, in turn, enable dysfunctional behavior on their parts. Those on the receiving end of abusive leadership are often caught up in the web of deception, as well.

Seldom will an abusive pastor acknowledge the hurt he has caused and willingly relinquish his post or change the ways he deals with his flock. Change must come, instead, from others in the congregation.

Curiously, however, it seldom does.

In none of the churches represented in the case studies I shared earlier in the book has there been any appreciable change in the manner in which pastoral authority is exercised. Current research into the relationship between abusive leaders and their followers tells us why.

As it turns out, there is something about human nature that causes us to tolerate—sometimes even willingly embrace—the harmful use of authority.

Compliant Congregations: The Allure of Toxic Leaders

The last phrase of the section heading immediately above is taken from the title of a book of the same name by Jean Lipman-Blumen. The subtitle says it all: "Why We Follow Destructive

Bosses and Corrupt Politicians—and How We Can Survive Them."[23]

Lipman-Blumen's burden throughout this important Oxford University Press monograph is to identify characteristics and tendencies in the populace at large—for our purposes, the congregation at large—that allow us to tolerate and even encourage abusive, dysfunctional leaders.

As it turns out, the reasons are manifold. Psychological dynamics that lead us to rally around toxic leaders include a subconscious longing for a parental figure later in adult life, the need for security and certainty in an unpredictable world, and a desire to feel chosen or special as we join together in community with others to support the noble vision of a bigger-than-life leader.

At a deeper level, people default to powerful, charismatic leaders out of a need for a godlike figure in their lives. In religious contexts this person can be a gifted, celebrity pastor who simultaneously serves as both God's representative and spiritual father to a willing, compliant congregation. Jesus was apparently well aware of this potentially destructive dynamic: "Do not call anyone on earth your father, because you have one Father, who is in heaven" (Matt 23:9).

External factors play into these psychological needs in significant ways, as well. The rapid pace of change—culturally and technologically—in America in recent decades renders many of us particularly vulnerable to the engaging charisma of messianic pretenders who assure us that everything will be okay. Add a serious crisis, and the majority commonly default to strong leadership with little concern for the integrity of those who lead them.

The classic example of a toxic leader finding widespread support in trying times is Adolf Hitler. Germany emerged from World War I in a crisis of national identity. The Germans had suffered defeat in the war and further humiliation at the hands of

---

23. Jean Lipman-Blumen, *The Allure of Toxic Leaders: Why We Follow Destructive Bosses and Corrupt Politicians—and How We Can Survive Them* (Oxford: Oxford University Press, 2005).

those who crafted the Treaty of Versailles. As Lipman-Blumen notes, "That left the German people dangerously susceptible to any Hitler who would promise to restore the nation's pride."[24]

Please don't misunderstand. I am not equating harmful church leaders with the likes of Adolf Hitler. I wish neither to sensationalize the problems in our churches, nor to trivialize the horrors perpetrated by the Nazis during Hitler's reign of terror.

My point is to underscore our widespread tendency as human beings to tolerate and enable the unhealthy and abusive use of power and authority in various social contexts. Hitler is an extreme and vivid example of this tendency.

Even where a leader responds to a threat or challenge in an admirable way, public reaction can tell us a lot about our felt need as human beings for a savior in the face of crisis.

Consider the following excerpts from an op-ed article about Mayor Rudolph Giuliani in the *New York Times*. The piece appeared on September 20, 2001, a little more than a week after 9/11:

> [Giuliani] moves about the stricken city like a god. People want to be in his presence. They want to touch him. They want to praise him. . . . On Central Park West, a woman searching for just the right superlative for the man who is guiding New York through the greatest disaster ever to hit an American city finally said he's not *like* a god, "He *is* God."[25]

Fortunately, Giuliani proved to be a relatively selfless, compassionate "God" throughout the crisis.

Sadly, this has not been the case in numbers of such incidents. Some of our gods turn out to be devils in disguise. And yet we continue to tolerate and even encourage strong leaders who misuse their power and authority.

---

24. Ibid., 89.
25. Bob Herbert, "The Right Answer," *The New York Times*, September 20, 2001, A31.

This is indisputably the case in our churches. Amazingly enough, with a single exception (Dr. Jeffrey Richmond, at Christ Community Church), every one of the abusive local church leaders chronicled in the earlier pages of this book remains securely in place in his paid position of pastoral leadership. This should give us pause, to say the least.

Why do these churches and their leadership boards put up with such behavior year after year? Lipman-Blumen's study, as summarized above, gives us some answers.

Lipman-Blumen also challenges us to no longer indulge or tolerate toxic leaders, and she offers some helpful guidelines to followers who have had enough and who want to free themselves from the control of abusive authority figures. Her suggestions range from quietly counseling and confronting an abusive supervisor to joining with others in the organization to overthrow the leader.[26]

Compliant—and, I would add, complicit—elders or deacons, who knowingly tolerate the abuse of pastoral authority, would do well to seriously consider Lipman-Blumen's suggestions. A better solution, however, would be to reduce the potential for abuse by redesigning the social context of church ministry in a way that encourages the healthy exercise of pastoral authority. It is to this project that we turn in the final chapter.

Conclusion

New Testament teaching about servant leadership is quite transparent where the use of ministerial power and authority is concerned. Reading texts like Acts 16 and Philippians 2 against the background of ancient history and culture only underscores the other-centered nature of Paul's cruciform vision for authentic Christian leadership.

Numbers of our pastors are, unfortunately, not responding in kind. This chapter was an attempt to explain why. The volatile combination of (a) emotionally needy, narcissistic leaders

---

26. Lipman-Blumen, *The Allure of Toxic Leaders*, 210-11.

appealing to (b) naively receptive followers in (c) corporate, institutional settings proves to be a set-up for the abuse of ministerial authority.

How shall we proceed? We cannot give our seminary students and pastors a second childhood, though we can probably do a better job of identifying and addressing emotional and relational dysfunction early in a minister's training. Nor can we do much to change the natural human tendency to gravitate toward powerful individuals who seem to be so ably in control.

We can, however, radically transform the social contexts in which we do church ministry. I will suggest in our final chapter that a key answer to the problem of authority abuse that plagues numbers of our congregations is a team of pastors who share their lives with one another, and whose oversight of God's people arises organically from the relational soil they enjoy as a leadership community of genuine brothers and sisters in Christ.

Questions for Reflection

1. How relationally vulnerable is your pastor with other people on the church staff? Others in the congregation? Do you think it is important for a pastor to have close friendships with a handful of other individuals in the church?

2. How would your church board (elders or deacons) define ministerial success? Are their criteria for success biblical? Are they sufficient? Why or why not?

3. Why do younger Christians tend to prefer a non-hierarchical, non-institutional approach to church? What are they reacting against?

4. In virtually every abusive church situation narrated in the book, the pastor remains in his position of authority. Why do some churches continue to tolerate unhealthy leaders like this? How should a church deal with an abusive pastor?

5. Summarize the pitfalls associated with a corporate approach to ministry. How can we avoid these pitfalls without sacrificing some of the positive attributes of a well-run institution, such as efficient organization or excellence in the execution of tasks and responsibilities?

_____

Recapturing Paul's Cruciform Vision for Authentic Christian Ministry

Leading in Community with Others

At its core, spiritual leadership must be relational in nature.
—Stacy T. Rinehart[1]

We have encountered a stark contrast between Paul's understanding of leadership and the ways that power and authority are often leveraged in our churches. The previous chapter sought to explain this disconnect between the biblical ideal and contemporary practice.

An unhealthy mix of (a) insecure, narcissistic leaders, (b) corporate models of ministry that give those leaders too much latitude, and (c) Sunday audiences enamored with self-assured, charismatic communicators has opened the door to the abuse

_____

1. Rinehart, *Upside Down*, 104.

of power and authority by numbers of persons in vocational Christian service.

Leaderless Communities?

Maji was a short-lived Christian community of some twenty to fifty persons in Birmingham, U.K. The group met for eighteen months or so as a "spiritual collective gathering point," according to representative Pip Piper.[2] Although not formally a church, the group's convictions aptly reflect the extremes to which some emerging Christians are willing to go in their attempts to dismantle top-down leadership structures:

> The leadership is organic and open. Everyone, whether they have been around and in relationship with people like myself for years or they have been here only twice, has equal access and voice to help shape the next gathering or to offer assistance and participation.[3]

Extreme approaches are understandable given the suspicion of authority in the culture at large and the unfortunate experiences many of us have had at the hands of hurtful church leaders. A leaderless congregation, however, proves to be neither scripturally sound nor pragmatically viable.

I need only to reflect on my past week in church ministry to be reminded of the danger of ceding my authority as a shepherd to the next person who walks through the doors of Oceanside Christian Fellowship.

Ken, a man for whom we had prayed for several years, became a Christian four months ago, much to the delight of Shannon, his believing wife. Three months later Shannon called to inform me that Ken's theological world had been rocked by a six-hundred-page book arguing that Jesus is not God.

2. Eddie Gibbs and Ryan K. Bolger, *Emerging Churches: Creating Christian Community in Postmodern Cultures* (Grand Rapids: Baker, 2005), 296.
3. Maji facilitator Pip Piper, cited by Gibbs and Bolger, *Emerging Churches*, 202.

Just last week we found out why. A recent attender had given the book to this bright but vulnerable new believer. He commended the book to Ken and informed him that it would stir things up among our church's leaders. Apparently that was his intention.

Now imagine the chaos that would have ensued in our church, if (with Maji's philosophy of leadership) we had allowed this proselytizing heretic "to help shape the next gathering or to offer assistance and participation" after he had attended OCF "only twice."

Kets de Vries rightly observes that "human beings must do one or the other—lead or follow—in whatever social context we find ourselves."[4] It is the nature of human community to organize itself into leaders and followers.

Like the Maji community, we might pretend we have no leaders. But leaders will arise to fill the vacuum we create with a "leaderless" approach to church ministry. And they may turn out to be the wrong kind of leaders.

As we saw in the previous chapter, narcissistic persons are driven by nature to lead. If we fail to identify, develop, and install leaders that we select, unhealthy leaders will appear on their own, more than willing to take control. The magnetic attraction that exists between narcissism and power virtually guarantees as much.

The leaderless church is not an option. Paul appointed elders in each of the communities he established. And Scripture has provided us with clear guidelines for identifying those whom God has raised up to lead his church (1 Tim 3; Tit 1).

Powerless Pastors?

Kester Brewin acknowledges the need for leaders. But he continues to exhibit emerging Christianity's distaste for institutional authority when he commends "a model of leadership that

---

4. Kets de Vries, *Leaders, Fools, and Impostors*, 2.

has very little *power*." Brewin claims that "this naturally fits very well with the Christian tradition of servant leadership."[5]

The option sounds attractive. It would certainly help prevent the hurtful use of authority in the pastorate. Unfortunately, Brewin's suggestion is neither biblical nor workable. The idea of powerless pastors does not at all fit "the Christian tradition of servant leadership." Nor does it effectively address the problem of authority abuse.

Christ, in his preincarnate state (Phil 2:6), did not have "very little power." Quite the contrary. As we saw in chapter 5, Christ was clothed in a robe of divine glory. He enjoyed equality with God.

Luke's story of Paul and Silas in Philippi reflects the same dynamic. As the narrative in Acts 16 concludes, we discover that the missionaries possessed Roman citizenship all along—a significant social privilege in the colony, and one that could have saved them a lot of physical suffering, had Paul and Silas chosen to leverage their citizen status to avert the beating and imprisonment.

In neither Jesus's case nor Paul's, therefore, did a lack of power figure in the exercise of healthy servant leadership. Instead, the key in both cases was the manner in which Paul and Jesus chose to leverage the relative degrees of authority or social capital they did possess.

Jesus "did not consider equality with God as something to be used for His own advantage" (Phil 2:6). Paul treated his Roman citizen status in a similar, other-centered way.

Both Jesus and Paul willingly assumed slave status for the benefit of others, and they did so from respective positions of power. This, in a nutshell, is the biblical model of servant leadership.

Not only does "a model of leadership that has very little power" lack biblical support, but Brewin's approach also proves

5. Kester Brewin, *Signs of Emergence: A Vision for Church That Is Organic/Networked/Decentralized/Bottom-up/Communal/Flexible/Always Evolving* (Grand Rapids: Baker, 2007), 115.

ineffective in practice. It might seem that dispersing power throughout the whole congregation would dilute the potential for the misuse of authority. Experience, however, suggests otherwise.

The wholesale democratization of local church authority, which seems attractive to some of our emerging brothers and sisters, has been tried and found wanting by earlier generations of American evangelicals. Our younger brothers and sisters could learn a thing or two from the past.

Majority Rule?

A congregational form of government—where every member has equal input into the life and direction of the community at regular church-wide meetings—continues to characterize polity in numbers of evangelical churches.

There is certainly biblical warrant for congregational authority in some areas of church life. In 1 Corinthians 5:1–9, for example, Paul challenges the church as a whole to exercise its authority to discipline a member who persists in blatant, public immorality.

A polity that removes virtually all authority from church leaders, however, and places it in the hands of the congregation, often does little more than shift the vexing problem of authority abuse from the pastor to the people.

My first years in ministry were spent in a democratically governed church, where *Robert's Rules of Order* was used to facilitate the decision-making process. The outcome was anything but inspiring.

Robert's Rules of Order is a book "containing rules of order intended to be adopted as a parliamentary authority for use by a deliberative assembly." That's how Wikipedia defines this resource, at any rate.[6]

6. "Robert's Rules of Order," *Wikipedia*, last modified January 10, 2013, accessed January 13, 2013, http://en.wikipedia.org/wiki/ Robert%27s_rules_of_order.

I had never heard of *Robert's Rules* until I attended my first congregational business meeting at Community Baptist Church. The fact that our church called these gatherings "business meetings" should have given me pause to begin with.

Yet, as it turned out, the meetings were unlike any meetings I had attended in the several businesses where I had been employed before I worked in a church.

What occurred instead was something akin to a collective free-for-all. Every member had an opportunity to voice an opinion, and a moderator tried to keep a lid on it all. The church's pastors, who had little say in the proceedings, put on happy faces and prayed inwardly that the meeting would end quickly, before some irreversible damage was done either to relationships among those in attendance or to the church programs the staff had worked so hard to develop.

One fellow took it upon himself to be our church's parliamentary expert. Maybe you have one in your own congregation. Willy never missed a meeting. And he was always ready to pounce, whenever we deviated ever so slightly from the procedures outlined in *Robert's Rules of Order.*

Willy wasn't all that concerned with the issues at hand. He was there solely to insure proper parliamentary decorum. He apparently viewed it as his calling. To this day I think Willy had committed *Robert's Rules* to memory.

Following *Robert's Rules* can, in fact, help a "deliberative assembly" work through difficult and divisive issues. We might stop at this point, however, to ask ourselves whether God ever intended his church to be governed by a deliberative assembly.

The history of *Robert's Rules,* in this regard, is illuminating. The nineteenth-century American general who developed *Robert's Rules* did so to help "adversaries in a democratic polity" settle their differences by peaceful means. Jim Kitchens, who relates the story of *Robert's Rules,* summarizes:

> What we need to understand from this short history lesson is that the parliamentary procedures set out in Robert's Rules

assume an adversarial relationship between the parties seeking to come to a decision.[7]

"Parliamentary procedures" designed to deal with "an adversarial relationship" between contentious "parties" in a "deliberative assembly"—is this really how God wants us to make decisions in his family?

I think not. The Bible views us not as adversaries vying to get our way in the contentious context of a deliberative assembly, but as a united family of brothers and sisters in Christ.

Faithful adherence to *Robert's Rules of Order* might keep tempers under control at a Baptist business meeting. *Robert's Rules* will do next to nothing, however, to encourage Paul's cruciform vision for authentic Christian leadership.

In too many churches, the parliamentary solution to the abuse of pastoral authority simply transfers the dysfunctional exercise of power from the shepherd to the sheep. This should not surprise us, for in the final analysis, there is no way to eliminate power and authority from a social collective, be it a church, a business, or any group people, for that matter.

Where there are people, there will inevitably be individuals who wield power and authority in some capacity. How this power is used—not its presence or absence—distinguishes healthy from unhealthy expressions of pastoral authority.

A Community of Leaders

The way back to Paul's cruciform vision for authentic Christian leadership is to be found in a community of pastor-elders who relate to one another first as brothers[8] in Christ, and who then lead their church family out of the fullness of that robust relational solidarity.

I happen to think there is enough evidence in the New

---

7. Kitchens, *The Postmodern Parish*, 89.
8. The reader is encouraged to interpret the term "brothers" generically. I happen to serve on an all-male leadership team. Some readers will share leadership with persons of both genders.

Testament to make plurality leadership a norm for the people of God under the new covenant. It is not my intention, however, to offer another series of proof-texts for what I understand to be biblical church polity. I have made the case in brief elsewhere, and others have done a much more thorough job than I.[9]

The focus here is on function rather than form. Whether or not you happen to buy into plurality leadership as God's prescription for church polity, I hope to demonstrate that team leadership is "biblical" (in the broad, value-laden sense of the word), and that the plurality approach offers much hope for raising up healthy, effective pastoral leaders and for significantly curbing authority abuse in our churches.

One Church's Experience

I am privileged to serve alongside a remarkable group of pastors. We are officially an elder-led church, per our church by-laws. What makes the leadership of Oceanside Christian Fellowship exceptional, though, is not our formal church polity.

To be sure, as we saw in the previous chapter, some forms of church government naturally lend themselves to the proper exercise of pastoral authority. So a formal polity of team leadership like ours is a step in the right direction.

What makes the leadership of Oceanside Christian Fellowship so healthy, however—what gives OCF's leaders so much credibility in the eyes of our people, and what makes it such a delight to serve as a pastor in the church—is not our formal structure but, rather, the quality of relationships we share with one another as a pastor-elder team.

Community Generates Consensus

Except for the fact that three of us draw a paycheck every couple of weeks, OCF knows no distinction between its

---

9. See chapter 6 and Hellerman, *When the Church Was a Family*, chapter 9. For a more thorough treatment, see Alexander Strauch, *Biblical Eldership: An Urgent Call to Restore Biblical Church Leadership*, rev. ed. (Colorado Springs: Lewis and Roth, 1995).

seminary-trained pastors and those on our board whom other churches might refer to as elders or (in churches without elders) deacons. Indeed, in order to discourage the kind of minister-versus-layperson mentality traditionally associated with the terms "pastor" and "elder," all nine of us are designated as "pastor-elders," and we encourage our church to view us that way.

Our weekly meetings are the key to the success of the whole enterprise. OCF's pastor-elders gather together for an hour-and-a-half each Wednesday morning. We have no business agenda. We share our lives and pray for one another, and we go through the prayer requests our people submit each week.

OCF currently has eight pastor-elders and one "in training" (see below). Our tenure ranges from three years on the team to more than twenty. I have been part of the team for seventeen years. You can imagine the kind of community we have developed by faithfully meeting and praying for one another for so long on a weekly basis.

Over the years we have shared in countless joys and sorrows, big and small. We welcomed four new children and several grandchildren into the world. We fervently prayed for shaky marriages in our extended families. And we grieved together when one of our brothers lost his wife to a long battle with cancer.

We generally reserve decisions and actions related to church programs and ministry for another context, meetings that we hold one Saturday each month. It is at the Saturday gatherings that the community we cultivate on Wednesdays pays big dividends to our church family as a whole.

Power plays? Authority abuse? Not a chance. Brandon, Denny, Ed, Stan, Dan, Carlos, Michael, John, and I know each other too well—and we love each other too much—to let anyone get away with politicking or posturing. It is really quite amazing what happens when decision-making arises organically from a relational soil of mutual trust, respect, and admiration.

We struggle through the same kind of overwhelming challenges that confront other church leaders. Disgruntled and divisive church members, immorality, financial crises, a major building program, hiring and firing staff—we've seen it all. And like any team comprised of opinionated leaders, we have had our share of strong disagreements along the way.

The community we cultivate on Wednesdays, however, allows us to tackle church crises on Saturdays—and push through divergent viewpoints to consensus—in ways that we never could, if we were a typical church board, devoid of caring relationships, meeting monthly solely to do church business or, perhaps, to rubber-stamp the limited vision of a sole pastor figure. Among OCF's pastor-elders, community is the bedrock of consensus:

Does This Really Work?

People who are new to OCF, and to our team leadership model, repeatedly ask, *How does this work out in practice, when a difficult and potentially divisive decision must be made?*

There are no absolutes where the decision-making process is concerned, and different groups of individuals will inevitably interact with one another in different ways. At OCF, our pathway to consensus typically runs as follows:

1. We each weigh in with our convictions or opinions about the issue at hand.

2. We listen carefully to each person's viewpoint and to the rationale for his perspective.

3. We seek to be highly sensitive to the general direction the discussion is going, trusting that the Holy Spirit is super-intending the process.

4. A pastor-elder whose viewpoint becomes increasingly out of step with the trajectory of the discussion willingly defers to the growing consensus of the group.

5. Once a decision has been made, we unanimously own it.

And, of course, we pray our way through the process. Not once, during my tenure on the board, have we ever had to vote formally on an issue.

God's Perfect Will?

Here is a final observation that will perhaps strike a number of readers as counterintuitive: the way we make decisions as a community of leaders is at least as important to God as the ultimate decisions we make. Indeed, I have become convinced over the years that God is generally more concerned with the process than with the outcome of our Saturday leadership meetings.

I often find it difficult to discern God's will when we are making decisions in our meetings. Perhaps you have the same experience in your own ministry. While some decisions are clear-cut, it seems that in most situations there are probably a number of viable alternatives, several of which would be pleasing to God. In still other situations, I suspect that God has no prefer-ence at all.

Persons who believe otherwise, and who seek vigilantly to ascertain God's perfect will for every key decision, run the risk of completely missing a biblical reality that is indispensable to healthy team leadership. In contrast to the lack of clarity often associated with the decision itself, God's will for the relational integrity of the process—humility, mutual respect, brotherly love—is crystal clear throughout the Scriptures.

It is, of course, quite Western to be preoccupied with outcome at the expense of process. But I don't believe it is biblical.

Indeed, it has been my experience that the Bible seldom speaks directly to the decisions that face us in church ministry. Scripture always speaks directly, however, to the manner in which we are to go about making those decisions together.

The upshot of all this for decision-making by consensus is that I am less and less inclined to confuse my personal convictions with the will of God on an issue, and I am increasingly willing to defer to group consensus when I represent the sole minority opinion at one of our Saturday planning meetings. My brothers on the board take the same approach. We are quite confident that if OCF's pastor-elders engage the process with integrity, God will be pleased with the outcome.

Relationships with the Church Family

So far, our discussion has focused on our relationships with one another as Oceanside Christian Fellowship's pastor-elders. What about the rest of the church? How do the people of OCF view their leaders?

With a great deal of confidence, it seems. A recent tally of several hundred members voting on our leadership teams (pastor-elders and deacons) and 2010-11 budget came up with 100 percent "Yes" votes on each and every ballot.

The only "exception" was Eric, one of our small group leaders. Eric voted in the affirmative on all counts, but he wrote us a little note suggesting that pastor-elder Stan had better "work on his spiritual walk."

Eric is one of our church family's most notorious pranksters. And our people are well aware of the quality of Stan's spiritual life. So we all got a kick out of Eric's attempt to bring a bit of levity to the otherwise uneventful annual voting process.

Credibility Factors: Gaining the Trust of Our People

When I think about the confidence our people have in OCF's pastor-elders, three credibility factors come to mind: (1) we are careful to select persons for our team who meet the biblical quali-fications for elder; (2) we make decisions openly and transparently before our people; and, as outlined above, (3) OCF's pastor-elders share our lives and lead our church together, in community with one another. Let's consider each of these factors in turn.

Credibility Factor #1: Spiritual Maturity

After nearly a year of searching, my previous church finally called a new senior pastor in 1986. John was a wonderful choice. He was a godly man with great wisdom, who, as it turned out, would gently but firmly lead a traditional Baptist church through a difficult time of cultural adjustment during his five-year tenure as our pastor.

Pastor John nearly gave up on us, though, early in the game. At his first leadership meeting, during his first week on the job, John had to interrupt a "discussion" among our deacons that be-came so heated that it threatened to escalate into some kind of physical altercation.

As you might gather, the church was not always careful about the kind of men it appointed to serve as deacons (we had no el-ders). Some of these fellows had learned to forcefully promote their agendas in the secular workplace over the years, and a couple of them had apparently brought those skills to the table at Pastor John's first deacon meeting.

I warmly recall the moment, some months later at an annual business meeting, when it came time to approve a new slate of leaders. Our by-laws required us to have eighteen deacons. The moderator tried in vain to get enough nominations and willing volunteers from the floor. Finally, a seminary student in the con-gregation raised his hand.

After he was given the floor, the young man innocently in-quired, "Are we recruiting additional deacons because we have a quota of eighteen spots to fill, or because we think that we have some men here who are biblically qualified, but who have not yet stepped up to the plate?"

For one precious moment a holy silence descended on that

Baptist business meeting. It was all I as a pastor could do to keep a straight face and contain my delight.

Becoming a Pastor-Elder at OCF

OCF has no set quota of pastor-elders. Nor do we rotate elders on and off our board according to some arbitrary timetable. We take great care, moreover, to recruit elders who meet the biblical qualifications for the office (1 Tim 3; Tit 1) and who share OCF's culture and philosophy of ministry.

Our board invites a potential pastor-elder to meet with us on Wednesdays and Saturdays for a full year before any formal commitment is made on the candidate's side or ours. Only after we are assured that the man (a) meets the requirements for elder as laid out in the New Testament, (b) embraces our relational approach to leadership, and (c) has the blessing of his wife and children, do we extend a formal invitation to join the board.

At the end of the year, when the candidate responds in the affirmative, we submit his name to the church for a vote of affirmation. Although we are always open to informal suggestions from our people, we take no nominations for pastor-elder from the floor in any formal congregational meeting. We do not even hold such meetings.

The practice of spiritually mature individuals enjoying an extended tenure as pastor-elders at OCF has resulted in our leaders gaining a great degree of credibility among the congregation as a whole.

The matriculation process described above faced its greatest challenge when we added Michael Martin to our board. Michael came to us as the pastor of a small African American church that merged with OCF in early 2011. How would Michael's people respond to an Anglo church requiring their dearly loved, highly gifted pastor—who had served as their shepherd for more than a decade—to spend a year at OCF as a "pastor-elder in training," as we refer to our new recruits?

I was assigned the daunting task of justifying our process to a group of twenty or so persons from Michael's church during our New Members Class. But it was Michael who, in the final analysis, convinced his people of the value of what we require. Michael is sold on team ministry. And he was highly supportive of the process for becoming a pastor-elder at OCF. Michael knows very well how absolutely essential social capital is to the plurality model of shared leadership.

And lest there remain any lingering doubt that Michael was somehow singled out in this regard, we currently have a fellow in the pipeline who has been in vocational Christian ministry for the better part of four decades. Over the years, John has served as (a) an associate pastor of a large church in Dallas, (b) the senior pastor of a congregation in Southern California (where John mentored me in my first staff position), (c) part of a church planting team, and, currently, (d) the chairman of the Bible Exposition department at Talbot School of Theology. But right now John is a "lowly" pastor-elder in training at Oceanside Christian Fellowship.

Nobody gets a free pass at OCF. Not even a seasoned veteran with a PhD in biblical studies and twenty-two years of pastoral ministry under his belt. Why? Because after more than a decade of experience with shared leadership, we are convinced that real **consensus** only arises in a healthy way from genuine **community**. The deep sibling relationships we share with one another as OCF's pastor-elders have proven to be the key to the whole team enterprise.

Brandon, Michael, and I have the formal training, and we do most of the Sunday preaching. You might think that our people would view us as the "spiritual giants" of OCF's pastor-elder board. Not by a long shot.

Several months ago, some of our high-schoolers got together to watch the 1973 horror film *The Exorcist*. When the movie was over, one of the young ladies in attendance blurted out, "If that happened around me, I'd want Joe to be there. . . . No! I'd want Stan to be there. He's . . . he's . . . he's like Moses!"

Apparently Pastor Stan has garnered more spiritual credibility in this teenager's eyes than Pastor Joe—even though Pastor Joe does a good portion of the Sunday preaching at the church and Pastor Stan does not. Pastor Joe would not have it any other way.

Character Comes First

The need for church leaders to satisfy and publicly demonstrate the biblical qualifications for leadership came home in a pointed way when our founding pastor, Ron, resigned from the board.

It is our understanding at OCF that the qualifications for pastoral leadership ought to be grouped together and prioritized as follows: (1) character, (2) biblical/theological knowledge, (3) giftedness. As I discovered when Ron resigned, some people in our church arrange these priorities in precisely the opposite order.

In 2000, Ron's wife left him and filed for divorce. Ron is a brilliant communicator who has since been restored to pastoral ministry. At the time, however, it was clear to OCF's elders that Ron did not meet perhaps the most important New Testament character qualification for pastor-elder: the one related to the spiritual health of a minister's family. An elder, Paul told Timothy, must be a person who "manages his own household competently" (1 Tim 3:4).

The morning we read Ron's letter of resignation I was accosted by a member who insisted in no uncertain terms, "You *cannot* silence that gift!" Relevant verses from the Bible did nothing to convince the man otherwise. For this individual, giftedness trumped character.

As evidenced by the examples narrated earlier in the book, numbers of churches and leadership boards tolerate or ignore problematic character flaws in the relational lives of their pastors, simply because these pastors happen to be inspiring leaders or gifted communicators who attract crowds and fill offering plates on Sunday morning.

However, pastors who rely on gifts rather than character to gain credibility with their people essentially turn the biblical pattern upside down. Giftedness, in the final analysis, proves to be a poor foundation for ministerial respect and credibility.

I suspect that much of the confidence our people have in OCF's leaders arises from the fact that we do our best to prioritize character above giftedness, whenever we are forced to choose between these two qualifications for pastoral leadership.

This approach to leadership does not always make for the most scintillating dog-and-pony show on Sunday morning. Frankly, our preaching at OCF is not quite as rhetorically engaging as it was when Ron was our primary communicator.

We are convinced, however, that prioritizing spiritual maturity above giftedness honors God. And we have seen it provide our congregation with a great deal of relational hope, as well as increased trust in OCF's team of leaders.

Credibility Factor #2: Transparency

A second key to healthy church leadership is an open and honest line of communication between pastors and their flock. The congregation I now serve began as a church plant back in 1986. Transparency was a core value from the beginning. It became a defining issue for OCF leaders during my first few months on the job.

Joann and I had followed the progress of Oceanside Christian Fellowship quite closely for ten years before I came on staff in 1996. The services during that first decade had great teaching but less-than-inspiring music. Ron, who started the church, was a great communicator, but he never had an ear for music.

We sang "Father Abraham" with the kids in the service one Sunday when Joann and I visited during the late 1980s. Cute but hardly inspiring. And that was about all the music we had that morning.

In February 1996, I joined Ron as a team pastor at OCF. I had been a candidate the previous December, and I'll never forget how surprised Joann and I were with the worship. There had been gradual improvement in this area over the past several years, but what we heard that first Sunday I preached in the church was quite impressive.

OCF now had a full worship team, led by a highly gifted guitar player named Sam, who clearly knew how to bring the people of God into the presence of God. Co-leading with Sam was an accomplished pianist named Ellen.

I soon learned why the team sounded so good. Sam and Ellen were seasoned pros. They had served in a large Calvary Chapel for nearly a decade and then spent the next four years leading worship for a church in the Vineyard movement. Ellen had a master's degree in piano performance from USC, and Sam was an accomplished guitarist with a natural gift for worship.

Sensitivity to the Holy Spirit + top-rate musicianship + years of experience—no wonder this worship team led us into the throne room of God that morning!

I could hardly wait to start my job in a church so well positioned to reach the surrounding community. I mentioned to Ron how excited I was about the future of the church, now that his great teaching was complimented by such meaningful worship.

Ron's response did not strike me as particularly enthusiastic. I later found out why.

I attended my first elder meeting soon after I came on board in early 1996. The main item on the agenda that day was terminating Sam. I was shocked. "Guys, do you know how good you have it with a worship leader like Sam?"

As it turned out, the twenty minutes or so of song-leading on Sunday mornings was the only thing Sam did well. He was a gifted musician, but he was administratively challenged, to say the least. Pastor Ron found it next to impossible to work together with Sam to plan the Sunday services.

On the musical side of things, moreover, it turned out that Ellen was the half of the duo that did all the work. Ellen found new songs, learned the music from the CDs, wrote up the chord charts, made the overhead transparencies, recruited and worked with the soundmen, purchased the equipment, and provided musical direction for the worship team. Sam fronted the band on Sundays and attended the team's Thursday night rehearsals.

The problem with the arrangement was that the church paid Sam—not Ellen—$2,000 per month as our part-time worship director. Frustration among the leaders had been mounting for some time before I came on the scene. The elders were ready to terminate Sam.

Well, the last thing I wanted to do was go back to "Father Abraham" on Sundays, so I said to the board, "Give me some time with Sam. Maybe I can help him get organized and do a better job with his time and his gifts."

Six months later nothing had changed. I had to agree that we needed a new leader. It was fair neither to the congregation that was footing the bill, nor to those who were doing his work, for Sam to be pulling in a paycheck for an hour or so of song-leading each week.

But how do you fire a pastor? Sam was not officially a pastor, but he had certainly become a shepherd to our people as he led them into the presence of the Lord each week.

Most of our Sunday attenders, moreover, saw only the positive side of Sam's ministry among us. As you can imagine, the congregation warmly appreciated Sam's weekly contribution to their spiritual lives.

One of our elders had an idea. "Instead of informing the church that we are terminating Sam," he suggested, "let's ask him to write a letter of resignation."

"We'll make Sam a deal. Our by-laws require us to give a terminated employee two weeks' severance pay. We'll offer Sam three months' pay, if he'll write us the letter. That way damage control in the church will be kept to a minimum. What do you think, guys?"

"Nope. Been there. Done that," I immediately replied.

I had been in enough church settings where staff terminations were publicly "spun" as resignations, and I'd had more than my share of the duplicity. It usually went down something like this.

An All Too Common Scenario

John and Sue Rainey experienced great fulfillment in their

role at Redlands Bible Church. The couple served RBC as co-directors of the church's small group ministry.

Associate Pastor Derrick had encouraged the couple to join a small group several years ago when they first began attending the church. Before too long, John and Sue found themselves co-leading the group with another couple. A year later Pastor Derrick asked the Raineys to consider taking charge of the churchwide small group program.

The couple signed on, and the arrangement turned out to be a fruitful and happy one for both the Raineys and their church family. John and Sue met with Pastor Derrick and his wife, Lucy, on a regular basis and, as an unexpected bonus, the mentoring relationship morphed into a genuine friendship between the couples.

The Raineys had found an ideal place to use their gifts, RBC's small group ministry was thriving, and for the first time, John and Sue had a meaningful relationship with another mature Christian couple in the church.

Things began to unravel, however, when a letter was read to the congregation near the end of the service one Sunday. The letter was written by Derrick and read as follows:

> *Dear Brothers and Sisters,*
>
> *It is with a combination of heartfelt sadness and great anticipation that I announce my resignation from my ministry as Associate Pastor of Redlands Bible Church, effective immediately.*
>
> *For some time Lucy and I have sensed God's Spirit moving us to consider a new ministry, and the time is right for us to wrap up the good work that God has given us to do here at RBC. RBC's small group ministry is doing quite well, and my other areas of responsibility are in able hands, as well.*
>
> *Lucy and I treasure the years we have had with you, and we wish you God's best, as you continue to love and serve him.*
>
> *Your Servants in Christ,*
> *Derrick and Lucy Sanford*

John and Sue were caught completely by surprise. They

didn't know quite how to react. They certainly wanted to affirm the role of God's Spirit in the Sanfords' lives, "moving us to consider a new ministry," as Derrick had put it. The Raineys were rather troubled, however, by the suddenness of it all.

Pastor Derrick seemed to be doing a great job at the church, and he appeared to be enjoying his work, as well. The Raineys had benefited tremendously from Derrick's mentoring, and they treasured their friendship with Derrick and Lucy.

It was the friendship with the Sanfords, in fact, that made the sudden resignation so hard to accept. John and Sue had just spent an evening with the Sanfords a week ago Saturday. Why hadn't Derrick and Lucy told the Raineys about their plans? The Raineys felt rather hurt hearing the news, for the first time, with everyone else in that large Sunday gathering.

And then there was the content of the letter. It was rather vague. Was there, in fact, a new ministry for Derrick and Lucy in another church somewhere? If so, the letter gave no specifics. The Raineys couldn't help but wonder if perhaps there was more to this than they had heard in Derrick's letter that Sunday morning.

There was. Associate Pastor Derrick Sanford did not submit his resignation. He was fired. And then he was strongly encouraged to write a letter to "spin" his termination as a Spirit-led decision to resign on his part.

What had transpired behind closed doors in the church office, far away from the public context of Sunday ministry, was, indeed, a very different story than the one reflected in Derrick's letter of resignation.

John and Sue, of course, were aware of none of this. And since the Raineys were not ones to stir up trouble in the church, they refrained from inquiring and tried to encourage the Sanfords, trusting that God was in control.

Derrick Sanford and his family soon left Redlands Bible Church, and a search committee was formed to find another associate pastor to take Derrick's place.

Maybe you have found yourself in a situation like John and

Sue Rainey's. Or perhaps you're an associate pastor who has written a letter like Derrick Sanford's to a former congregation.

Or maybe you're a senior pastor (or the chairman of a church board) who has asked a staff member whom you've fired to spin his termination publicly as a resignation.

The story above is fictional. But only the names. For just such a scenario plays itself out, again and again, in local Southern California congregations with which I am all too familiar.

This is why—returning to the story of Sam, the worship leader—I immediately resisted the suggestion from my fellow elder that we should frame Sam's termination as a resignation and compel him to write the church a nice letter to that effect by offering to extend his severance package.

How, then, *do* you fire a pastor? With honesty, openness, and transparency before the congregation, assuming that the reasons for the termination are legitimate in the first place, as they were in Sam's case.

I had discovered in my six months or so at the church that OCF's elders had garnered a tremendous amount of respect and trust with the flock over the years. I told the guys that I felt it was now time to cash in some of that social capital.

"Let's be up-front with the congregation," I said, "and let the chips fall where they may." After some discussion, the elders agreed. We determined to be as honest as we could with the church, without unnecessarily compromising our people's view of Sam or our sense of gratitude for his ministry among us.

We wrote a letter informing our people that we appreciated where Sam had taken the church musically, but that we were terminating our arrangement with Sam because his administrative skills no longer satisfied the demands of the job. And we extended Sam's severance package to help meet his needs while he sought another position. We had next to no negative fallout from the congregation.

OCF's pastor-elders try to exercise this kind of transparency and openness with our people wherever we can. We keep the church informed about important decisions, and our people have access to the way we spend our money, right down to the line items on the annual budget that enumerate our staff's salaries.

Some issues, of course, demand confidentiality, and our folks understand that. In fact, I think it is because we are open and honest where we are able to be, that our people generally exhibit a great deal of trust in us in those areas where we find it necessary to keep sensitive information to ourselves.

Given the hermeneutic of suspicion of authority that characterizes the culture at large, there will always be a handful of persons in every church who do not trust their leaders. We have ours at Oceanside Christian Fellowship. A policy of honesty and transparency as outlined above, however, goes a long way toward gaining the confidence of the people we lead as God's shepherds.

Credibility Factor #3: Community Among Leaders

Ministry is no easier for me today than it was thirty-three years ago when I accepted my first paid position in a church. It is, however, a lot less complicated.

It would likely have become simpler much earlier in my pilgrimage as a pastor, if I had just listened to Jesus. Jesus boiled the whole Old Testament down to two basic commandments:

Love the Lord your God with all your heart, with all your soul, and with all your mind. This is the greatest and most important command. The second is like it: Love your neighbor as yourself. All the Law and the Prophets depend on these two commands. (Matt 22:37–40)

There it is. A simple, twofold job description for the ministry of a local church pastor. I am to encourage my flock to love God and to love others.

Simple on paper. But what does this look like in practice? Let's take the first commandment. How will I know when the people of Oceanside Christian Fellowship are loving the Lord with all their heart, soul, and mind?

Their time alone with God? The way they spend their

money? The movies they choose to watch? The kinds of beverages they consume?

Love for God certainly manifests itself in the relative vitality of our devotional lives. And I would not want to minimize the importance of sound financial habits or moral purity as evidence of a living faith.

Yet the Bible does not identify a Christian's devotional life as the primary indication of love for God. Nor do personal morality or financial generosity make the cut.

Instead, Scripture turns repeatedly to the quality of our relationships—particularly with our fellow Christians—as the foremost evidence of genuine love for God. Jesus put it like this: "By this all people will know that you are My disciples, if you have love for one another" (John 13:35).

The New Testament unequivocally maintains that healthy human relationships are to be the natural and indispensable response to God's great work on our behalf in salvation history. Here are just a few of the familiar "one anothers" from the Bible:

- Love one another (John 13:34)

- Show family affection to one another (Rom 12:10)

- Be in agreement with one another (Rom 12:16)

- Let us no longer criticize one another (Rom 14:13)

- Accept one another (Rom 15:7)

- Instruct one another (Rom 15:14)

- Serve one another (Gal 5:13)

- Be kind and compassionate to one another (Eph 4:32)

- Forgive one another (Eph 4:32)

- Submit to one another (Eph 5:21)

- Encourage one another and build each other up (1 Thess 5:11)

- Be hospitable to one another (1 Pet 4:9)

Because our love for God is evidenced primarily in our love for others, there is a sense in which the first great commandment ("Love the Lord your God") cashes out, in practical terms, primarily in the way we relate to our fellow human beings ("Love your neighbor as yourself").

Paul saw this clearly: "The entire law is fulfilled in one statement: Love your neighbor as yourself" (Gal 5:14).

The apostle elaborates in Romans 13:8–10:

> [T]he one who loves another has fulfilled the law. The commandments: Do not commit adultery; do not murder; do not steal; do not covet; and whatever other commandment—all are summed up by this: Love your neighbor as yourself. Love does no wrong to a neighbor. Love, therefore, is the fulfillment of the law.

It is the second of Jesus's two great commandments (Matt 22:37–40) that becomes the mark of the Christian and the primary tangible evidence of the reality of our relationship with God.

Suddenly my twofold job description as a pastor has become even simpler. I am called as a pastor to encourage and equip my people to engage in healthy, sacrificial, mutually edifying relationships with their fellow human beings in response to what God has done for us in Christ—that is, to love one another.

Pretty straightforward, at least in theory.

You Cannot Lead Where You Will Not Go

But here's the rub. Just where do I get the credibility, Sunday after Sunday, to tell my people to love one another, if I am a CEO senior pastor who answers to no one during the week? If I answer to no one in the church office, how can I credibly tell others that they need to answer to one another in the pews?

I can't. Not with any real integrity, at any rate.

The seriousness of the problem cannot be overstated, yet I suspect that few church leaders give it much thought. What we have in the corporate model of ministry is a pastor who relates intimately to no one in the church, but who nevertheless exhorts his people to engage relationally with each other.

The glaring disconnect that inevitably results threatens to undermine the most basic virtue of the Christian life: our love for one another in the family of God.

Maybe this is why so many pastors and boards remain content to take the corporate approach and evaluate the success of their ministries by Sunday attendance and financial viability. Neither criterion requires anyone in the church—leaders or followers—to engage in healthy, mutually edifying interpersonal relationships.

Community is at the very heart of the Christian faith. And community in our churches must begin at the top.

Michael Frost and Alan Hirsch write unequivocally about the need for church leaders to model the kind of community that we so often extol in our Sunday messages:

> [W]e need to recognize that an authentic community can only be founded on changed relations between people; and these changed relations can only follow the inner change and preparation of the people who lead, work, and sacrifice for the community. In other words, it must begin with leadership.[10]

This is hardly rocket science. A pastor who has no genuine brothers in his congregation will lack the prophetic platform necessary to challenge others in the church to humbly engage in the

---

10. Michael Frost and Alan Hirsch, *The Shaping of Things to Come: Innovation and Mission for the 21st-Century Church* (Peabody, MA: Hendrickson, 2003), 156.

kind of surrogate sibling relationships that God intends for his people.

This disconnect proves particularly problematic in a culture where people are cynical about their leaders, and where church-goers are highly attuned to any perceived disparity between a pastor's "Sunday talk" and his "weekly walk." Frost and Hirsch elaborate:

> We simply don't believe that people in the "crap-detector" generation, savvy people who understand what it means to be constantly targeted by hundreds of thousands of clever sales messages, are going to follow other people who don't live out their messages. If leadership fails to embody the message, no one is going to follow. Leaders, you cannot lead where you will not go; you cannot teach what you do not know.[11]

Strong words, to be sure. Yet as we all know, the principle is inviolable: "you cannot lead where you will not go." And this will be particularly the case where risky, vulnerable interpersonal relationships are concerned.

Consider, in contrast, the credibility inherent in a community of leaders (a) who share their lives together as brothers in Christ, (b) who share the public ministry of their church, and (c) whose people see their pastor-elders sticking it out and making peer relationships work at the top in the real world of day-to-day pastoral ministry.

Here brotherly love—that central Christian virtue—is modeled by church leaders. And a preaching pastor suddenly possesses all the credibility he needs to challenge his people to join him in enthusiastically embracing Jesus's primary charge to His followers: "Love one another as I have loved you" (John 15:12).

Conclusion

At the outset of our discussion, I promised not to present a list of texts from Scripture favoring a specific church polity. I said

---

11. Ibid.

that I hoped, instead, to convince you that team leadership is biblical, in the broad, value-laden sense of the word. In the three Credibility Factors outlined above, I believe I have done just that.

What is more biblical than *Spiritual Maturity* (Credibility Factor #1)? Except for specific pastoral gifts (like teaching), the qualifications for pastor-elder laid out in the New Testament are character qualities to which all Christians are to aspire. As leaders, we had better be modeling these character qualities for our people.

Where better for a pastor to cultivate spiritual maturity than among an intimate group of peer leaders in the church, who help each team member to maximize his strengths and to come to grips with his shortcomings, and who hold each other accountable for the way authority is exercised in the community?

And what about *Transparency* (Credibility Factor #2)? Transparency is an expression of the basic Christian character trait of honesty. It finds its theological basis in the truthfulness of God himself.

We cannot even begin a relationship with God without being honest with ourselves about our sin and our need for a Savior. And transparency remains an indispensable key to maintaining good relationships with God and with others, in the home and in the church, throughout our Christian lives.

It only makes sense, then, that transparency should particularly characterize the ways in which pastors and church boards relate to their congregations. And this is much more likely to occur if pastors and board members themselves are in open, mutually transparent relationships with their fellow leaders.

Finally, as we saw above, community—healthy surrogate sibling relations among God's people—is to be the primary evidence that we truly belong to Jesus (John 13:35). What could be more biblical, in this regard, than practicing and modeling *Community among Leaders* (Credibility Factor #3) with a team of pastor-elder peers?

As it turns out, plurality leadership is an eminently biblical option. Indeed, team leadership more readily contributes to the cultivation of the virtues reflected in our three Credibility Factors—churchwide—than any other approach to church life and structure. And these virtues represent the very heart of biblical Christianity.

In contrast, neither the business model, consisting of a CEO pastor with his board of deacons, nor a democratic, congregational system of church government, does much to encourage the biblical values and character qualities outlined above. In fact, as we have seen throughout the pages of this book, these common approaches to church organization and power relations exhibit systemic shortcomings that too often lead us in precisely the opposite direction.

God's church is to be led by a plurality of pastor-elders who relate to one another first as family members in Christ, and who function only secondarily—and only within that primary relational context—as vision-casting, decision-making leaders for the broader church family. A genuine community of leaders offers great promise to those who long to recapture Paul's cruciform vision for authentic Christian leadership.

Questions for Reflection

1. A subheading in this chapter reads *Community Generates Consensus*. What does the author mean by this? How are *Community* and *Consensus* related to one another where team leadership is concerned?

2. The heart of the chapter considers three key Christian character qualities: *Spiritual Maturity, Transparency*, and *Community*. Why are these qualities important for both leaders and followers in the church (discuss them one at a time)?

3. How does plurality leadership encourage spiritual maturity (among leaders and followers) in ways that other leadership models do not?

4. How might team leadership foster a congregational culture of openness and transparency in ways that a senior pastor approach to church government might not?

5. In what ways does a community of leaders encourage healthy relationships among members of the broader church family? Can a senior pastor effectively encourage community in the church to this degree? Why or why not?

CONCLUSION

Some Final Thoughts and Challenges

> *"You call Me Teacher and Lord. This is well said, for I am.*
> *So if I, your Lord and Teacher, have washed your feet, you*
> *also ought to wash one another's feet. For I have given you an*
> *example that you also should do just as I have done for you."*
> —John 13:13-15

I trust that our survey of Rome's honor culture has illustrated the value of these background materials for understanding the biblical text. The social world of Paul's readers in Philippi sheds much light upon the countercultural nature of the self-humiliation and subsequent exaltation of Christ, as portrayed in Philippians 2:6–11.

In a society where competition for honor set the ground rules for virtually every public encounter, Christ willingly exchanged equality with God for slave status, finally submitting to the utter humiliation of a Roman cross (2:6–8)—all to reconcile wayward human beings to our Creator God.

In response, God affirmed Christ's culturally anomalous approach to power and authority by exalting him to the highest place, thereby guaranteeing that Jesus—not Caesar—would ultimately be publicly honored as "Lord" by every creature "in heaven and on earth and under the earth" (2:9–11).

Philippians 2:6–11 is to be understood as Christology in the service of ecclesiology. Paul intended his portrayal of the humiliation and exaltation of Christ to foster a Jesus-like perspective among members of the church in Philippi who possessed relative degrees of status in the community: "Make your own attitude that of Christ Jesus" (2:5). The message would have been especially pertinent to leaders ("overseers and deacons," 1:1) who exercised authority in the church.

It is a long way from Roman Philippi to modern America. We minister today in a setting that is quite different from the ancient Mediterranean world of early Christianity.

The cultural distance between Paul's world and ours becomes shorter, however, when we consider the basic contours of human nature and the good news of the gospel. Some things are time-less—like the example of Jesus in Philippians 2.

The perennial challenge is to figure out how to contextualize the enduring truths of the Bible in our own socio-cultural matrix. The regrettable phenomenon of authority abuse in our churches suggests that we are doing a less-than-adequate job along these lines, where pastoral leadership is concerned.

Rob Moll, in a recent *Christianity Today* article, reflects as a young adult on "a surprising number" of youth group friends who were at one time committed to Christ, but who have now left the faith. The common thread? "Each tended to have had some experience in which Christian leaders acted as hypocritical, power hungry, judgmental, or arrogant elites."[1]

Paul's Challenges

Paul, too, had his hands full trying to convince his contemporaries to use their social capital in the service of others. Leading like Jesus did not come naturally to persons who had been socialized from infancy to vigorously compete with one another for public acclaim.

Paul apparently recognized that the example of Jesus, in and

---

1. Rob Moll, "Saved by an Atheist," *Christianity Today* 54:8 (2010): 4.

of itself, was not enough to convince Christians in Philippi to leverage their status in an other-centered manner. What was needed was an alternative social context, a way of doing church that would subvert the relational priorities of Rome's honor culture and, instead, engender a Jesus-like approach to authority on the part of leaders and other persons of influence in the church at Philippi.

To this end Paul embarked on a twofold strategy: (1) the Philippians were to see themselves as members of a new family, and (2) leadership was to be exercised in community with others.

The strategy was brilliant on both counts. First, framing the church as a surrogate family had the potential to subvert Rome's honor culture, since persons in the Mediterranean world competed for honor only with representatives of other families. At home the honor game was off-limits.

To become a follower of Jesus in Philippi was to join a new family. Former adversaries in the struggle for social status in Philippi became brothers and sisters in Christ. Contending for honor was no longer socially acceptable. God's children were to "consider others as more important" than themselves (Phil 2:3).

Second, Paul's take on leadership would have discouraged the self-promoting use of status and authority among the Philippian Christians, as well. Paul's churches in the New Testament all reflected plurality leadership. The description of the leaders at Philippi—"overseers and deacons" (1:1)—is a case in point.

We gather from Paul's life and ministry that team leadership was highly relational, rather than merely formal or structural in orientation. Paul enjoyed a rich sense of community and camaraderie with his coworkers. We may assume that he intended the elders he appointed in his churches to relate to one another in a similar fashion.

The church as a family. Relational team leadership. Paul's twofold approach to community life and ministry would have gone a long way toward ensuring that the Philippians would resist the values of the dominant culture and, instead, use their social capital in a Jesus-like manner as they interacted with one another in their local church fellowship.

Our Challenges

We have much to learn from Paul and his missionary strategy. Ours is not a traditional honor-shame society. Yet the relational priorities of the dominant culture in America today are equally at odds with the pattern of behavior modeled by Jesus in Philippians 2. Cruciform living turns out to be countercultural in just about any social environment.

Recent trends in American evangelicalism have made it particularly difficult to remain true to New Testament leadership values and priorities. In many instances we have traded biblical ecclesiology for a secular paradigm of hierarchy and institutionalism.

The corporate approach to congregational life has led all too often to an insecure, narcissistic leader acquiring unilateral authority over the rest of the community, enabled by a church board whose metrics for ministerial success do nothing to curb the unhealthy behavior of their gifted but relationally challenged leader. The systemic weaknesses of what we might call "corporate ecclesiology" have converged to open the door to the abuse of power and authority by numbers of persons in vocational Christian service.

In one important way we are very much like the early church. The example of Jesus, in and of itself, has been insufficient to guarantee servant leadership in our communities. Like the Philippians, we need a social context for ministry that is different from the world around us, a way of doing church that will provide the checks and balances necessary for healthy pastoral leadership in our congregations.

I have suggested that the pathway back to Jesus-like leadership begins with a plurality of pastor-elders who relate to one another first as family members in Christ, and who function only secondarily—and only within that primary relational context—as vision-casting, decision-making leaders for the broader church family. A genuine community of pastors offers great promise to those who long to recapture Paul's cruciform vision for Christian leadership.

Contextualizing Paul's Vision

It remains to consider how to apply what we have learned to our current ministry settings. The guidelines below are general by design. I do not pretend to have a plan that will suit your specific congregation.

For all our similarities as Christians, each local church takes on a culture of its own. The pathway back to New Testament leadership values and practices will look different in your church than it does in mine. What follows is intended to provide a point of departure as you begin the journey.

I have targeted my suggestions at two groups of readers. Some of you answer (or will answer) to others in your ministry. You might serve as an associate pastor in a multi-staffed church. Or you may be a seminary or Bible college student anticipating an entry-level position in a multi-staffed church upon graduation.

Other readers serve as senior (or sole) pastors. A head pastor generally has much more latitude than associate staff to determine the future of his church, with respect to both philosophical values and weekly programming.

The different roles of associate and senior staff present distinct sets of opportunities and challenges for persons determined to recapture Paul's vision for relational team leadership. We will consider each in turn.

Those Who Answer to Others

I spend much of my time in an academic setting. My primary calling as a professor is to provide my students with the tools necessary to develop a set of biblical, transcultural values about Christian community and leadership—values that can serve as their ecclesiological ideals, so to speak, for a lifetime of church ministry. The relational approach to the pastorate commended in this book is an example of just such an ideal.

Ideals, however, are both dangerous and fragile commodities. They are dangerous in the hands of the strong among us. I have in mind those willful, uncompromising individuals who have all the answers in their twenties and thirties, but who lack the wisdom, maturity and sensitivity to contextualize their ideals in the messy world of day-to-day ministry.

Ideals are fragile, however, in the hands of the weak among us. Other graduates leave seminary and soon become so captivated by the American trinity of efficiency, growth, and pragmatism—principles enthusiastically advocated at many pastoral leadership conferences—that they quickly cave to culture and abandon their biblical ideals in favor of the latest trends in church growth.

We must avoid each of these extremes. Wisdom demands a mediating approach, as we seek to apply the Bible to the real-life world of church ministry.

Ideals and Reality: Holding on Without Selling Out

I encourage my students never to abandon their values, but to revisit them and refine them throughout their years in ministry. I also remind our graduates that there is no perfect church.

The simple fact is that our ecclesiological ideals—as biblical as they may be—will never be fully realized in any church setting. We must learn to live in the tension of the already/not yet.

Paul's vision for authentic Christian leadership is a case in point. The concept of a team of pastors, whose leadership arises naturally out of mutually edifying peer relationships, will not even be on the radar screen of most churches looking to hire recent seminary graduates.

The challenge for those of us who are determined to stay true to our biblical ideals in this area will be to discern the degree to which we can implement relational team leadership in a way that does not irretrievably compromise the unity and mission of our particular congregation.

Earlier I related my "aha moment," when I first encountered the biblical data reflecting plurality leadership in the New Testament. I served at the time in a Conservative Baptist church that had a long heritage of one-man leadership. The senior pastor's philosophy of ministry was so institutional that he warned young seminarians like myself not to make friends with anyone in our future congregations.

It would have been foolish and divisive to attempt to champion an agenda of relational leadership, churchwide, in a setting like this. Yet I was quite unwilling to let go of my newfound biblical ideal.

A great option presented itself. My wife and I led a college-career group of about sixty young people, and I began to implement what I was learning about early Christian community in that context.

We began with a topical study of the church in the New Testament. Sunday after Sunday, for several months, I taught on the mission of the church, the ordinances of the church, church discipline, spiritual gifts, and, yes, plurality leadership.

At the end of the series I informed the group, "Joe is not going to teach every Sunday anymore. Nor am I going to lead this group alone. I am going to ask some of you to become part of a new leadership team. I will train you to study and teach the Bible with me on Sundays."

Before too long, we had formed a team to lead the group, and four of us shared the Sunday teaching. I trained two of our older collegians in biblical hermeneutics and lesson preparation, along with an adult volunteer who had been with the class for a number of years.

The shared teaching proved to be the crucial component. The group suddenly realized that the new team was not simply a planning group, recruited to organize activities under the sole authority of the College Pastor. We were a genuine plurality of spiritual shepherds, teaching the Word on Sundays and praying for the group during the week.

The ideal, however, was only partially realized in my ministry as a College Pastor. My age, along with my formal staff position and years of training and experience, meant that our team was not, without qualification, a team of equals.

We did not experience the kind of peer relations, for example, that I currently enjoy as one of eleven pastor-elders at Oceanside Christian Fellowship. But we made significant strides in the right direction, and the group benefited tremendously from the transition to shared ministry.

The point here should be quite transparent. This side of eternity we will never see our biblical values fully realized in the context of ministry. This will especially be the case for newly minted seminary graduates who assume associate roles in senior pastor-led congregations.

In many situations junior staff can, however, find a place to implement their values, regardless of the structure and culture of the church as a whole. That place may be a Sunday school class, cell group, or ministry team of some kind.

Our task is to exercise the wisdom to do what we can, when we can, with the precious people whom God has given us, without undermining the unity and ministry of the broader church body.

Advice for Your First Job Interview

For my student readers, here is a key bit of advice that I give to those who are looking for their first associate staff position. Follow it, and you may very well save yourself a whole lot of grief.

In an ideal world a seminary graduate would look for a church that (1) specifies plurality leadership in its by-laws, (2) utilizes a shared teaching rotation in the pulpit in each service, and (3) has a team of pastors who share life together and who lead the church out of that relational context.

Unfortunately, the above combination—biblical though it is—will prove virtually non-existent to a first-time ministerial candidate plying the job market. There is, however, one "non-negotiable" in the mix. It is a modified version of the third criterion.

My advice, in this regard, is straightforward. I encourage my students to accept an associate staff position only if the senior pastor of that church engages in meaningful, transparent relationships with a handful of other persons in the congregation.

In the course of the interview process, you will likely be given an opportunity to ask your own questions about your potential employer. Here, for my money, is the crucial one to ask, where your future job satisfaction is concerned: *Does the senior pastor of this church have close friends in the congregation?*

The answer you receive will be your best indicator of whether or not the culture of leadership among the staff will be genuinely relational, or merely institutional, in nature, whatever might be the church's formal governmental structure.

It is not hard to see why. A senior pastor who is relationally engaged with others in the church will be much more likely to model and encourage transparency and healthy relationships among the church staff. And he will be much less likely to abuse his authority in manipulative, hurtful ways.

Here is another question you should ask at the interview: "What is the average tenure of associate staff at the church?" The abuse of pastoral authority and frequent staff turnover seem to go hand in hand in some institutional church settings.

When It's Time to Leave

Many students at Talbot School of Theology already serve as associate staff in congregations in the greater Los Angeles area. Most find themselves in nurturing, mentoring relationships with their pastoral supervisors.

As the case studies from chapter 7 indicate, however, dysfunctional leaders and the abuse of spiritual authority have irretrievably compromised staff relations in numbers of our students' churches. Sadly, there are times when our biblical values become wholly incompatible with the ministry context in which we find ourselves.

Each year I have several students ask, "When should I just give up, get out, and find another ministry?"

No one can answer that question for you. But you had better not ask it alone. Godly counsel is always helpful and clarifying, if not ultimately determinative. Some of us leave too soon. Others probably remain in unhealthy situations too long.

I have changed church families only once in my thirty-seven years as a Christian. I do not take such a decision lightly.

Back in 1996, however, I left the Conservative Baptist church described above after twenty years of ministry, when it became clear, through a change of senior pastors, that my ecclesiological convictions were no longer a fit for the direction the church was taking. I could not in good conscience stay and support a philosophy of ministry that contrasted so sharply with the values and practices outlined in the earlier pages of this book.

In some situations, finding a place—anywhere in the church—to cultivate biblical priorities related to leadership and community becomes an altogether fruitless endeavor. Then it is time to get out.

Those Who Answer to No One

If you are the sole or senior pastor of a church, and you have read this far, you have likely become weary of the traditional model.

Perhaps you struggle with the sense of isolation that comes from one-man leadership. Or maybe you are finding yourself more and more uncomfortable with the criteria for success advocated by a church board that takes an institutional approach to ministry.

Whatever the situation might be, I hope you have found the ideas you encountered here potentially renewing and refreshing. The good news is that you, as the head pastor, have an opportunity to gain churchwide support for your convictions about Christian community and leadership in ways that an associate pastor does not.

If you serve in a congregation with a long history of one-man leadership, you will still face some daunting challenges. The expectations of your people are increasingly at odds with your ecclesiological ideals. Where do you go from here?

What we do not need is another set of church programs. Indeed, our structures and programs often obstruct, rather than encourage, the kind of community—among leaders and followers—advocated in this book.

I find it helpful, instead, to go back to the New Testament to remind myself that the keys to effective Christian leadership are twofold: teaching and modeling.

I need to explain to my people *what* needs to be done. I need to show them from Scripture *why* it needs to be done. And then I need to show them *how* it's done, by example.

In the present connection, this means that I must expose my congregation to the biblical contours of church leadership through the teaching ministry of the church, and I must model a relational approach to ministry in my own life as a pastor.

Teaching Them the "What" and the "Why"

We see from the lives of Jesus and Paul that there is an indispensable cognitive component to spiritual formation. Jesus taught extensively during his earthly ministry, and Paul's letters are full of instructions about church life and leadership.

Do not underestimate the power of the pulpit to change the thinking of your people about the way we do church. A well-crafted set of sermons on leadership in the New Testament will do much to prepare the soil for a cultural shift in your congregation's philosophy of ministry.

It will help to combine Sunday teaching with more specific instruction tailored to your church board. Consider reading and discussing *Embracing Shared Ministry* with your leaders. Several chapters of the book are now required reading for elders-in-training at Oceanside Christian Fellowship. We feel that this will help our new brothers to get up-to-speed on our philosophy of ministry sooner rather than later.

The combination of a sermon series, along with more focused training of church leaders, will go a long way toward educating your people about relational team leadership.

The Spirit Bears Witness

Where the cognitive component of discipleship is concerned, I find great encouragement in the fact that this is ultimately the Holy Spirit's project, not my own. God wants his people in community—including his shepherds. We may be assured that God is on our side in this endeavor as we teach our people.

We do not have to do cartwheels or twist arms to persuade our congregations to embrace this radically new way of thinking about church leadership. The Holy Spirit will do that for us if the material we present is truly biblical. The combination of the Word and the Spirit has been indispensable to renewal throughout Christian history, and this will continue to be the case until the Lord returns.

I suspect that this is especially true of the topic at hand. The great irony here is that numbers of your people are likely already experiencing the kind of relationships that you lack as a pastor. They see firsthand the value of the surrogate sibling bonds that the Holy Spirit naturally cultivates among God's children. It may not be as difficult as you think to convince your people that you as leaders ought to enjoy the same kind of Christian community that members of the congregation have been experiencing all along.

Those who resist your teaching will generally be lone-ranger types who have their own problems opening up and sharing their lives with fellow believers in the church family. A person who struggles with intimacy, and who has developed strategies for keeping others at a distance in his or her own life, will likely not respond positively to the idea of a community of leaders in the church, especially if that person has been socialized to buy into a corporate model of ministry.

It should go without saying that the convictions of such individuals should not be allowed to determine a congregation's approach to leadership and its philosophy of ministry.

Showing Them How It's Done

We spent a good deal of time in chapter 9 lamenting the dilemma of the senior pastor who answers to no one, but who nevertheless challenges his people to engage relationally with one another. We need not revisit in any detail the hypocrisy involved in this glaring disconnect between what a pastor says on Sundays and how he lives his life the rest of the week.

We will assume, at this point, that you are a pastor who longs to develop meaningful relationships with a handful of people in your congregation. You plan to preach about community and you intend to model it in your own life and ministry. Where do you begin?

Ideally, with your staff (or lacking an associate staff, with members of your church board or a handful of other leaders in the congregation). Indeed, if your people do not see you relating in a healthy way with other leaders, they will soon gather that all those Sunday platitudes about team leadership really do not work in the day-to-day life of church ministry.

You will need to exercise care, however, as you begin to develop relationships among staff persons who are accustomed to operate with an institutional mind-set. Here is a way *not* to begin:

Hey, guys, we are going to begin to function differently around here. I want us to work together as a team, planning and leading the church as a plurality of leaders.

This strategy looks fine on paper. It is likely doomed to failure, however, because at present you almost certainly lack the social capital necessary to lead the church as a genuine community of pastors.

As we saw in the previous chapter, consensus arises from community, not the other way around. The journey to effective team leadership does not begin with decision-making and church programming. It begins with meaningful relationships. You might try something like this, instead:

Hey, guys, we are going to begin to function differently around here. I want us to start cultivating some meaningful relationships among us as a staff. Beginning next month we will meet together and pray for one another for an hour or so every Thursday morning. No planning. No church work. Just prayer for our families, and some sharing and accountability about our personal relationships with the Lord.

Depending on where you begin relationally with your staff, it may take months, or even years, to develop the kind of openness and transparency necessary to function as a genuine community of leaders. You yourself may even need to initiate the process by apologizing for the manner in which you've handled staff relations in the past.

Whatever the case, you, as the pastor, will set the tone for the relational integrity of the team. Your staff will open up and trust one another only as you lead the way—a risky proposition, to be sure, but the only pathway, in the final analysis, that holds much promise for truly transforming your own life and ministry, and for renewing the culture of your church.

Only when you have established a significant degree of trust and community among your staff will you be ready to lead the church together as a genuine team of pastors. We now come face to face with what will likely be a senior pastor's greatest challenge: giving away significant portions of the ministry.

Genuine plurality leadership will find the lead pastor becoming but one of several voices that determine the community's vision and make key decisions. But collective leadership goes beyond vision-casting and decision-making. Members of the pastoral team should share the teaching ministry of the church on Sundays, as well.

The change to shared decision-making will likely prove least problematic. Most church planning goes on behind the scenes. Weekly attenders generally will not know whether decisions in these areas are made by a single leader or by a team of pastors.

Teaching is another story entirely. The weekly sermon is the most public aspect of a pastor's ministry. For many pastors it is the highlight of their week. A transition to a team of Sunday teachers will likely be the most difficult part of "giving away the ministry," for both a pastor and his congregation.

Yes, Even the Pulpit

Pastors typically derive a great deal of satisfaction and

self-esteem from their role as the Sunday sage. Here the temptation to ignore a biblical ideal in favor of longstanding cultural norms will be almost irresistible.

The expectations of the flock will reinforce the reluctance to share the pulpit. Most congregations prefer to hear a single voice on Sundays, at least until they are taught—and experience—otherwise. All this means that it will take great determination on the part of the senior pastor, along with a thorough education of his congregation, to share the pulpit with associate staff on a regular basis.

Be assured, however, that sharing the Sunday teaching is all worth the effort. Nothing will do more than a plurality of voices in the pulpit to convince your people that they truly belong to a team-led congregation.

I recognize that not all elders contributed equally to the teaching ministry of the New Testament churches. In 1 Timothy 5:17, for example, "those who work hard at preaching and teaching" appears to be a subset of "elders who are good leaders." Note, however, that even this subgroup contains more than one individual.

The point is not to quibble over whether or not every pastor-elder should be in the preaching rotation. It is to emphasize the fact that your people will only be fully convinced that genuine community exists at the top level of leadership when they see those leaders sharing the teaching ministry of the church.

The latter reality recently manifested itself in my own church family. As I mentioned earlier, Brandon, Michael, and I do the great majority of the preaching at Oceanside Christian Fellowship. In spite of this, most of our people view the remaining five pastor-elders in the church as our ministerial peers. But not everyone is on board, as we discovered during the recent addition of a Saturday evening service.

The new service began with a monthly pilot program during the summer of 2010. We transitioned to weekly Saturday services that fall. One of our fellow pastors, Carlos, filled the pulpit for the June kick-off service.

No one had a problem with the fact that neither Brandon nor Joe preached at that first Saturday night service (this was before Michael joined the rotation). It was just fine that Carlos brought the message. When it was discovered that Brandon and I were both planning to be out of town for the occasion, however, some grumbling arose.

Apparently, it was not enough for Carlos, along with two of our non-preaching pastors, Denny and Ed, to represent the pastoral team in support of the new service. Brandon or Joe needed to be there, as well. So we quickly rearranged our vacation schedules to enable one of us to be present that evening.

I suspect that things would have been different had all OCF's pastor-elders shared the pulpit in the years prior to the launch of the new service. Brandon and I would likely not have been missed at all.

Carlos will increasingly participate in our teaching rotation, and Denny and Ed preach occasionally, as well. Sharing the pulpit equally among the seven of us, however, will continue to prove impractical for reasons of both giftedness and availability. So we, like you, will continue to live in the tension of the already/not yet, where full plurality leadership is concerned.

The point of this discussion should not be missed. Shared Sunday teaching is perhaps the most fundamental aspect of an authentically relational approach to ministry. Give away the pulpit—even for one Sunday a month—and your people will begin to believe that you truly are leading the church in community with your surrogate siblings on the pastoral staff.

Conclusion

Few of us become pastors because we want to serve ourselves. We graduate from seminary sold out to Jesus and ready to serve his church. Our intentions are commendable. Our motives are pure.

Then something goes seriously wrong along the way. The church begins to grow, but you, the pastor, do not.

People from the surrounding community fill the pews to listen to you preach about relationships. At the same time, deep-seated emotional insecurities prevent you from connecting in any meaningful way with the many persons in your own church family.

As attendance and giving soar, biblically illiterate board members with an institutional mind-set affirm a ministry that is relationally bankrupt but numerically and financially robust. "Atta-boy, Pastor, you're doing a great job here."

In such a setting you find it increasingly easy to buy into a corporate mentality that allows you to enjoy your position of authority and esteem, while remaining relationally isolated from others in the church family, including your associate staff. The atmosphere in the church office becomes more institutional than relational, and staff come and go.

Spiritual maturity, transparency, and community—those basic biblical benchmarks of healthy Christianity—have all but vanished from day-to-day ministry at the top level of church leadership. In their place arise the subtle manipulation of others in the service of the senior pastor's personal agenda and, in a worst-case scenario, the blatant abuse of pastoral authority.

No one chooses to go down this path. We desire, instead, to follow in the footsteps of Jesus. As the case studies related in the earlier chapters indicate, however, the above scenario continues to play itself out in church after church in America today.

It is not hard to see why. In the final analysis, instances of authority abuse in our churches can be traced to the violation of one of the most basic principles of the Christian faith—one that determines the life trajectory of every person who names the name of Jesus: *We cannot follow in the footsteps of Jesus alone. We need each other to be faithful to Jesus.*

Isn't this precisely what we tell our people from the pulpit, Sunday after Sunday? That the Christian life is not meant to be lived alone, in isolation from others in the church family? That God has designed us for community?

Pastors know better than anyone what happens to people in our churches who withdraw from Christian fellowship and try to follow Jesus on their own. Lone rangers don't stand a chance against the temptations of the world and its values. Compromise is inevitable.

Conversely, those of us who serve as God's shepherds also know that the members of our flock who are relationally connected with one another are the ones who generally experience the richest and most productive Christian lives.

The correlation between Christian community and spiritual vitality is hardly coincidental. We grow together or we don't grow much at all.

Do we really think it will be different for those of us in vocational Christian service? How is it that we have somehow come to assume that God's church ought to be run by a single individual who answers to no one?

Given what we have learned about community and leadership in early Christianity, does it really make biblical sense to believe that a professional minister who is closely connected to no one in his congregation should unilaterally determine the future of a whole church family?

Experience confirms what the Bible teaches. God has not equipped us to navigate the temptations and challenges that come with pastoral authority on our own. God has designed us to be in community with one another as ministers of the gospel.

The way back to Paul's cruciform vision for authentic Christian leadership begins with a group of pastors who share life together, who genuinely love one another, and who lead their church, as a team, out of the richness of the soil of those peer relationships. May God grant us the wisdom and the courage to walk down this enriching and paradigm-changing pathway.

Questions for Reflection

1. You are part of a church board that wants to implement the values you have been exposed to in this book. Where do you begin? How do you bring your pastor on board? Your congregation?

2. In view of what you have read, what advice would you give young seminarians looking for their first job as an associate pastor in a large church? What should they look for in the senior pastor? The church board?

3. You are a gifted leader and preacher who planted a church that has quickly grown to eight hundred members. Now you desire to change to a more biblical, team approach to ministry. How do you go about it? Come up with a game plan.

4. What are some legitimate reasons for leaving a church? What are some unacceptable reasons?

5. How would you evaluate your church in view of the values and practices advocated in this book? How might you improve along these lines?

BIBLIOGRAPHY

Barnett, Paul. *The Second Epistle to the Corinthians*. NICNT. Edited by Gordon D. Fee. Grand Rapids: Eerdmans, 1997.

Barton, Carlin A. *Roman Honor: The Fire in the Bones*. Berkeley: University of California Press, 2001.

Beck, Roger. "The Mysteries of Mithras." In *Voluntary Associations in the Graeco-Roman World: Issues in Function, Taxonomy, and Membership,* edited by John S. Kloppenborg and Stephen G. Wilson, 176–185. London: Routledge, 1996.

Brewin, Kester. *Signs of Emergence: A Vision For Church That Is Organic/Networked/ Decentralized/Bottom-up/Communal/Flexible/Always Evolving*. Grand Rapids: Baker, 2007.

Danker, Frederick W., ed. *A Greek-English Lexicon of the New Testament and other Early Christian Literature*. 3rd ed. Chicago: University of Chicago Press, 2000.

Dorcey, Peter F. *The Cult of Silvanus: A Study in Roman Folk Religion*. Leiden: Brill, 1992.

Edwards, Mark J., ed. *Galatians, Ephesians, Philippians*. ACCS New Testament 8. Downers Grove, IL: InterVarsity Press, 1999.

Esler, Philip F. "Family Imagery and Christian Identity in Gal 5:13 to 6:10." In *Constructing Early Christian Families: Family as Social Reality and Metaphor,* edited by Halvor Moxnes, 121-49. London: Routledge, 1997.

Fagan, Garrett G. *The Lure of the Arena: Social Psychology and the Crowd at the Roman Games*. Cambridge: Cambridge University Press, 2011.

Fee, Gordon D. *Paul's Letter to the Philippians*. NICNT. Edited by Gordon D. Fee. Grand Rapids: Eerdmans, 1995.

Flower, Harriet I. *Ancestor Masks and Aristocratic Power in Roman Culture*. Oxford: Clarendon, 1996.

Frost, Michael, and Alan Hirsch. *The Shaping of Things to Come: Innovation and Mission for the 21st-Century Church*. Peabody, MA: Hendrickson, 2003.

Garnsey, Peter. *Social Status and Legal Privilege in the Roman Empire*. Oxford: Oxford University Press, 1970.

Garnsey, Peter, and Richard Saller. *The Roman Empire: Economy, Society, and Culture*. Berkeley: University of California Press, 1987.

Gibbs, Eddie. *LeadershipNext: Changing Leaders in a Changing Culture*. Downers Grove, IL: InterVarsity Press, 2005.

Gibbs, Eddie, and Ryan K. Bolger. *Emerging Churches: Creating Christian Community in Postmodern Cultures*. Grand Rapids: Baker, 2005.

Glancy, Jennifer A. "Boasting of Beatings (2 Corinthians 11:23-25)." *JBL* 123.1 (2004): 99-135.

Harper Brad, and Paul Louis Metzger. *Exploring Ecclesiology: An Evangelical and Ecumenical Introduction*. Grand Rapids: Brazos, 2009.

Hartley, L. P. *The Go-Between*. New York: NYRB Classics, 2002.

Hawthorne, Gerald F. "In the Form of God and Equal with God (Philippians 2:6)." In *Where Christology Began: Essays on Philippians 2*, edited by Brian J. Dodd and Ralph P. Martin, 96-110. Louisville: Westminster John Knox, 1998.

Hellerman, Joseph H. *The Ancient Church as Family*. Minneapolis: Fortress, 2001.

———. "Brothers and Friends in Philippi: Family Honor in the Roman World and in Paul's Letter to the Philippians." *BTB* 39.1 (2009): 15-25.

———. "μορφῇ θεοῦ as a Signifier of Social Status in Philippians 2:6." *JETS* 52.4 (2009): 779-97.

———. *Reconstructing Honor in Roman Philippi: Carmen Christi as* Cursus Pudorum. SNTSMS 132. Cambridge: Cambridge University Press, 2005.

———. "Vindicating God's Servants in Philippi and in Philippians: The Influence of Paul's Ministry in Philippi upon the Composition of Philippians 2:6-11." *BBR* 20.1 (2010): 85-102.

———. *When the Church Was a Family: Recapturing Jesus' Vision for Authentic Christian Community*. Nashville: Broadman & Holman, 2009.

Hengel, Martin. *Crucifixion In the Ancient World and the Folly of the Message of the Cross*. Translated by John Bowden. Philadelphia: Fortress, 1977.

Herbert, Bob. "The Right Answer." *New York Times*, September 20, 2001, A31.

Hurtado, Larry W. "Lord." In *Dictionary of Paul and his Letters*, edited by Gerald F. Hawthorne et al., 560-69. Downers Grove, IL: InterVarsity Press, 1993.

Huxley, Aldous. *Ends and Means: An Inquiry into the Nature of Ideals and into the Methods Employed for Their Realization*. San Francisco: Harper and Brothers, 1937.

Kets de Vries, Manfred F. R. *Leaders, Fools, and Impostors: Essays on the Psychology of Leadership.* San Francisco: Jossey-Bass, 1993.

Kitchens, Jim. *The Postmodern Parish: New Ministry for a New Era.* Herndon, VA: Alban Institute, 2003.

Kloppenborg, John S. "Collegia and *Thiasoi.*" In *Voluntary Associations in the Graeco-Roman World: Issues in Function, Taxonomy, and Membership,* edited by John S. Kloppenborg and Stephen G. Wilson, 16-30. London: Routledge, 1996.

Lendon, J. E. *Empire of Honour: The Art of Government in the Roman World.* Oxford: Clarendon, 1997.

Lenski, Gerhard E. *Power and Privilege: A Theory of Social Stratification.* New York: McGraw-Hill, 1966.

Lewis, Naphtali, and Meyer Reinhold, eds. *Roman Civilization: Sourcebook II: The Empire.* New York: Harper Torchbooks, 1966.

Lipman-Blumen, Jean. *The Allure of Toxic Leaders: Why We Follow Destructive Bosses and Corrupt Politicians—and How We Can Survive Them.* Oxford: Oxford University Press, 2005.

Littlejohn, James. *Social Stratification.* London: Allen & Unwin, 1972.

MacMullen, Ramsay. *Roman Social Relations: 50 B.C. to A.D. 284.* New Haven: Yale University Press, 1974.

Malina, Bruce J. *The New Testament World: Insights from Cultural Anthropology.* Louisville: Westminster John Knox, 2001.

Malina, Bruce J., and Jerome H. Neyrey. "Honor and Shame in Luke-Acts: Pivotal Values of the Mediterranean World." In *The Social World of Luke-Acts,* edited by Jerome H. Neyrey, 25-65. Peabody, MA: Hendrickson, 1991.

Malina, Bruce J., and Richard L. Rohrbaugh. *Social-Science Commentary on the Synoptic Gospels.* Minneapolis: Fortress, 1992.

Martin, Dale B. *Slavery as Salvation: The Metaphor of Slavery in Pauline Christianity.* New Haven: Yale University Press, 1990.

McKenna, David L. "The Ministry's Gordian Knot." *Leadership* 1:1 (1980): 45-51.

McLean, B. Hudson. "The Place of Cult in Voluntary Associations and Christian Churches on Delos." In *Voluntary Associations in the Graeco-Roman World: Issues in Function, Taxonomy, and Membership,* edited by John

S. Kloppenborg and Stephen G. Wilson, 186-225. London: Routledge, 1996.

Moll, Rob. "Saved by an Atheist." *Christianity Today* 54:8 (2010): 38-40.

Morgenthaler, Sally. "Leadership in a Flattened World: Grassroots Culture and the Demise of the CEO Model." In *An Emergent Manifesto of Hope,* edited by Doug Pagitt and Tony Jones, 175-88. Grand Rapids: Baker, 2007.

Moxnes, Halvor. "Honor and Shame." In *The Social Sciences and New Testament Interpretation,* edited by Richard Rohrbaugh, 19-40. Peabody, MA: Hendrickson, 1996.

O'Brien, Peter T. *The Epistle to the Philippians.* NIGTC. Grand Rapids: Eerdmans, 1991.

Oakes, Peter. *Philippians: From People to Letter.* SNTSMS 110. Cambridge: Cambridge University Press, 2001.

Pilhofer, Peter. *Philippi, Band 1: Die erste christliche Gemeinde Europas.* WUNT. Tübingen: J. C. B. Mohr, 1995.

———. *Philippi, Band 2: Katalog der Inschriften von Philippi.* WUNT. Tübingen: J. C. B. Mohr, 2000.

Platt, David. *Radical: Taking Back Your Faith from the American Dream.* Colorado Springs: Multnomah, 2010.

Rapske, Brian. *The Book of Acts and Paul in Roman Custody.* Vol. 3 of The Book of Acts in Its First Century Setting. Grand Rapids: Eerdmans, 1994.

Richardson, Cyril C., trans. and ed. *Early Christian Fathers.* New York: Macmillan, 1970.

Rinehart, Stacy T. *Upside Down: The Paradox of Servant Leadership.* Colorado Springs: NavPress, 1998.

Saller, Richard. "Status and Patronage." In *The Cambridge Ancient History,* edited by Alan K. Bowman et al., vol. 11, 817-54. Cambridge: Cambridge University Press, 2000.

Salmon, Edward T. *Roman Colonization under the Republic.* London: Thames & Hudson, 1969.

Shelton, Jo-Ann, ed. *As the Romans Did: A Sourcebook in Roman Social History.* New York: Oxford University Press, 1988.

Stegemann, Ekkehard W., and Wolfgang Stegemann. *The Jesus Movement: A Social History of Its First Century.* Translated by O. C. Dean Jr. Minneapolis: Fortress, 1999.

Strauch, Alexander. *Biblical Eldership: An Urgent Call to Restore Biblical Church Leadership,* rev. ed. Colorado Springs: Lewis and Roth, 1995.

Tauber, Michelle, Elizabeth McNeil, and Cathy Nolan. "Jackie's Style." *People* 55:18 (2001): 52.

Tellbe, Mikael. *Paul Between Synagogue and State: Christians, Jews, and Civic Authorities in 1 Thessalonians, Romans, and Philippians.* Stockholm: Almqvist & Wiksell International, 2001.

Treggiari, Susan. "Social Status and Social Legislation." In *The Cambridge Ancient History,* edited by Alan K. Bowman et al., vol. 10, 873-82. Cambridge: Cambridge University Press, 1996.

Walker-Ramisch, Sandra. "Graeco-Roman Voluntary Associations and the Damascus Document: A Sociological Analysis." In *Voluntary Associations in the Graeco-Roman World: Issues in Function, Taxonomy, and Membership,* edited by John S. Kloppenborg and Stephen G. Wilson, 128-45. London: Routledge, 1996.

Webber, Robert E. *The Younger Evangelicals: Facing the Challenges of the New World.* Grand Rapids: Baker, 2002.

Wilde, Oscar. *The Picture of Dorian Gray.* New York: Modern Library, 1998.

Wright, N. T. "A Fresh Perspective on Paul?" *BJRL* 83.1 (2001): 21-39.

Zanker, Paul. *The Power of Images in the Age of Augustus.* Translated by Alan Shapiro. Ann Arbor: University of Michigan Press, 1988.